TONY BLAIR

THE MODERNISER

Jon Sopel

BANTAM BOOKS

LONDON · NEW YORK · TORONTO · SYDNEY · AUCKLAND

TONY BLAIR
The Moderniser

A BANTAM BOOK : 0 553 50387 1

Originally published in Great Britain
by Michael Joseph Ltd

PRINTING HISTORY
Michael Joseph edition published 1995
Bantam edition published 1995

Set in 11 on 13pt Monotype Bembo
by Phoenix Typesetting, Ilkley, West Yorkshire

Bantam Books are published by Transworld Publishers Ltd,
61–63 Uxbridge Road, Ealing, London W5 5SA,
in Australia by Transworld Publishers (Australia) Pty Ltd,
15–25 Helles Avenue, Moorebank, NSW 2170,
and New Zealand by Transworld Publishers (NZ) Ltd,
3 William Pickering Drive, Albany, Auckland.

Reproduced, printed and bound in Great Britain by
Cox & Wyman Ltd, Reading, Berks.

To Max and Anna

Contents

Photograph Credits

The Author and Publishers would like to thank the following people and organisations for permission to reproduce the photographs in this book:

1, 3, 4, 5 Courtesy of the Blair family; 2 Ross-Parry Picture Library; 6 Dr Geoff Gallopp; 7 *The Times*, 15 *The Times*/Peter Brookes; 9 John Burton; 10 Press Association/Neil Munns, 17 Press Association/Tim Ockenden; 11 *Independent*/John Voos, 12 *Independent*/Brian Harris; 13 Mirror Syndication International; 14 BBC.

The Publishers have made every effort to contact the owners of illustrations reproduced in this book; where they have been unsuccessful they invite copyright holders to contact them direct.

Acknowledgements

When I recently told someone in my local pub that I was writing a biography of Tony Blair, he looked at me aghast: 'He hasn't died has he?' was his half serious, half mocking reply. But having seen that supermodels feel able to write their autobiographies in their early twenties, and that sportsmen rarely wait until their thirties it seemed that Blair's first forty-one years were ripe for appraisal.

This is not an authorised biography, nor did I want it to be. So I have not had the benefit of rifling through Tony Blair's filing cabinets of letters and papers, but nevertheless I must put on record my thanks to him for the time that he has given me, and in particular my thanks to his office staff, particularly Anji Hunter, for fielding my requests for this or that crumb of additional information.

Thanks too must go to the countless friends and associates whom I have badgered to 'dish the dirt' on Blair. It is either a mark of their loyalty, my failure, or the blamelessness with which Tony Blair has conducted his life that I have come up with so little in that department. But in helping to give me a rounded picture of the character and personality of Labour's new Leader, I am very grateful to his friends from schooldays onwards, and his political friends and opponents in the Commons.

The judgements made here are my own, but I was given priceless help in writing this book by my editor Louise Haines: her advice and constructive criticisms were invariably spot on. Thanks too to my researcher Catherine Rimmer who has tirelessly ploughed through old Hansards, press cuttings and speeches. I am also extremely grateful to Bill Bush, the indefatigable head of the BBC's Political Research Unit, who has been a frank critic and a good friend.

But I reserve the greatest thanks for my wife, Linda, and our two children who have had to put up with a husband and father who has spent the past few months locked away in his study writing, while normal families had summer holidays and went out together. But it struck me that the privations of the Sopel family must be put into context. On one occasion when I went to interview Tony Blair at his home in his constituency, he arrived at 5 p.m. on Friday evening to be greeted by an endless stream of requests to do this or that. His children arrived with the nanny later that evening while he was meeting local Party workers in the Labour Club, and he didn't get to see them until the following morning. Immediately after breakfast he went straight into a Saturday morning constituency surgery, made a speech to the local flower society, and came back home to find another procession of people waiting to see him and a *Panorama* crew wanting to film him looking relaxed. He then had to pen a speech that he was making that evening, and eventually, late on Saturday afternoon, we sat down to talk. It was a normal weekend for Tony Blair. He was concerned though about how my family were putting up with me spending so much time writing a book and he asked whether his name had become a swear word in my house. I told him it had. To which he replied, 'Not half as much as it is in mine.'

Jon Sopel
Hampshire
January 1995

CHAPTER 1

A Silver Plated Spoon

'I was never a radical when I was young for fear of being a
Conservative when I grew old.'

Robert Frost

No sooner had Tony Blair MP been installed in the suite of
offices that goes with the job of being the Leader of the
Opposition, than a call came from Buckingham Palace. He was
invited to attend both a rehearsal in the Cabinet Office and also
the ceremony in which the Queen would swear him in as a Privy
Councillor, one of the highest honours that the British establishment bestows upon a politician.

It is an extraordinary occasion. Those present have to move
in a crab-like fashion, either walking backwards or sideways, so
that at no point does anyone turn their back on the Queen – the
height of bad manners. Everyone stands, to make it as uncomfortable as possible for those attending; and also to ensure that
business is transacted quickly so that Her Majesty is not detained
for a moment longer than necessary. People walk out of rooms
backwards; flunkeys in powdered wigs are on hand. It is the
British establishment at its oddest and most ritualised.

When the Right Honourable Anthony Charles Lynton Blair
MP emerged from the Palace blinking into the daylight to be
driven by his chauffeur back to the Commons, he said to one of
his staff with a twinkle in his eye, 'So that's how the English
upper classes keep themselves entertained.' It was a typical Blair
comment: mildly irreverent, laughing slightly at convention, but
stopping well short of causing offence. But it must have been an
even more extraordinary occasion for the Queen herself. For

there standing before her was the man most likely to become the tenth Prime Minister with whom she has dealt during her reign. But, most startling, the man who aspired to be Britain's next Prime Minister and First Lord of the Treasury hadn't even been born when she ascended the throne in 1952.

The young Queen Elizabeth had been head of state and defender of the faith a little over a year when an Edinburgh couple, Leo and Hazel Blair, announced the birth of their second son, Anthony, on 6 May 1953. He was born into an upwardly mobile family – and an uncertain world. Stalin had just died and telegrams from Winston Churchill were flying across the Atlantic as he and Eisenhower squabbled about whether or not they should travel to Moscow to meet the Soviets as the West waited to see who would replace 'Uncle Joe'. On the day of Blair's birth, Churchill was locked in a top secret meeting of the Defence Committee of the Cabinet, called to discuss how to protect Britain's interests in Egypt should the Soviet Union or Egypt mount any pre-emptive strike against British forces in the Suez Canal zone.

It is worth noting, because Blair is a politician free of the pre-occupations of a previous generation. He is post-war, very nearly post-Cold War, and free from the ideological baggage that had shaped the parameters of political debate in the 1960s and 1970s. He grew up seeing only the failure of the brand of socialism practised on the other side of the Iron Curtain. He was an adolescent fifteen-year-old during the revolutionary upheavals of 1968. And his entry into politics came as Britain was decisively turning its back on the corporatist, collectivist solutions that had been offered by Labour hitherto. Blair represents a new generation of politicians, a product of the 1960s, but, more significant than his youth and modernity, is the fact that he stands so far apart from the traditions and roots of every other Labour Leader who has preceded him: Jim Callaghan, the former union man, was able to open his arms expansively and talk about 'this great movement of ours'; Neil Kinnock was a romantic Bevanite left-winger who, when he became leader, hung across one of the oak panelled walls of the shadow cabinet room a giant, scarlet embroidered Welsh mineworkers' banner with a tableau depicting one of the great struggles of yesteryear; John Smith was a right-winger and member of the Solidarity group whose mix of ethical values, strong Christian base and gritty Scottish background made him a highly reassuring, even predictable figure to those who did not share his political outlook. And certainly there are no pictures in the Blair family's attic of the young Tony dressed in shorts standing on the doorstep of Number 10 Downing Street as Harold Wilson had done when he was a boy.

Blair is not hewn from the rock of previous leaders. He stands outside many of Labour's traditions, and causes consternation, alarm and excitement in roughly equal proportions in his efforts to articulate a new, more pluralist language for left-of-centre politics in Britain. He doesn't talk wistfully of bygone days, conjuring up folklore memories of comrades on winter mornings huddling together around a brazier outside the factory gates or the historic battles on the picket lines as organised labour fought against the power of capital to bring that socialist dream one step closer. Blair wears none of the Labour movement's campaign medals, nor bears its battle-scars. As he stands before an audience of Labour activists and union fixers, the pre-eminent feeling is that he is not one of them. He feels no need to seek to justify the events that resulted in the Winter of Discontent – he simply condemns what happened. He bears no malice towards those who sought to destroy the Labour Party when they formed the SDP – that piece of recent history was before his time, and he understood their unhappiness. And, while Tony Blair has studied more closely than many the history of his political forebears, he believes passionately in change. He has sought to position his politics as an ally of modernisation, and has little time for those who seek to turn the past into a collection of musty holy relics.

★   ★   ★

Tony Blair was born into a politically aware and increasingly politically active family. His father Leo's first port of call was with the Young Communist League. With the growth of Fascism on the Continent before the outbreak of war, Leo Blair, like so many young men of his generation, saw the world in stark terms. On one side were the 'baddies': the Nazis, black-shirts and brown-shirts; on the other were the forces of good: the Communists. It wasn't until many years after the war that the true extent of the oppression in the totalitarian Soviet Union became apparent. Fired by a youthful idealism, Leo Blair became Secretary of the Young Communist League by the time he was sixteen, attending conferences in London. A year later he left school and went to work as a copy boy on the *Daily Worker* in Glasgow. But that job did not last long as the Second World War had now started, and the then Home Secretary, Herbert Morrison, closed it down for being too pro-Communist. The propaganda machine of the War Cabinet had not yet transformed Stalin into cuddly 'Uncle Joe'. Leo then went to work for the Glasgow Corporation where he served as a clerk in the Public Assistance Department until he joined the army in 1942.

Leo Blair had been adopted by a Govan shipyard rigger and his wife when he was only a few months old. They lived in the upstairs part of a privately rented house where the rent was five shillings a week. The total weekly income was only around eighteen shillings a week because Leo's elderly step-father was seldom able to work in the shipyards. Their flat consisted of a kitchen and one other room. The lavatory, which was downstairs, was used by eleven people.

With the phoney war over, Leo enrolled in the army, joining the Royal Signals. He went in as a Private, and came out as an acting Major. He had a good war. But because there was such a shortage of signals officers, he was unable to return to 'civvie street' until November 1947. Immediately afterwards he went to work for the Inland Revenue, but was determined above all to complete the education that a mixture of war, the need to earn a wage, and the rigidities of the pre-war class structure had

4

interrupted. Blair enrolled as a law student at Edinburgh University from where he graduated in 1952. Leo Blair was now motoring up the social scale. He was appointed a tutor in the Law Department, wrote a PhD, and a promising career as an academic was beckoning.

He had also married and started a family. His bride to be, Hazel McLay, was the daughter of a small Glasgow businessman who owned a few butchers shops. She was a shy, slight, demure woman who came originally from a small 'c' conservative protestant farming family in Donegal. While her husband was away pursuing his career, she raised the family with stoicism and good humour, instilling in all of them a sense of family loyalty and duty that has endured. She was also possessed of a deep social conscience, caring passionately about the suffering of others less fortunate than her family. They had three children; Bill is the eldest, then came Tony three years later, and Sarah the youngest was born three years after that. They all followed in their father's footsteps and became lawyers. Bill is now a Queen's Counsel specialising in banking law, while Sarah works in legal publishing. In one of those odd coincidences, Tony Blair has produced a carbon copy of his own family. He and Cherie (also a lawyer) had two sons, Euan and Nicholas, and then a daughter, Kathryn, but each spaced two years apart.

But the rags to riches story of a young man pulling himself up by his bootstraps to take his place in middle class society is more complicated than that. It is also etched with extraordinary personal sadness and pain. Leo, who was born in August 1923, was dumped when he was a small child on a Mr and Mrs James Blair who lived on the Clyde. His real mother, Celia Ridgeway, was a music hall dancer, occasional actress, and, during the First World War, a voluntary nurse. After he had been left with the Blairs, Leo saw his real mother only once more, when he was thirteen. His mother had come from a wealthy West Sussex landowning family, marrying first when she was seventeen. From that marriage came two daughters, Jenefee and Pauline. Pauline Harding, now nearly ninety, lives in Ealing, West London where she still keeps a photograph of her mother – and Tony Blair's true paternal grandmother – on her mantelpiece.

> Mother was always away and she didn't often answer our letters. Our father was wicked to her. He used to knock her about, though I suppose he was fed up with her carrying on.[1]

Her 'carrying on' led to the break up of that marriage. She remarried. Her second husband, Hugh Wilson, was a commercial photographer in Ealing, but Pauline remembers how that marriage went the same way as the first.

> He grew more and more upset because he knew she was having affairs. Then we heard that our little brother Leo was born, and Hugh knew it couldn't be his. It was rotten for him and so he divorced her and moved out.[2]

Leo was the product of a liaison with an actor, Charles Parsons, who was known on the stage – and to his friends – as Jimmy Lynton. He and Celia Ridgeway toured the regional theatres, Jimmy Lynton doing comedy, Pierrot performances and straight acting. Leo Blair was born in Filey, Yorkshire. When he was three, his parents formalised their relationship and Celia Ridgeway embarked upon her third marriage. But Leo was now long settled into his life with his foster parents, so that his real parents could pursue their peripatetic lifestyle unhindered.

None of this was known to any of Leo Blair's children until midway through Tony Blair's leadership campaign in 1994. It was a bombshell to the family. When one journalist contacted Bill Blair about what had been reported, he replied 'the names Charles Parsons and Jimmy Lynton don't mean a thing to me.' The article was based on an interview with Pauline whom Leo Blair had last heard from before the onset of war. It is hard to exaggerate the sense of shock that he must have felt as Leo read the *Daily Mail* piece. The dust and cobwebs had been blown from a chapter of his life that he had buried in his subconscious. He now found these hidden memories splashed across the pages of a national newspaper. But what was reported was only a part of an incredible story.

Leo Blair, having not told his children about his background, would not speak to journalists as they pressed for details about his parents. But his reticence can now be explained for there was much that Leo did not know himself until he was reunited with his half-sister in the latter part of 1994.

When Leo was a child growing up on the Clyde, there may not have been visits from his blood relations, but there was a regular exchange of correspondence. His parents and half-sisters would send birthday cards and presents, and gifts would arrive at Christmas too. They even exchanged Easter cards. His real parents would also send him a modest amount of money. The young Leo kept these reminders of his real family in a biscuit tin under his bed. It was a collection of letters, mementos, cards and photographs that he had built up over the years.

But on one home visit during the war, Leo went to the biscuit tin to find the contents had gone. His step-mother had burnt everything in a bid to remove all trace of Leo's real background just after he had enlisted. When he challenged her to explain what had happened, she explained that she was in effect his real mother as she had reared him from when he was a tiny baby. Leo Blair, now a slight, frail man with a deep throaty voice, and an accent that bears the imprint of the many places he has lived – part Scottish, small part Geordie, but unmistakably educated – talks about this traumatic episode with remarkable compassion and understanding. 'You have to understand,' he says in a gentle and almost soothing tone, 'that she had had two miscarriages, and had come to realise eventually that she was never going to have a child of her own. My step-mother wanted me for herself without the constant reminder that I was in fact someone else's son.'[3]

Then something else happened that seemed to confirm to him that his step-mother was justified in her actions. During the war, the stream of letters dried up. There was no explanation given and none sought. Not another word of communication was heard from either his parents or his half-sisters. Leo concluded that he had simply been forgotten. 'I thought they had lost interest in me', he says without emotion, but with unintentional poignancy. As a foster child farmed out to another family it must have been an easy and obvious conclusion to reach. Why after all, the foster child must think, would you dump me if you truly loved me. And not wanting to upset his foster mother he never went in search of his roots. A year after he returned from the army in 1948, Leo changed his name by deed poll from Leo Augusta Parsons, to Leo Charles Lynton Blair. In his surname at least he had eradicated his past, if not in the middle names.

Those names were drawn from both his father's real name, Charles Parsons, and stage name, Jimmy Lynton. Both were passed on to Tony, but without any explanation. Those two names were the only reminder, the only clue, as to Leo's background. But having read the *Daily Mail* article, arrangements were made for Pauline Harding to meet her half-brother. They met at the home of Leo's eldest son, Bill, in Islington. Also present was Jenefee, who died a few months later, early in 1995, and the Blair children. It was a strange and emotional reunion. For Leo it was the awkward rediscovery of a family that he had consigned to the deepest recess of his mind. For Leo's children, it was not so much a rediscovery as a discovery. Two elderly ladies of whom they had known nothing were suddenly in Bill Blair's drawing room piecing together a family history that the Blair children had hitherto thought unremarkable. But what Leo Blair heard that day explained something that had lain unexplained and uninvestigated for almost fifty years.

Leo learnt that the reason that he never heard again from his real family was because of something else that his step-mother did in those fraught years during the war. As she came to terms with the fact that she had now passed the age when it was possible for her to have a child of her own, so she systematically set about making sure that Leo belonged to nobody else. At the same time as burning all his correspondence that he had faithfully kept in his biscuit tin, she wrote to Celia Ridgeway and Charles Parsons to inform them that their son had gone missing, and was presumed lost in action. It was news that his real parents would have greeted with a mixture of upset, and perhaps even relief – after all his mother had visited him only once, and but for the ritual sending of cards, there was little to suggest that they had made much emotional room for him in their lives. But the one feeling that would not have emerged was surprise. In wartime many thousands of families across the land were drawing the curtains early after receiving that knock on the door that told them that a loved one had died in action. And so Leo's real parents pulled down the blinds on the son they had abandoned. They mourned his loss, but, as Mrs Blair had correctly assessed, they sought to find out no more. For half a century his real family thought he was dead; for half a century Leo Blair thought they had abandoned him.

For a man entering his seventies this has been an extraordinary amount to come to terms with. Stones have been overturned in his life that have lain undisturbed for half a century simply because of the success and fame of his middle child. But if there is hurt, bitterness, betrayal even, then these emotions are brilliantly concealed. Leo Blair has an armful of reasons to resent both the actions of his real parents and the deceit of his foster parents. But this small, slightly frail old man has no time it would seem for such things: his dominant feelings are relief and indeed happiness. He is relieved that at last he has come to understand why after the war he never heard from his real parents again, and happy to find there is an older half-sister who can paint in parts of his life story that he should have known about but never did.

When Leo got married after the war, home was a modest bungalow in Edinburgh's Paisley Terrace. Bill and Tony were brought up there while Leo Blair was a tutor at Edinburgh University's law department. But when Tony was only eighteen months old, Leo was offered a job that he could not, and would not, turn down. He had been offered a more senior academic post at Adelaide University in Australia. They lived in the Southern hemisphere for nearly four years (Sarah, the youngest, was born there) before Leo decided to return, this time to another teaching job, at Durham University.

With social elevation came political conversion; Leo left behind his pre-war radicalism and switched his support to the Conservative Party. The experience of the Cold War, and the recognition of what was happening in the gulags in Stalin's Russia forced many erstwhile communists to re-evaluate their politics. That, combined with the self-reliant 'can-do' enthusiasm which he found in Australia, brought him into close affinity with the right in British politics.

And in Durham, Leo was branching out both professionally and politically. Having taught law since graduating, he wanted to practice, and in 1961 he was called to the bar. The same year he was made chairman of the Durham Conservative Association. The family had by now moved into a flat in a house within the precincts of the Cathedral. Leo was a meritocrat who saw the keys to social mobility lying in education, and both sons' names were put down for the Choristers School attached to the Cathedral.

Leo was the classic ambitious, self-made-man Conservative. Tony Blair has described him as

> a gut Conservative. He disliked the patrician Tory Party. He was keen on the Thatcher revolution. I understood where my father was coming from because he was totally self-made. The sort of Tory represented by Norman Tebbit I completely understand and I understand where they come from and why they believe what they believe. In a sense they were the first generation to be helped by a more collective society, but then rebelled against it, and started to believe it was holding people back, and in some senses they were right.[4]

For this ambitious young father the sky seemed the limit. Leo Blair had been made chairman of the Durham Conservative

Association, and was becoming one of the leading Tories in the North East. He was in demand as an after-dinner speaker and was a betting certainty to secure the nomination for the nearby parliamentary constituency of Hexham. Blair remembers barely seeing his father in the early years.

> Dad had a flourishing legal business and was always lecturing around the country. He was also an astute self-publicist, appearing regularly on regional television. I am sure I saw less of him then than my children see of me now.

That he barely saw his father in his early years did not deter Tony Blair from entering politics, but it would later make him acutely aware of the importance of spending whatever free time he had at home with his children. Conservative politicians passing through the North East would stay with the Blairs – some of them, like Michael Spicer, are still in the Commons, although apparently none has made the connection between Leo Blair the aspiring Tory and the boy whom they met in Durham who has gone on to become the Leader of the Opposition. Leo was very much the coming man. Extrovert, charming and bursting with energy, he seemed to be the model Conservative, a walking advertisement for social mobility and on a trajectory that made thoughts of reaching high office seem not only plausible but probable.

The Choristers School is set in a large sturdy medieval building just a short walk across the cobbles from the imposing nine-hundred-year-old cathedral. It has been in that spot, serving the cathedral with choir boys, since pre-Reformation days. Tony Blair was very much at home there. One of the masters who taught him says that the thing everyone who taught Blair remembers about him was his smile. 'He had an almost impish smile; it could light up a room. And when I see him now on television, that smile has not gone.' The young Tony was much more outward going than his older brother, Bill, who had also been at the school. The dark-haired – and much shorter – older brother was less extrovert and flamboyant, playing his cards close to his chest, although academically bright. Tony by all accounts was the model well-rounded pupil. He played cricket for the first XI, and rugby for the first XV; he acted in school productions, sang in the choir, gained a good grounding in Latin and stood out from the herd.

But while Tony Blair was an impressionable ten-year-old at the Choristers School, disaster struck, turning the world of this ambitious family upside down. His father had suffered a massive stroke and had to be rushed to hospital. That morning the young day-boy was dropped off by his anxious mother. 'Please will you look after him?' she said to the headmaster, Canon John Grove. 'We simply don't know what is going to happen to Leo.' As she rushed to be at his hospital bedside, it was left to Canon Grove to explain to Tony what had happened to his father. Canon Grove recalls that, while the young boy was deeply upset, he showed a control of his emotions that belied his years. Later that morning he led Tony into his book-lined study, which is at the back of the school overlooking the gardens and the banks of the river. After sitting the boy down in one of the two armchairs in the room to talk about what the ramifications might be, they both knelt and said prayers together. That afternoon Blair's mother returned to the school to pick up her son. Blair remembers it vividly.

> We were outside playing games when the gate opened and my mother came rushing over. 'The news is better,' she said. 'He's going to be all right. He's going to live.'

Canon Grove has no doubt that this whole experience had a profound impact on Blair, bringing him into contact with the power of religious faith for the first time, a faith that, although it has flickered, has never been extinguished and which now burns brightly.

But what none of them knew that day was what kind of life Leo would be able to lead, and what impact his illness would have on the rest of the family. It was catastrophic.

> We are a very closely knit family. But it was as though all the security that as a youngster you take for granted and think will be there for ever had been shattered in an instant. On an emotional level, I was suddenly made aware that nothing is permanent. You think as a child your parents are indestructible; that they will live for ever. But there was my father, unable to speak, having been lucky to survive.

In fact it would be another three years before Leo regained the power of speech, and, for a man who had made his living out of the oratorical skills of a barrister and lecturer, this was a devastating blow. Financial security went the same way as the emotional blanket that had enveloped the family until the illness. Tony's mother had never worked – and Leo was adamant that she would not start now. 'He had very fixed ideas about that sort of thing,' recalls Blair, 'and even though she wanted to get a job to tide the family over this difficult period, he wouldn't hear of it.' The family had by now moved to a modern detached house, which in estate agents' argot might just be described as an 'executive-style' house, on the outskirts of Durham. The four-bedroomed house in Hill Meadows is a trim, unflashy property, in a street full of other similar houses. It was a comfortable family home, but there was nothing grand about it.

Hazel was the foil to Leo's confident, extrovert and thrusting manner. Tony Blair adored his mother, and he says now that she was the cement that kept the family together and so close, particularly during the upheavals of Leo's illness. Children have very little sense of comparative wealth. They don't think in terms of the aristocrat in his castle being wealthier than the manual worker in his council house. But what children are aware of is any sudden change in their own domestic arrangements. And Blair was acutely aware of the financial straits constraining the family. New school uniforms became hand-me-downs, treats became more rare and foreign holidays that had been planned were shelved as the family struggled to meet their existing commitments. Blair is careful not to exaggerate the privations suffered:

> We were never poor, but it was a big change from what had gone before. And I suppose it made me aware that there were lots of people who, for whatever hardships we might have been suffering, were a lot worse off than us.

Unable to work, Leo Blair would never have been able to afford the fees by himself to keep Bill and Tony at Fettes College in Edinburgh, but Hazel Blair's father stepped in to pay the bulk of the fees, and Tony himself won a modest scholarship.

But it wasn't always obvious that the young Blair would go his own way politically. Just before he left the Durham Choristers School the masters organised a mock election to coincide with the 1966 general election. So while Blair's current deputy, John Prescott, was standing in his first proper parliamentary election as the Labour candidate in Southport, the precocious thirteen-year-old was the Conservative candidate at his prep school's mock election! But on polling day itself Blair was sick and someone else had to stand in and wear the blue rosette. Canon Grove recalls the episode with a broad grin: 'I think the fates intervened and said to the young Blair "You can be a Conservative this far, but no further." '

Blair fitted in easily at the Choristers School and was happy there, but the illness of his father dominated the home life of Blair and his older brother, Bill, and younger sister, Sarah. Leo's political ambitions had been dashed. And instead of being the patriarch who seemed to be heading for the stars, he was stuck at home, unable to work and frustrated beyond imagination, as everything he had worked towards had turned to dust. He was a year off his fortieth birthday. From that moment on, Leo Blair would have to learn to transfer his ambitions to his three children. Throughout all this, Hazel, the practical and down-to-earth daughter of a Glasgow butcher, nursed him patiently and lovingly, but, just as Leo was starting to show signs of improvement, so Tony's younger sister fell seriously ill. Sarah, who was yet to reach her teens, was diagnosed as having a form of infantile rheumatoid arthritis, called Still's disease. She spent two years in hospital as doctors battled to stabilise her condition using toxic immuno-suppressive drugs which have other side effects. The disease erodes the cartilage and eventually burns out the joints. And now, although only in her thirties, her health has never really returned and she has already had to undergo a hip-replacement operation.

Blair smarts at the suggestion made by detractors that because he went through public school, Oxbridge and the Bar his was the archetypal silver-spoon upbringing.

People read that I went through the private system, finishing at Oxford, and think that it must have been a bed of roses. Don't get me wrong, it was a happy childhood, but it also seemed as though I was spending every spare minute in Durham hospital, visiting either my father or sister . . . and there was a lot of worry and uncertainty attached to that.

A carefree childhood it wasn't, but no-one who knew Blair from that period believes it overburdened him or dragged him down. There was a well developed serious side to him, yes. But the testimony of those who knew him suggests that he never lost a sense of fun or the ability to enjoy life. According to one friend, it was not that he was frivolous, it was just that he had a sense of perspective.

At Fettes College in Edinburgh, the scholarship boy found himself in a completely alien world. Like many thirteen-year-olds leaving home for the first time to go away to board, he had to cope with all the usual upheavals of packing a trunk and learning that what limited emotional comfort there was would come from a matron, not his mother and father. His brother, Bill, was

15

already at the school, but that aside there was nothing else to remind him of the human warmth of home. Fettes College has often been described as 'Eton in a kilt'. But it wasn't the great Scottish landowners who sent their children to the school, it was more for Edinburgh's merchant class. The school perched ostentatiously on a hill imperiously looking down on the surrounding area is an extraordinary architectural confection, combining the building styles of a Loire chateâu, Bedlam and Disneyland rolled into one. It is a dizzying mass of spires and domes.

But when Tony Blair arrived there in 1966 it was a school locked in a time warp. As one of Blair's contemporaries of the period put it, 'Fettes hadn't accustomed itself to the idea that it was no longer training boys to go out and run an empire or fight on the Western Front'. It was not uncommon for public schools in the mid-1960s to offer a harsh environment, but Fettes was more backward than most. There were rules for everything. Rules laying down how many buttons on your chocolate and magenta blazer had to be done up, rules setting out at what age you could walk with your hands in your pockets, rules forbidding any pupil to walk on the grass, rules decreeing how short hair had to be cut. But there was one practice above all that shocked the fresh-faced thirteen-year-old when he arrived, and would have a profound impact on the young Blair's views on authority – and that was fagging.

The school was divided into six houses, and he was sent to 'Kimmerghame'. It was a primitive place. The large three-storey stone house with the school crest – a bee with the motto 'industria' beneath it – built into the front wall, had been put up at the turn of the century and had changed little in the intervening years. There were no carpets, and the walls were whitewashed. It was cold and draughty. Blair shared his dormitory with about fifteen other boys. Privacy amounted to two pieces of vertical hardboard and a metal bar across the top holding the makeshift walls in place, in which space there was enough room for a bed and chest of drawers. The boys called them horse-boxes. Kimmerghame is about three hundred yards down the hill from the main school in the south-west corner of the school grounds. But it wasn't the spartan conditions or the unmodernised building that Blair found unacceptable, it was the extraordinary practice of fagging, which was the one part of the furniture of public school life that Blair resented bitterly.

It still brings back uncomfortable and pained memories for the Labour Leader; one of the aspects of school life he displays a marked reluctance to discuss. Senior boys or prefects were entitled to march into dormitories or study areas and shout 'Fag!', and the juniors would be expected to drop whatever they were doing and jump. Blair was a 'dedicated' fag to one of the house and school prefects, Mike Gascoigne, who is now the senior partner in an eminent Edinburgh law firm. Gascoigne who thought 'it was damned useful' that if you had to see a master, you could instantly call on a fag to come and polish your shoes, had no doubts about the worth of the system. The idea was that juniors learnt discipline and a sense of service. He explained what Blair, the fag, had to do:

> They were generally fairly light duties. Blair would clean my shoes, blanco my army belt and polish the brass on it. If I couldn't see my face in it, he would have it thrown back at him. He would also, if it was a games afternoon, lay out my rugger kit on the bed for me, or my whites if it was cricket. I would also have him run errands for me, so he would take messages down to the housemaster, or to other parts of the school. We would also summon fags like Blair to the prefects' room. There was always a requirement for toast, but we insisted that it had to be one inch thick, no thinner no thicker, with lashings of butter and marmalade. And Blair would steam into the adjoining kitchen where he made particularly good toast, and would also brew us up powdered coffee. [5]

Gascoigne remembers Blair as being a model fag.

He was a fresh-faced boy with a willing disposition. He was cheerful, not mopey like so many other juniors who had left home for the first time. And there was never any truculence or unwillingness: he was willing and efficient.

All boys were called by their surname, and prefects had to be addressed as 'sir'. Blair fagged for Gascoigne for two terms before the older boy left Fettes to go to university. But there was also a darker side to fagging, for prefects were empowered to thrash the younger boys, almost at will, and acted as judge, jury and executioner of the punishment.

The new boy was deeply unhappy and found himself on the wrong end of a prefect's caning on a number of occasions. And although Gascoigne says he can't ever recall having had cause to beat Blair, that is not how the Labour Leader remembers it. Eventually Blair grew so unhappy and felt so powerless to change anything that he packed his bags and ran away from school. It resulted in his father being summoned to see the headmaster, with Blair's father explaining the source of his son's unhappiness, and the headmaster expressing concern that while Blair was bright, he had to knuckle under and accept the school's disciplinary regime.

Blair looks back on the period with toe-curling horror. He was miserable beyond belief, and found the cheerful 'gung-ho' barbarism of people barely four years his senior horrifying. He begged to be moved from this house, away from the petty rules and summary justice. Needless to say Blair's recollection of his life as a fag could not be more different from Gascoigne's. It would be another twenty-five years before the two, oppressor and oppressed, were to see each other again. Blair, now a member of the Shadow Cabinet, had been invited to speak as guest of honour at a function organised by an Edinburgh lawyers' dining club. He had his revenge. Early on in the evening he had spotted someone in the audience whom he recognised. Eventually the penny dropped that this was the prefect from Fettes: it was Gascoigne. And in a departure from his text, Blair spoke of how pleased he was to see so many people whom he recognised, and in particular someone from his alma mater. Blair pointed to Gascoigne and, to general amusement, expounded humorously on the rigours he had endured as Gascoigne's fag.

In the highly disciplined and structured environment of an old-fashioned and rigid public school, Blair had started to question, and very quickly he was set on a collision course with authority. He now jokes that his opposition to fagging and the petty rules that strangled individuality was his first act as a modernising politician.

At school I was somewhat rebellious and I questioned things. And I always questioned things. I was never an out-and-out rebel, but I was a rationalist in the sense that, if certain things were wrong, I would say so.

A close friend of Blair's at the time, Nick Rydon, recalls that the school was like a prisoner-of-war camp: 'Frankly, when we were there at the end of the 1960s it was easier for a Westerner to travel unhindered across the Soviet Union than it was for a Fettesian to get into the centre of Edinburgh.'[6] The school had a twelve-foot perimeter wall, and, just to deter any would-be Steve McQueens from attempting a great escape, the college authorities would occasionally pull surprise assemblies, where the bell would ring unexpectedly after lessons, and everyone had to gather for roll call. Rydon recalls how they went once to play a hockey match against a borstal team in Rumbling Bridge, Clackmannanshire. After the game the students from one of Scotland's premier public schools were told they should stay behind and talk to the cream of Scotland's young criminal fraternity. Comparing notes, the borstal boys were aghast at how much stricter and more repressive the regime was at Fettes!

In that context Rydon says he and Blair, and others like them, 'either rebelled and kicked against the system or went stark raving mad.' Blair eventually succeeded in moving out of the old-fashioned school house where he had been a fag to one that had been purpose built. In terms of Fettes it was trailblazing, heralding an approach to public school education that is now the norm. Out went some of the more ludicrous rules, and in came a more liberal regime under which academic excellence was given the highest priority. Arniston House under the headship of Dr Eric Anderson seemed to usher in a realisation that perhaps it was time for Fettes to move into the second half of the twentieth century. But that didn't stop Rydon and Blair from sitting in Arniston and imagine re-enacting scenes from Lindsay Anderson's cult film *If*, which had just been released. In it, a group of disaffected public schoolboys break into the college's armoury, and lead an armed insurrection against the school authorities, gunning down and blowing up the masters in the school quad. Fettes too had more than a hint of the imaginary school in that film, with its combined cadet force which was compulsory for the first two years, which Blair, like all the other boys, went through.

The alternative after those two years was to do community work via a scheme called 'outside service'. Whether it was because of Blair's burgeoning social conscience, or whether it was an easy way out of the square-bashing and gun-stripping, the teenager chose to help the less fortunate. But Blair also immersed himself in the work that the Chaplain of the college did to help the poor in Edinburgh. The Very Reverend Ronald Selby Wright, a former Moderator of the Church of Scotland, ran summer camps for children from the City's Canongate slums, and Blair was one of his volunteer helpers.

In many ways Fettes bears obvious comparison with that other celebrated Scottish public school, Gordonstoun. With the publication of Jonathan Dimbleby's authorised biography, it became apparent that the heir to the throne spent a miserable few years. But at Gordonstoun the strict disciplinary regime was the product of an ideology of how to turn a child into a man. The school's founder, the late Kurt Hahn, had clear ideas about how to shape and mould a young person. The Hahn philosophy was that you educated the whole child in mind and body, while teaching the individual the need to serve others. At Fettes, there was no such idealism in the school's approach to discipline. Strict rules, rigidly enforced were there simply because they had always been there.

Blair's housemaster at Arniston, Dr Anderson (who also taught at Gordonstoun, which could give him the unique distinction of having taught both the future King and the future Prime Minister), recalls the errant pupil with affectionate exasperation.

> He was unforgettable. He was one of those people whose presence in the room was always noticeable. At times a pain in the neck, but fundamentally great fun to have around. He was intensely argumentative and every school rule was questioned. He could uphold his side of the debate about the rights and wrongs of everything better than any boy in the school. I think I would have guessed that he would become a top barrister in his time, but not that he would go into the Labour Party. [7]

Indeed, many of Blair's skirmishes with the powers that be resulted in further clashes with the school establishment. Another contemporary remembers how the other boys all thought Blair was rather brave in his blatant challenges to authority. Alastair Campbell, now an Edinburgh lawyer, by virtue of the closeness of names in the alphabet sat next to Blair in class.

> He thought for himself which, you have to understand, was something that was rather frowned upon. He was no respecter of authority, which in its own way was admired by all the other boys in the class. His hair was always a bit too long, but never outrageously so, and he would look scruffy. He would sit with either shoulders slouched or his head cocked back. He really knew how to show that he was pissed off with the masters without actually saying so. [8]

But for all the pettiness of Fettes, Blair came eventually to enjoy his time there. He and Dr Anderson (for whom Blair had the greatest respect, believing here was one master who recognised that public schools must either change and modernise, or wither and die) were to work together extremely closely on many of the school drama productions that the college undertook. While still only fifteen he won the part of Mark Antony in *Julius Caesar*. From there he went on to play the lead in R.C. Sherriff's First World War drama, *Journey's End*. The school magazine, *Fettesian,* noted approvingly that the college had been 'very fortunate in having so experienced an actor as Blair for this central figure.' He also sang tenor, performing pieces of Mozart during the Founder's Eve concert in 1968. His former music teacher Michael Lester-Cribb recalls: 'Certain members of staff found him rather trying. But I found his attitude very refreshing and thought him a rather stimulating person to have around the school. Everyone knew who he was even if they didn't have direct contact with him.'[9]

Another close friend of Blair's at Fettes was Chris Catto who is now a doctor in Folkestone. It was while he was staying at Catto's parents' house in Forfar during the summer holidays that he became friendly with a girl a year younger than him, Anji Hunter – she was fifteen. She came from what can only be described as an exotic colonial background. Her father was a rubber plantation boss in what was then Malaya, and when the family moved back to Scotland when Anji was ten, their Chinese servant came too. The family lived in a mansion with extensive grounds in Brechin near the Cattos and she and Blair became close friends. And, although educated at the sister school to Fettes, St Leonard's, she spoke in the rounded tones of someone who has seldom left the Home Counties. She was a free spirit with a zest for life. Attractive, but not beautiful, striking but not overwhelming, Anji and Blair were never boyfriend and girlfriend, but they were to lay the foundations of a friendship that summer which has developed into an exceptional closeness. Twenty-five years on from when they first met, she is now the head of his private office in the Palace of Westminster in what has become a fascinating political relationship.

Blair was also remembered at school for his easy charm, and relaxed manner. It was not surprising in that context, therefore, that, when the school decided it should experiment with co-educationalism, the first girl it admitted into the sixth form should end up as Blair's girlfriend. Amanda Mackenzie-Stuart, daughter of the High Court judge and cross-bench peer, Lord Mackenzie-Stuart, remembers Blair warmly:

> It was the first time I had felt that sort of thing and, all right, I was his girlfriend. He was so bright, so engaging – and very funny. He could get away with teasing the masters, and, looking back, I suppose it was because he was cleverer than most of them. We spent a lot of time together. We used to go for long walks, go for a coffee in a café and talk for hours. He was not really into politics at that time – it was more Led Zeppelin and Cream – but I was never surprised that he joined Labour. That was always there.'[10]

The two are still close friends, having gone to each other's wedding and kept in touch ever since. Blair was also taken under the wing of Lord Mackenzie-Stuart, who invited Blair back to his home for dinner, where the judge and the sixth form student would sit up late discussing politics and ideas. But for all that Blair took part in school debates no-one remembers him as a budding politician. In addition, his irreverence and pushing at the boundaries of what was permissible and what was not should not lead to the conclusion that he did not fit in. Blair was not an outsider in a strange and alien world; he protested within the confines of acceptability. He was a rebel who had yet to find his cause. No-one from Fettes can remember Blair having any over-all shape to his political views. He hated petty rules, but wasn't anti public school *per se*. He was interested in Third World issues, and had a strong sense of injustice, but that had not converted him to socialism.

23

Blair stayed on at Fettes after his A levels to study for Oxbridge. This surprised some of his friends who were starting at Scottish universities because, while he had been thought of as bright, he wasn't thought of as that bright. He won a place at St John's to read law.

For the aspirant politician there is nowhere better than either Oxford or Cambridge. All the routes are well signposted, the pathways to glory well travelled. For the putative Labour MP, there is a whole series of musts at Oxford: a prominent role in the Oxford Union, ideally ending up as President. There are the student newspapers, *Cherwell* and *Isis,* where thought-provoking articles on this or that aspect of Government policy have been a good way of getting noticed. Then there is the University Labour Club, or, of course, if their concerns seem a tad trivial or disconnected from the real world, there is the Oxford Labour Party, which takes in the working-class areas around Cowley and the car plant there, which at the time Blair was at Oxford was a hotbed of political activism.

Blair the undergraduate went into the Union only once. He never wrote for *Cherwell,* although one of the parties that he threw was apparently such 'riotous good fun' that the editor thought it worth a mention in the gossip column. He was never a contributor to *Isis,* but one of his productions did make it into its illustrious pages: 'The St John's revue was written, produced and performed by people with little or no experience in this medium, and bearing this in mind it was really quite a remarkable achievement . . . Blair being particularly good in his more extrovert, almost slapstick roles.'[11]

Student politics at that time was dominated by the campaign to force the University authorities to provide a united students' union building. But the activities of the Labour club were a complete turn off:

> I couldn't be bothered with that. I have always had a fairly practical turn of mind and student politics at Oxford, at any rate, never seemed very practical. Instead I generally

enjoyed myself, performed in revues, sketches and played music. I have always been crazy about rock music.[12]

Needless to say he didn't join the local Labour Party either. In fact there is precisely nothing from what Blair joined or did at Oxford to suggest that he had even the faintest glimmer of a political ambition in him. There are no tales of Blair sitting with friends writing on the back of an envelope, as Michael Heseltine reportedly did when he was at Pembroke College, Oxford, his timetable for political advancement culminating in being made Prime Minister. And certainly he didn't make as many ripples in the River Isis as his contemporary of the period, Benazir Bhutto, who was the star of that generation of Oxford undergraduates.

Blair loathed the falseness and pretentiousness of many of those around him. He wanted no part in the affectations of the would-be prime ministers and was repelled by those who were so ambitious that you could smell it on their breath. That was not and never has been Blair's way. Looking back he says he felt as if he never really belonged at Oxford:

I think, like all big institutions, far from being intellectu-ally invigorating, it is actually rather stifling. There was very little room for fresh or original thought. And those that were thinking only seemed to be doing so as a means to further whatever career they intended to pursue. So when I look back at my time at Oxford I have extremely fond memories of the friends I made there, but all the time I was at Oxford I felt like an outsider.

Blair also met up at Oxford with Anji Hunter again. She was at the sixth-form college St Clare's studying for her A levels. It was through her that he met a strikingly beautiful woman, Susie Parsons, who some of Blair's contemporaries say looked like the actress Wynona Rider. The student from St Clare's was regarded by all Blair's male contemporaries as quite the best looking woman in Oxford, and was much coveted by the other men in college. They went out together for most of the first year, although Blair had a string of girlfriends during his undergraduate days. Blair was much sought after. Six feet tall, with clear blue eyes and athletically built, he has the classic broad shoulders tapering down to a narrow waist. Then he had a mop of thick sandy brown hair, which nowadays is rather thicker at the back of his head than it is at the front. One friend remembers the amusement caused when the Blair family made a visit. All the other members of the family are a good six inches shorter than him, with black hair. Blair spent the rest of the term being ribbed that he must have been the product of the milkman. But there is one physical resemblance that Blair has with his father that is striking, and that is his smile.

One of the more intellectual students whom Blair went out with briefly was an American, Mary Harron, now a freelance television producer working in New York. She was the features editor on *Isis,* and knew all of the people who were on their way up the greasy pole. But, she said, Blair wasn't one of them. 'He didn't seem terribly ambitious, and certainly wasn't one of those trying to cut a dash in the political arena.' She remembers their brief relationship with affection.

> Even before he became an MP and famous I always thought of Tony as the only 'nice' person that I ever went out with at Oxford. He was very good looking, in a kind of sweet way, and wasn't at all predatory. He was very different from most of the guys I knew, but I guess I fell for him because he was cute. [13]

Blair's early days at Oxford were spent enjoying himself and doing what was required to get through the course work for his law degree. He took a lot of stick from friends for spending so much time poring over his books in the library. Marc Palley, Blair's best friend from Oxford (Blair was his best man and is godfather to one of Palley's children), recalls all this with a smile. 'He was very trendy with a vile synthetic skin coat. He worked hard, was a natural sportsman and had all the best looking women running after him. It would have been very easy to hate this guy.'[14] Blair had a full social life at St John's, as a prominent member of the Archery Club, which had absolutely nothing to do with bows and arrows and targets, but everything to do with having a good time. It was a glorified dining club which occasionally aped the antics of the Oxford of *Brideshead Revisited*. After one dinner they sat on the sixteenth-century ramparts throwing champagne glasses down on to the grass beneath. But Blair was never really part of that set, even though he had no difficulty fitting in from time to time.

His relationship with one girl landed him in trouble with the college authorities. St John's had strict rules on how long a member of the opposite sex was allowed to stay in the bedroom of a male undergraduate. He and Marc Palley were summoned by the senior and junior deans to answer the charge that women had been in their rooms beyond the witching hour. They produced as circumstantial evidence a lipstick that had been found in Blair's room. 'Oh, that's mine,' responded Blair with a completely straight face. Palley to this day insists, with a somewhat less straight face, that they were innocent of all charges! But Blair's frequent brushes with authority at Fettes had left him well equipped to deal with this minor incident. Palley and Blair became extremely close, later going on to share a house in Oxford in their final year together, and in London after they had both gone down.

Blair also played in a rock band, the Ugly Rumours. Mark Ellen, who went on to present BBC2's *The Old Grey Whistle Test* and now edits a rock magazine called *Mojo,* describes Blair's stage appearance in the sort of detail that Blair himself would probably rather forget:

> Tony Blair enters stage left. Reading from top to bottom he has the long hair with the rather severe fringe and a slightly medieval look about him. Sort of like the Three Musketeers. A T-shirt that can only be described as hoop

necked, possibly even trumpet sleeved which stopped just beneath the ribcage leaving a large acreage of rippling bare torso. And beyond that there were the obligatory purple loons, topped off by the Cuban heeled cowboy boots.[15]

His father recalled going to collect his son from Oxford and seeing an undergraduate with hair halfway down his back wearing a black coat with a scarlet lining. 'I wondered who the hell it was. Then he said, "Hi, Dad".'[16] He was recruited to the band by the guitarist Adam Sharples, now a rather serious minded economist at the Treasury who it is hard to believe ever did anything as frivolous as play in a rock band.

Blair's audition for the band took place in Adam Sharples's room in Corpus Christi. Sharples had seen Blair perform in the revues at St John's and thought here might be somebody who could lend a little glamour and presence to their somewhat lacklustre stage craft. Mark Ellen recalls: 'We were rather tragic, and had precisely zero presence on stage. We were yards of unconditioned hair in cowboy boots.' The night before the audition, Blair contacted Sharples to find out what music the band played. When he turned up the next day it was clear that Blair had been burning the midnight oil, as the lyrics to each of the songs had been painstakingly transcribed in longhand by the would-be lead singer. The rest of the group were astonished, but it was a typically Tony Blair thing to do: if you are going to do something, better do it well or not at all. Meticulous preparation and attention to detail would later become a hallmark of his political career. So Blair was seated in an armchair, while a microphone was plugged into Sharples's puny stereo system and he was asked to perform. Ellen remembers that Blair went through the whole routine of dancing and waving his hands in this small room overlooking the quad in Corpus Christi while Sharples played acoustic guitar, Jim Moon the drummer bashed an upturned green metal wastepaper basket and Mark Ellen played his bass guitar without amplification. The Rolling Stones it was not, but Blair got the job as lead singer.

The 'set' consisted of a mixture of laid back West Coast sounds, like the Eagles 'Take it Easy' and the Doobie Brothers' songs 'China Grove' and 'Long Train Running'. They did two Rolling Stones numbers: 'Honky Tonk Women' and the raunchy 'Live With Me'. The encore on the rare occasion that one was accorded the band was 'Johnny B. Goode'. Blair insists that no recordings of the band have survived (and other members of the band are saying that too), but at least one of those present at Blair's fortieth birthday party recalls Cherie playing a tape of a discordant rock band that seemed to be the Ugly Rumours. After Blair was elected Labour Leader and there was a surge of interest in his past as the lead vocalist in the Ugly Rumours, Blair sent Ellen a postcard with the simple message: 'You see, we've made it big at last.' Blair's role model in the band was Mick Jagger. He would strut on to the stage, à la Jagger, punching the air and wagging his finger at the audience. His performance was much admired. Another person who remembers it well is the junior Social Security Minister, Alistair Burt, who was a couple of years below Blair at St John's:

If you would have said to me that Tony Blair was going to become a rock star then I would have believed you – he had long hair, a shirt undone to his navel, and he did a terrific Jagger impression; if you had said to me that he was going to become the next leader of the Labour Party then I would have thought you were mad. But then if you would have said that I was going to end up as a Conservative minister, I wouldn't have believed that either![17]

Ellen, who had now started going out with Anji Hunter, remembers Blair's insistence on proper preparation getting them into trouble with the authorities at Corpus Christi before one of their gigs at the college: Blair insisted on a full rehearsal, and so a power cable was run down from a room in the college to an underground car park. The noise and vibration sent various members of the college into a rage, and the power was duly cut off. Ellen recalls him as being completely fearless and without embarrassment: at a concert in St John's the drummer lost all his kit into the audience, and, while the débâcle was sorted out, Blair did an impromptu stand-up routine to keep the jeering and booing students at bay. Their finest hour came at the Corpus Christi 'alternative' ball, which had been instigated by Adam Sharples in protest at the prices charged for the proper ball. There was a string quartet, a 'trad' jazz band and the Ugly Rumours. For a grand finale, Blair brought this strange amalgam of musicians of variable talent together for a joint rendition of Mick Jagger's 'Live With Me'.

But there were some of the trappings of being a rock star that Blair had nothing to do with. There was never any shortage of drugs in Oxford during the early 1970s. Like most universities in Britain at the time, there were extremely few people taking hard drugs, but it was almost impossible to get through college without having smoked at least one marijuana joint. One friend from that period said, 'It was hard to go to a party around Oxford without seeing someone in a corner rolling a joint and passing it around.' But Blair, unlike his Rhodes scholar Oxford predecessor Bill Clinton, not only never inhaled, he remarkably never put a spliff to his lips. He insists he never 'did' drugs: 'The one thing my father really drummed into me was never to take drugs . . . and anyway,' he said with a smile, 'I was doing so many other things that I never needed to.' Blair smoked nothing more heady than cigarettes, and because he was a hard-up student, they were mostly other people's. None of Blair's friends ever recall seeing him with a joint in his hands either. His student life seemed to be sex, no drugs and lots of rock and roll. 'I think wine, women and song would be a more discreet description,' says Geoff Gallop, an Australian Rhodes scholar who was studying politics, philosophy and economics at St John's with Blair, and who would play an important part in Blair's political development.

CHAPTER 2

Political Awakening

'To the University of Oxford I acknowledge no obligation; and she will as willingly renounce me for a son, as I am willing to disclaim her for a mother.'

Edward Gibbon (1737–1794)

For all the fun of wine, women and song, Blair was intellectually restless. His course in Jurisprudence made him work hard, but it failed to satisfy. He had no desire for the posturings of the Union, but he wanted something which would allow him to express what one Oxford contemporary remembers as 'an overdeveloped social conscience'. David Fursedon who was in St John's with Blair and later went on to share a flat in North London says, 'At Oxford he was listening to all sorts of ideas, and was very much an idealist believing naïvely in the absolute goodness of others. He was a bit of a bleeding-heart liberal.'[1] Through Blair's association with Geoff Gallop, who is now a Labour MP in Western Australia and still in close contact with the Labour leader, the undergraduate came into contact with a group of overseas students who were to satisfy Blair's thirst for ideas and discussion. Gallop was then a member of the International Marxist group, one of what used to be called the '57 Varieties' of Trotskyist groups that proliferated during the 1970s. Blair was never sufficiently interested in joining any of these organisations, but he was interested in the ideas they espoused. Blair is a voracious reader, and he read the various 'set texts' of Marx, Lenin and Gramsci that were *de rigueur* for any student revolutionary who wanted to talk about dialectical materialism and sound convincing, but nothing that he read at that stage led him into direct political activity.

Gallop and Blair had met through Blair's production of a comic revue in which the Rhodes scholar played the role of the archetypal drunken Aussie. Gallop then introduced Blair to another Australian, Peter Thomson. Thomson was an ordained priest, a radical theologian, thirty-six years old, a dab hand at tennis, a profound thinker and able to drink most of his younger undergraduate friends under the table. He was also slightly better off than his younger companions, so he became the provider of coffee, tea, cigarettes and intellectual stimulation. Thomson had come to St John's to fulfil a lifetime ambition to study theology at Oxford. He recalls meeting Blair and thinking of him as a lost soul:

He was a very sensitive person, and clearly someone who wanted to stand up for the underdog, but he found it difficult to abide all the stuffiness and posturing of Oxford, and I think his life kind of lacked purpose and direction. Beyond getting a degree, I don't think he knew what he was doing at Oxford, and I think he felt unsatisfied.[2]

Marc Palley was also a member of this group. Palley had come from a highly political background, but not in Britain. His father Ahrn Palley had been the sole white voice of opposition in the Salisbury Parliament when Ian Smith declared UDI from British rule for Rhodesia on 11 November 1965. His opposition on the day of UDI led to him being evicted by the Serjeant at Arms, and, as he was led away, he famously called out: 'This is an illegal assembly: God Save the Queen!' Another member was Olara Otunno, a practising Christian who went back to his native Uganda to become Foreign Minister and was a candidate for Secretary-General of the United Nations. What all these people with the exception of Tony Blair had in common was that they were all from overseas, and quite unaffected by the strictures of the English class system.

They were all left of centre, and they all (with the exception of Marc Palley who is a Jewish-born atheist) had to a greater or lesser extent an interest in Christianity. Thomson is a man of rare enthusiasm and charisma, and he became a sounding board for the younger students, particularly in matters theological. Blair's Christian education had been formal to the point of stifling. At Fettes every boy had to attend chapel twice a day and his best friend from school, Nick Rydon, remembered that if a boy had any religious conviction when he went there, the manner in which it was force fed would have been enough to squeeze the faith out of him. Christianity, Blair remembers, was an unfashionable thing to be interested in at Oxford. But Blair, for all the outward signs of 'trendiness', never did anything because it was 'in'; and, through the Svengali figure of Thomson, Blair's eyes were opened to a religious faith and an interpretation of the scriptures that were to transform his thinking. Thomson introduced Blair to the works of philosophers who sought to explain the 'social' side of Christianity. The bulk of these theologians had been writing in the 1930s and 1940s, like the Archbishop of Canterbury of that period, William Temple. Many of them were socialists as well, and they sought to explain faith in a demythologised sort of way. It was a period of great radicalism for English theology, and Blair was captivated. Thomson recalls:

His eyes were popping out of their sockets as he read all this stuff. You see, Blair had been exposed to Christianity as a young chap, but he never realised it had been put into a philosophical context, and I think it was through this holistic approach that Tony started to make sense of both his political and religious views.

The early 1970s also saw the start in Latin America of 'liberation theology', with Catholic, particularly Jesuit preachers changing their mission from one of simple religious enlightenment to social action and 'praxis'. Thomson would speak to Blair about how there was much more to Christianity than just the 'vertical beam' of faith that came down from the heavens, but the 'horizontal beam' too, which translated Christianity into the need for social change to tackle poverty and deprivation. Thomson also introduced Blair to the ideas of an obscure Scottish philosopher, John Macmurray.

Macmurray's books, like *Persons in Relation* and *The Self As Agent,* sought to marry socialism and Christianity. Blair became fascinated by his work and it introduced him to an idea that would later become central to his political thinking, the notion of 'community', as Thomson, now a fifty-eight-year-old cattle rancher in his native Australia explains:

> The idea of community started there, and it wedded beautifully with our concept of religion. What we were on about was developing community – a sense of co-operation rather than a debit and credit ledger thing: if you do this for me, then I'll do that for you, which is the general norm of society. We were trying to develop a sense of community where people were connected to something – that is, the welfare of one another – and, although that seems wishy-washy, it actually works. And it has a definite religious base.[3]

Spurred on by Thomson, whom Blair found 'spellbinding', a group of them travelled in 1974 to Scotland and met John Macmurray shortly before he died. These ideas find voice nowadays through the American Communitarian Movement, Amitai Etzioni. The central proposition is that individual rights and responsibilities must be properly balanced, and that this new settlement must take place in the context of the community. The significance of this in terms of traditional socialist thinking is that it marks a shift from the left's assumption that the state will always provide, towards an emphasis on voluntary action.

Coincidentally, Geoff Gallop, who then took an orthodox Marxist view that religion was a distracting opiate, nevertheless found that Macmurray was a key figure in his PPE studies. As Gallop studied Karl Marx's early works, it turned out that some of the first translations of Marx from German into English had

34

been done by Macmurray. Back in Oxford, Blair was prepared for confirmation by the assistant chaplain of St John's, the Reverend Graham Dow, now the Bishop of Willesden. It was a former Labour general secretary, Morgan Phillips, who said that socialism owed as much to Methodism as it did to Marx, and that is certainly true of the socialist approach that Blair would later develop. Blair is not a pulpit politician, although there are times when a certain piousness and 'preacheyness' takes hold. When he was made Leader his speech had overtones of the hymns 'Jerusalem' and 'I Vow to Thee, My Country' as phrases from these and other hymns were woven seamlessly into the text of his address. At the end of his speech he spoke of the importance that hope had played in South Africa: 'They have changed it through courage and compassion and intelligence; but most of all through hope, the small, broken moments of hope, that forever are worth an eternity of dull despair.'

But Blair the politician never saw the Church as another outlet for his political ambitions. He has never sought a seat on the General Synod and has never thought it his place to lecture Bishops on what they should be doing. His faith is private, but there is no doubt how important the teachings of Christ are in informing what he calls 'ethical socialism'. And there is no doubt how important his faith is on a day-to-day basis. He became at Oxford a practising Christian through intellectual commitment which ignited a lingering childhood faith. He still is.

Twenty years on there was a most vivid illustration of that Christian devotion midway through his leadership campaign in scenes that were both hilarious and tense. He had just attended a hustings meeting and it was early Sunday evening. As Blair came down from the rostrum, a gaggle of people were waiting to see him. But the normally courteous Blair was brusque. He told Anji Hunter that he wanted to leave Southport immediately. She rounded up the helpers and, with the Merseyside MP, Peter Kilfoyle, at the wheel of a rather dilapidated Ford Sierra, the reason became clear. Blair had not had a chance to go to church that morning and was anxious to get to Holy Communion. After driving a few miles, a church spire was spotted from the brow of a hill. It was some way in the distance and appeared to be surrounded by thick woodland. With the clock ticking ever closer towards 6.30, the time that the assorted brains of the Blair campaign had guessed the service would start, it was not long before they were completely lost. Kilfoyle executed U turns on motorways, he screeched round corners and at last the church hove into view. The relief on Blair's face was accompanied by hilarity. The church was in a village called Bickerstaffe. 'It must be Rodney's church,' said Kilfoyle (Rodney Bickerstaffe is the engaging deputy leader of the public service union, UNISON, and was a supporter of Prescott for the leadership). Blair rushed in just as the service was starting. When the vicar looked up and saw that among the dozen or so wizened matrons he also had the next leader of the Labour party in his congregation, he completely lost his place in the service. (While Blair prayed, his staff wandered around the churchyard, only to find that next to the gravestone of Agnes Bickerstaffe was the final resting place of a Jacob Prescott. Kilfoyle, not exactly oozing Christian compassion, murmured, 'And we'll bury them in the leadership contest too.')

Blair at Oxford was by now becoming much more sure of his left-of-centre view of politics. But, despite the turmoil of the final moments of Edward Heath's period in Downing Street, with the three-day week and the miners' strike, Blair was still not tempted into direct political activity beyond voting for Labour in the two 1974 general elections. But in the mid-1970s, as Blair's student days were drawing to a close, a new and dangerous political force had come on to the scene, the National Front. Feeding parasitically on unease stirred by the number of immigrants entering Britain from former Commonwealth countries, the NF sought to exacerbate those racial tensions. Counterdemonstrations were organised, and Blair went on a couple of them. It was not the height of political radicalism but it was Blair's first political activity. However, the political ingénue with his long hair and afghan coat was mistaken for a student revolutionary, and as Blair, Thomson, Gallop and others stood in front of a police line outside Oxford Town Hall, a group of policemen moved against them. According to Thomson, 'Tony was grabbed and physically picked up by the police, and thrown through the air like a leaf. He was incredibly shaken up by the whole affair – he had never experienced anything like it in his life.' Blair was roughed up by the police for doing nothing in particular and they all went back to Thomson's flat to recover, with Blair's respect for the law not exactly enhanced by what he had been through.

Blair left Oxford having gained an upper second and went home to Durham, with a place at Bar school fixed for the autumn. But it was a family in crisis that he found. His mother had been diagnosed earlier as having cancer of the throat, and her condition had suddenly deteriorated. Within two weeks of Blair's graduation from Oxford, she was dead. The sense of shock was profound. It had just seemed inconceivable to Blair that the woman who had held the family together when first his father and then his sister was ill would no longer be there to look after them.

It's a very strange experience that, even though it is obvi-ous that death must be a possibility, you somehow exclude it from your own mind when it's a part of your own family. So it came as a shock, even though, when looking back on it, it was absolutely crazy that it came as anything other than inevitable.[4]

Peter Thomson had stayed with the Blairs in Durham during his time in Britain. He says her death 'knocked the socks off Tony'. Thomson says that she was a very different character from Leo.

He was in some ways a hard man. He'd made his way in the world having pulled himself up by his bootstraps. He was very private and very contained and wouldn't talk

37

about emotions. Mrs Blair, on the other hand, was the sort of woman who you felt you wanted to hug after a short meeting . . . and it was absolutely clear that she doted on Tony and that Tony adored her. She also had a really deep social conscience and I think Tony has turned out to be the type of human being that she would have wanted him to be.

Leo remembers his son's reaction to her death: 'He was very solicitous towards me, very kind. He was a very loving son. His mother adored him.'[5]

In coping with the death of a loved one there is invariably a kaleidoscope of emotions – a feeling of loss, of distress, even of anger and betrayal. But Blair remembers in the midst of his profound grief feeling strangely galvanised.

I think the death of someone very close to you does act as a spur to you, because as well as your grief for the person your own mortality comes home to you. And you suddenly realise – which often you don't as a young person – that life is finite, so if you want to get things done you had better get a move on.

Blair acknowledges that the experience made him grow up quickly, and perhaps take a more serious view of life than many of his peers.

This sense of having to get a move on manifested itself in a practical way when he came down to London to study for his Bar exams. He moved into a basement flat in Ifield Road, Earls Court with his long-standing friend from University, Marc Palley, and resolved immediately that he wanted to become active politically. To join the Labour Party at that stage, one had to be a member of a trade union, but Blair managed to sign up even though it would be some years later before he joined the Transport and General Workers Union. Redcliffe Ward, which is one of the areas within Chelsea Labour Party, had grown dormant and inactive. One of the old-timers in the constituency, Sandy Pringle, decided it was time to breathe new life into it. Pringle sent out a mailshot to some people who had joined but had never been that involved. One of them was Tony Blair, and within a short period of time he soon found that the price of his enthusiasm was that he was co-opted into being ward secretary. He held this post for about a year. Palley, though sympathetic, never joined, and he watched in wonder as his friend would go out evening after evening irrespective of the weather to attend meetings and deliver leaflets. But Palley now noticed that there was a more serious and brooding side to Blair following the death of his mother. He would come home late and sit up reading the Bible in bed. The next morning Blair would be up at the crack of dawn so that he could keep abreast of his course work, and later, when he qualified as a barrister, his caseload.

The Labour Party that Blair joined had started to crumble. Even though Harold Wilson had won his fourth general election, and Labour were back in power, the moribund ward that Blair had joined was symptomatic of the state of the Party nationally. At the top Blair saw a governing body with ministers like Healey, Callaghan and Jenkins who were household names, but beneath them a party of activists that seemed to be a million miles away from what the Government of the day was doing, thinking and saying. And to avoid embarrassing policy defeats at Party conferences, the Party leadership came to rely ever more heavily on the block votes of the Union barons as the only means of keeping the much more radically left-wing grassroots at bay. Blair was never part of that radical London left that wanted to take control of the Labour Party from the leadership, and which found voice in Ken Livingstone's GLC, with its support for every trendy ginger group going. But he wasn't an apologist either for the way the Party's high command had turned a blind eye to what the foot soldiers were doing.

The Labour Government was lurching from crisis to crisis. It was governing with a wafer-thin majority. Within a year of Blair joining the Labour Party, Anthony Crosland, the intellectual giant of his generation, was declaring that the party was over for public expenditure and the creditors from the International Monetary Fund had moved in to cast a wary and damaging eye over the accounts. Blair thought the leadership had been negligent while the activists had gone off the rails. At a demonstration some years later Blair bumped into Sandy Pringle again. By now Blair was actively looking for a seat, but Pringle told him, 'There's no point touting yourself around the London constituencies, you don't wear the right badges in your lapel.' It was shrewd advice.

But after his bar exams, Blair delayed his search for a pupillage and went off to France for a few months. He left with no particular goal in mind other than to get a job, improve his French (he is fairly fluent) and have a good time. But he talks about the experience as being important in shaping a certain aspect of his political outlook. He worked first of all as a barman at the Hotel Suffren de la Tour very close to the Eiffel Tower, and then did some clerical work for one of France's biggest insurance companies. Britain was by then a full, if not an enthusiastic, member of the Common Market, having a year earlier voted in the referendum to stay inside the EEC. It meant that Blair was able to pitch up in France, without a work permit or anything else and seek employment. Blair says his French sojourn converted him to being an enthusiastic supporter of the European Community, although these views were so brilliantly camouflaged as to be unrecognisable when some years later he stood in his first parliamentary elections and apparently followed unquestioningly the party line that Britain should withdraw from the Common Market.

When Blair returned he fixed his mind on finding a set of chambers where he could advance his legal career. His political involvement was taking up an ever increasing amount of his time and this helped shape the direction in which he wanted his work as a barrister to develop. He applied to join the chambers of Alexander Andrew Mackay Irvine QC, at Number 2 Crown Office Row. Blair says the reason he applied to join Irvine's chambers was because he was a leading Labour lawyer, having done a lot of work for the unions and the Labour Party. That is a partial explanation. There was also a generous helping of 'old boys network' at play. A friend of Blair's father, Colin Fawcett, who was a silk on the Northern Circuit, asked Irvine if he would meet Blair. Blair sent Irvine his CV. 'I remember being not overly impressed. His qualifications were perfectly respectable, but there was nothing about him that stood out on paper.' Irvine also explained that he only ever took on one pupil each year, and he had just taken on a young Merseyside woman, Cherie Booth, whose CV positively shone, having been the cream of her year at the London School of Economics and having come top in the annual bar examinations, easily beating Blair.

But Irvine was so bowled over by Blair's enthusiasm – and desperation to get this particular pupillage – that after a short period of time in which he was subjected to Blair's persuasive charm, Irvine relented and took him on. Derry (as he is known to everyone) is a solidly built handsome man. He has thick, straight, dark brown hair brushed back, and he has the physical bearing of one who probably played as a rugby front row forward, although the lack of physical scars suggests otherwise. Irvine is flattering about Blair's skills and talents, but he had no idea what Blair's politics were when he took him on, and wasn't much interested.

> He was a brilliant lawyer. A complete natural. He had a tremendous talent for assimilating very quickly complex factual material and I have no doubt at all that he would be a QC by now if he'd stuck with the law. He was a fantastically fast gun on paper, producing high quality legal opinion with remarkable fluency and speed.[6]

Blair did some work in the industrial relations field, for unions and local authorities, but Irvine says that attempts to portray Blair as a 'Labour lawyer' are wide of the mark. 'He was an all-rounder,' he says, 'with a significant commercial practice.'

They worked together on a case in Louisiana, which involved

litigation concerning the export to the United States of a pre-fabricated town. Blair was also Irvine's junior on a huge case of litigation involving the Bank of Oman. The bank was owned by a wealthy Arab sheikh. Blair had done much of the paperwork on the case, but the court found against the bank, and Irvine suggested that Blair fly out to the Middle East to see the sheikh to determine whether he wanted to appeal against the court's decision. Blair flew out to Abu Dhabi alone, and was taken to the sheikh's palace by bodyguards with sub-machine-guns over their shoulders, in a bullet-proof Mercedes. Flanked by the four armed guards, Blair was taken into an enormous room with just a throne in it. The sheikh appeared and took his place on the throne. He looked down at the young English barrister and said in faltering English: 'Does the English legal system apply the principles of truth and justice?'

Blair, surprised at this, said, 'Yes, of course.'

At this, the sheikh waved his hand dismissively at Blair, and said, 'Then our cause will prevail.' The sheikh then ordered the bodyguards to escort the startled lawyer back to the airport. Blair flew back to England on the next flight.

Blair is flattering about the role that Irvine played in shaping him both politically and intellectually.

> His contribution to my intellectual development was enormous. I never quite engaged intellectually at Oxford and my schooling was very much the schooling that gets you through exams. You know, you can pass exams without really thinking.

Blair credits Irvine with teaching him how to think.

> He taught me how to analyse and confront problems and how to marshal arguments in debate. He showed me there was no point simply reading a book and reproducing its ideas, what was needed was the confidence to question them.

He was a hard task-master, always pushing Blair to the limit. He instilled in the young barrister the importance of meticulous preparation, something that has stayed with Blair at Westminster. He has also become the single most important figure in Blair's political career. If anyone is scratching around, looking for a mentor figure in Tony Blair's life, they need look no further than Derry Irvine. Blair still speaks to Irvine about twice a week, and the Blair family frequently take their holidays at Irvine's magnificent Scottish home in Clachan, Kintyre. All the way through Blair's rise in the Labour Party, Irvine has been a source of advice and support.

But his decision to take Blair on as a barrister also cast Irvine in a role that, despite his massive experience in both politics and the law, he had never undertaken before: that of matchmaker. Within a year of becoming pupils, Cherie Booth, the other barrister that he'd taken on in advance of Tony Blair, started to go out with Blair. And, after a courtship lasting three years, she became Blair's wife. David Fursedon, who shared a house in Primrose Hill, North London with Blair while he and Cherie were courting, remembers Cherie as being rather different from a lot of the other women that Blair had gone out with. 'Tony had gone out with a lot of women, who, while very pretty, weren't always that bright. Cherie was extremely bright, and clearly challenged Tony intellectually.'[7] Cherie Booth is the daughter of the actor Tony Booth, who became known to millions as the 'scouse git' in *Till Death Us Do Part*. They married in 1980. At their wedding in St John's College, one of the toasts was proposed by Lord Irvine, in which he described himself as 'Cupid QC'.

Cherie Booth (she practises under her maiden name) is still working and is regarded as one of the brightest employment and public law barristers of her generation, and was given the badge of establishment approval when she was made a Queen's Counsel early in 1995. She plays a prominent role in bar politics too, speaking out on a variety of issues like access to the legal profession for women. Indeed on one occasion, just after she had been made a QC, Tony Blair was startled to hear from one of his constituents at a Saturday morning surgery that his wife had appeared earlier that morning on the *Today* programme. Mr Blair insisted that the constituent must be mistaken, but when he spoke to his wife later that morning she confirmed that indeed she had been on the programme that the Labour Leader most likes to appear on.

She is also crystal clear about what she intends to do if her next move of house takes her to Number 10 Downing Street. At a reception in Blair's constituency to celebrate his becoming Leader, a less than politically correct local councillor ventured to suggest that she would be giving up work if her husband became Prime Minister. 'And can you tell me one good reason why I should?' came back the reply. Cherie Booth has always worked, taking precious little time off, even when she had just had her children. But Cherie points out that her mother always worked, as did her grandmother, and that she would find it hard to contemplate giving up work. Like many of the new breed of politicians' wives, Cherie is easily the main breadwinner, netting a six figure salary, and she tells friends that with an expensive home to run (local estate agents put a value of around £400,000 on the Islington house) and the additional costs they incurred after her husband became Leader, like entertaining and new clothes, she has no option but to continue to work.

But she is a 'political wife' too. At her husband's first Labour Party conference after he had been made Leader, she played a prominent, confident role. At some receptions she stood in for her husband, making speeches and looking entirely at ease in the role of Labour's First Lady. When her diary permits she accompanies her husband on visits to schools and factories, pressing the flesh and making polite small-talk. She will also sit at the top tables with the captains of industry or visiting dignitaries. For important occasions Blair's office will provide briefing notes on whom she will have to engage in conversation. For example on the occasion of the 50th anniversary of VE day, at a banquet at Guildhall, Cherie Booth sat next to the King of Swaziland.

Blair's office, as well as providing her with essential details like GDP of the country and potted history, gave guidance on the King's extensive marital history so that no *faux pas* would be committed over the hors d'oeuvres. She appears to relish the role, confiding that it gives her the chance to be nosey about other people's lives, whether it be heads of state or heads of schools.

Cherie is petite with large hollow brown eyes, high cheekbones and a smile that seems to go out in a straight line dissecting her small, expressive face. From afar there is a hint of vulnerability. She often looks hunted, occasionally haunted – perhaps a mark of her size – but close to she exudes authority and intelligence. Her eyes lock on to whoever she is talking to and perhaps from years of courtroom experience or simple assertiveness, she tends to command the direction of a conversation. She is slightly wary of strangers and is not given to disingenuous displays of flattery to those she does not know well. But she knows the rules of public life, and that means rubbing along with all manner of people. Some MPs say she can be charmless and cold; certainly she can show a sharp edge. But those close to Cherie dismiss her occasional coolness as no more than natural reticence and reserve. Some outsiders have described the Blairs as having a tempestuous marriage, but that is dismissed even more vehemently by their inner circle of friends who see them as extremely close and supportive of one another.

It was striking in their first sustained period in the public gaze, at the 1994 Labour Party conference, how close they seemed, with Cherie repeatedly reaching out to hold her husband's hand during the Sunday morning church service before the conference started. On other occasions her head would often come to rest on her husband's shoulder, and they would walk down corridors, arms entwined, although there was an impression that Mr Blair was feeling rather less tactile than Mrs Blair. The Blairs also dispensed with another piece of Labour etiquette at the conference. Breakfast was taken in their room, not in the restaurant with everyone else: the few moments of privacy they can have they guard jealously. But more striking was the extent to which

45

Cherie Booth had undergone an image transformation. In public she was always fully made up, and her wardrobe had been overhauled. Suddenly it wasn't just the political correspondents that were interested in the Blairs; in came the fashion writers, too.

But Tony Blair is extremely image conscious as well. During the 1994 conference, as he came down the winding staircase of the Imperial each morning, it was quite clear he was wearing face powder, so that his nose wouldn't shine on camera. And one of his aides once said half jokingly, that travelling in a car with Blair the item that gets most used is the passenger's vanity mirror. Detractors – some inside the Labour Party, others outside – have sought to portray Blair as the triumph of style over substance, but Blair takes the view that good presentation is the servant of serious politics. And to those ends Blair cares deeply about the way the Party comes across, and how he comes over, too. For this reason he is self-conscious to the point of vanity, but it stops short of narcissism.

The Blairs live in a large house in Islington with their three children. A clutch of relations live nearby, like Blair's older brother, Bill, and Cherie's sister, Lyndsey, which means there is an extensive support network for the children who all come and go from each other's houses with great regularity. The Blairs' house bears some of the scars of their stretched lifestyle, but, like Cherie herself, it seemed to undergo something of an image transformation when Blair became Leader. The hall which used to be the repository for football boots, school bags and bicycles has been lavishly re-done with wallpaper that gives an impression of a house made of stone columns. And the threadbare carpets have been replaced by trendy hessian matting. The three children are each two years apart: Euan, the eldest, Nicholas and Kathryn. They are close, even though Kathryn tends to get left out a bit because of the two older boys' obsessive love of football. One is devoted to Liverpool; the other to Manchester United.

If Tony Blair came into the Labour Party through intellectual convictions he discovered after he left Oxford, Cherie was born into the Party from a family steeped in Labour movement tradition. Her maternal grandfather was a miner and his lamp is still kept as a treasured family memento. He was a member of the Salvation Army, and Cherie's mother, Gale, was brought up as a non-conformist Christian in Ilkeston in Derbyshire. Cherie's father, in between his bouts of drinking, acting and carousing, has been a lifelong Labour Party member. His mother was a towering matriarch who came from a Merseyside Catholic working-class family, and it was her influence which ensured that Cherie and her sisters were brought up as Catholics, long after Cherie's errant father had left the scene. And in those Northern working-class families support for the Labour Party was as much a part of life as Mass on Sunday. Despite her mother's non-conformist background, Cherie was brought up a practising Catholic, something she has passed on to her children. In his autobiography, Tony Booth doesn't mention his daughters (there are seven from a variety of liaisons), but he dedicates the book to: 'The women in my life – especially Cherie, Lyndsey, Jenia, Bronwen, Sarah, Emma and Nancy – with my love and hopes for their forgiveness.'[8] Extraordinarily for an autobiography, his marriage to Gale is not even the subject of the most cursory passing comment, although it goes into great detail about how he lured his second wife, the late *Coronation Street* actress, Pat Phoenix. And, apart from the dedication in the introduction, that is the only mention that any of his children get. But Booth, now married to an American public relations consultant living in Manchester, is a vocal supporter, and turned up to cheer his son-in-law on at local meetings during the leadership contest. And he and Pat Phoenix, before she died, lent a little glamour to Blair's election campaigns by turning up to canvass in his constituency.

There have been attempts to portray Cherie as a Lady Macbeth-cum-Hillary Clinton rolled into one. In fact she is neither. Cherie is ambitious for herself, ambitious for her husband and immensely proud of her children, but juggling the demands of running a London home and a house in the constituency and three noisy and exuberant children with the pressures of being a high-flying barrister leaves little room for scheming and plotting her husband's path to glory, even if she wanted to. There was talk that soon after they got married a pact was agreed that whoever was elected first to parliament would be supported financially by the other. But even though Cherie was the first to be nominated to fight a Labour seat, in Thanet North – which she lost to Roger Gale, still the sitting Conservative MP – she was only there to wave the Labour banner in a no-hope seat. Cherie Booth's long-term ambitions were in the Inns of Court, not the Palace of Westminster. And Blair is dismissive of suggestions that there had been a deal. He said that, while he would have made a good, even a very good, barrister it was clear that Cherie was destined to become a quite brilliant advocate. Lord Irvine frowned when that was put to him. 'I think Tony is being falsely modest, saying that. He was every bit as brilliant.'

Blair in his six years at the bar built up an impressive list of commercial clients, but it was his contact with the unions and the Labour Party which further fuelled his political ambitions, and he started to think in the late 1970s for the first time that maybe his future would be at Westminster. The Labour Government by this time was on its last legs. Jim Callaghan was now Prime Minister and spent three years trying to govern with a non-existent majority, desperately trying to cobble together a majority with this or that minority party. Dubious deal-making had become the order of the day; the only political imperative was clinging to power, and in that sort of climate quaint notions such as a 'big idea' or a coherent political theme was lost in the raw battle for survival. The Labour Party was at the mercy of anyone who wanted to blackmail it, and some of those doing the arm-twisting were Labour MPs in pursuit of this or that policy. The Lib/Lab pact had been formed to stave off the inevitable votes of no confidence that would have heralded a general election. But it was the unions who delivered the fatal blow to Labour's limping administration. The very people whom the leadership used to rely on at conference to deliver their block votes against the radicals in the constituency parties had turned nasty themselves and had become part of the leadership's problem as they first baulked at and then destroyed Denis Healey's 5 per cent pay norm.

With inflation running at around 7.5 per cent, the pay claims that were flying in from the unions were way in excess of that. Ford car workers – always one of the benchmark pay settlements – demanded 15 per cent, and the public sector unions, who have always thought of themselves as the Cinderellas of the annual pay round, were pressing for a lot more than that. Local authority manual workers made the most audacious claim, asking for a staggering 40 per cent increase in pay. This unhappy cocktail was to lead to the Winter of Discontent, during which the rubbish piled up on the streets, the dead went unburied, and the image of the Labour Party as a party that was best able to manage harmonious industrial relations was to take a battering from which it would take a generation to recover. Denis Healey recalls: 'Each night the television screens carried film of bearded men in duffel coats huddled around braziers. Nervous viewers thought the revolution had already begun.'[9]

Blair's blessing as a politician today is that he was not a politician then. None of the baggage and infamy that attaches to that period of government can be linked to Mr Blair. In fact it was in the aftermath of Labour's defeat in 1979, when Mrs Thatcher won with a forty-one seat majority, that Blair decided his future was in politics. Blair knew that Cherie's father, Tony Booth, had been a long-standing supporter of the Labour Party (Booth, when he was arrested a little the worse for wear on a drink-driving charge, demanded that the police contact his friends Harold Wilson and Jim Callaghan), and even if his contacts did not quite extend to the highest echelons of the Party, there were others who might be able to help. Booth obliged. He put the up-and-coming barrister in touch with Tom Pendry, a Labour bruiser and MP for Stalybridge and Hyde since 1970. Blair remembers the occasion vividly. He recalls walking through the portals of the St Stephen's entrance, up the stairs, with the vast Westminster Hall where kings and queens have lain in state to his left, along what is now the corridor where members of the public wait to be seated in the Strangers' Gallery, and then into the imposing Central Lobby, with its ring of green leather benches and glistening domed mosaic ceiling. As the twenty-seven-year-old sat looking round in awe waiting for the badge messenger to call out Mr Pendry's name, Blair realised that he had become convinced of what he already knew: he wanted to become a politician. It was an ambition that stemmed largely from commitment, but as he sat in the Central Lobby and drank in its intoxicating atmosphere, he also felt a surge of excitement at the drama, power and glory that would be at stake in pursuing a political career.

Blair is a curious mix of politician. He entered politics out of conviction to change the world, or at least out of a desire to make Britain a better place to live in; and yet he is not a 'conviction' politician in the way that Margaret Thatcher was. She saw things in black and white and her sense of mission had an almost religious zeal to it. Blair is not much interested in chauffeur driven cars and the other trappings of office, but he feels the adrenalin of power. Blair tells friends with hand-on-heart sincerity that he doesn't actually think of himself as a politician. He has even confessed to disliking politics itself, but now that he has chosen his path he is not going to let much deflect him.

Ironically the moment that Blair came to the conclusion that he wanted to become a Labour MP coincided with the period that Roy Jenkins, David Owen, Shirley Williams and Bill Rodgers were reaching the decision that they could no longer face having anything to do with the Labour Party. Blair, who shared many of their views and beliefs, might have been thought of as a model recruit, but he says he never even contemplated leaving, even though there were many of his generation of Oxford-educated professionals who did. It is also worth remembering that, in the heady days of the winter of 1981 and spring of 1982, it really did seem as though the SDP might supplant the

Labour Party as the main voice of opposition to the Conservatives. For an ambitious young man, it seemed the place to be. But it was almost as though Blair, having spent so long deciding that it was the Labour Party that he wanted to join, wasn't going to be deterred because a rival force had come along.

> Although I agreed with the Gang of Four that there were things wrong with the Labour Party that had to be changed, I disagreed with their view that it was basically unchangeable ... If what I wanted was merely a career in Government, let us be clear that I would not have been joining the Labour Party and working through it. I joined it because I believed in it. And still do. And, although I have waged a relentless campaign to change the Labour Party, because I thought it needed changing, I have never actually doubted that it was the place for me to be.[10]

After Tony and Cherie had married in 1980 they set up home in Hackney, and became active in the local Labour Party there. But Tony and Cherie also became involved in the London Labour Co-ordinating Committee. It was a mainstream left organisation that was set up by Charles Clarke, who would later become Neil Kinnock's chief of staff when he became leader, and Jack Dromey, a Transport Union official who had come to prominence during the Grunwick film processing dispute during the 1970s and is now married to Harriet Harman. Their aim was to provide a forum outside of the ideological straitjacket of the Bennite left, which had now taken a grip on London Labour politics. It was the high tide of 'loony-leftism', and the London Labour Co-ordinating Committee was meant for those who felt oppressed by the ideological dictates laid down by the hard left. The Blairs were active supporters, both physically and financially. Clarke and Blair first met at Camden Town Hall, where the London LCC was launched. Clarke remembers Blair as being something of a political ingénu, but was to see in him that day personality traits that have been constant:

Tony was extremely green and very inexperienced in politics, but he was wanting to learn the whole time. He wanted to help. He wanted to give money. He wanted to know what he could do. He wanted to know how he could be most effective.[11]

After the general election defeat of 1979, the dominant right-wing Labour leadership was tired, dispirited and confused. Some seemed almost ashamed of their years in Government, while others bitterly blamed the unions for everything that had gone wrong. Tony Benn had been part of the Cabinet throughout those years and had lived apparently untroubled by the compromises and disarray that had marked the last years of the Labour government. But in Opposition he saw himself and quickly became the leader of the Left. The Left in the Party at large felt that the right-wing leadership had exposed themselves in Government as opportunistic centrists. And the solution they offered was easy: the Party had to become more socialist. They felt that the power of the Party Leader and the remoteness of the Parliamentary Labour Party from its activists combined to ensure that in Government Labour politicians ignored the Party in its various forms – Conference, the NEC, the constituency General Management Committees (GMCs). And so the post-election soul-searching became an argument about accountability.

The energetic forces of the Left wanted two reforms of Party democracy. They wanted individual MPs to be subject to re-selection during each parliamentary term. And, secondly, they wanted the Party Leader and Deputy Leader to be elected by Party activists and not by MPs alone.

The changes were dramatic. Reselection of MPs would mean that every MP would spend the Parliament looking over his or her shoulder, worrying about the views of the tiny number of activists who sat on their GMC. These activists had high opinions of themselves as the guardians of the Party's conscience, and invariably their views were way out of step with the average Labour voter. To be a Labour activist in the late 1970s and early 1980s almost guaranteed that you were at odds with the electorate. It involved giving up several evenings a month – there would be ward meetings, a meeting of the constituency Executive, a meeting of the GMC itself, possibly a local government meeting, a meeting of your faction, and all the paperwork that went with each occasion. Meetings drifted effortlessly into the night, were often bad-tempered, and were riddled with inaccessible jargon. This structure was a gift to the hard left (or headbangers as they were known to the other comrades). They had commitment, they had organisation, and, worst of all, they seemed to enjoy it. Ordinary mortals rapidly dropped out, leaving MPs with an antagonistic GMC. Under the proposed rule change it was going to be these people who would be prosecuting counsel and hangman for every MP accused of being a class traitor.

The proposed changes for electing the Leader and Deputy Leader were also intended to make them responsive to the demands of this activist élite. On the face of it, it seemed beautifully democratic – why shouldn't a Party be able to hold its Leaders to account? In reality it was not to be all Party members who would be involved, but just those activist obsessives.

A problem for the Right was that the proposals struck a chord across the Party. Many MPs were lazy, and did ignore their local Party members, sometimes justifiably, often not. The campaign for accountability was able to unite a wide range of forces – groups that could not possibly agree on a basket of policies. The umbrella group CLPD (Campaign for Labour Party Democracy) contained many strange bedfellows – Stalinists, 57 varieties of Trotskyists, Tribunites, the emerging 'soft left', old utopian socialists and peaceniks, and the individually ambitious who merely wanted to get rid of their sitting MPs so that they could replace them. The impetus for change was becoming unstoppable.

The right wingers who would later break away to form the SDP because they couldn't accept these constitutional changes (although there were other, more opportunistic, reasons that underscored their decision to form a new party) believed that it was part of a wider move to shift the Party irreversibly to the left, and announced that they were determined to fight. Unfortunately for them they had a weak hand; some of their leading lights were tarnished with having been ministers in Callaghan's Government, some were transparently ambitious, some defended the indefensible.

Tony Benn believed that if the Labour Party's structures were reorganised in such a way that MPs were accountable to the grassroots activists, then that would create a democratic party. But Blair believed passionately that this overlooked one critical principle: how to make the activists answerable to anyone other than themselves. That they were not, yet wielded this extraordinary power, led to that unbelievable document, Labour's 1983 general election manifesto, which Gerald Kaufman memorably called the longest suicide note in history. It called for withdrawal from the Common Market, massive nationalisation and renationalisation with much greater centralised planning of the economy, exchange controls, trade barriers: all weapons to create a siege economy. And the party set itself the wholly laudable but unrealistic target of reducing unemployment by two million in five years. Blair's conviction that the Labour Party needed to change stemmed from a time before he even arrived in Parliament. What he wanted was a Labour Party that was in touch with the real grassroots: the millions of ordinary voters who backed Labour at general elections. But one area where polling evidence showed that Labour was out of touch with the electorate was in the sensitive area of trade union reform.

After the Conservative victory in 1979 there was a huge appetite among the public for clipping the wings of the union barons. Tory moves to democratise the unions were popular in the country yet resented hugely in the Labour Party. But Anthony Blair (as a barrister, he practised under his less 'common man' name), although he now insists that he has always believed there was a good case for union reform, and did much in the run up to the 1992 general election to persuade the unions to accept some of the Conservatives' trade union reforms, was not always of that view. His verdict on Jim Prior's 1980 Employment Bill gave little clue of a moderniser waiting to break out: 'These proposals are not moderate. They are a concerted attempt to destroy the effectiveness of industrial action.' And Blair was writing again for the *New Statesman* a year later when Norman Tebbit as Employment Secretary was introducing further reforms: 'The clear intent of the proposals is to cut out any action which involves anyone other than the immediate parties. This is a draconian limitation on effective industrial action.'[12]

Tory legislation of the period no doubt acted as a recruiting sergeant for the hard left, even if it chimed with public opinion and the moderate union members who helped sweep Mrs Thatcher to power. But the extent to which the far left had taken a hold on Labour was now becoming a professional concern for Blair the barrister. 'Entryism' was the tactic by which revolutionary Trotskyist groups would join a democratic party with a clear mission to subvert its policies by essentially operating as a party within a party. Without the discipline that being in government imposed on Labour, constituency parties and trade union branches were ripe for entryism by determined and well organised groups that stood outside Labour's democratic traditions. And far and away the best organised and most determined was Militant. *Militant* was the newspaper sold at every Labour rally, on every picket line and even in town centres on Saturday mornings. But the Labour Party leadership knew that Militant was much more than a newspaper, and was a national organisation with a highly disciplined and extensive infrastructure operating within the Labour Party. The problem was how to weed out the hard core of activists.

After much agonising by Michael Foot, who was now Labour leader, about what to do – and indeed among the 'soft' Tribunite left there was some agonising over whether anything needed to be done at all – it was decided that the best way forward would be to set up a register of affiliated organisations, with the clear intention of declaring Militant ineligible to be a part of the

Labour Party. That would then, according to the plan hatched in Walworth Road between Michael Foot and the new general secretary, Jim Mortimer, leave the party free to expel its leaders – the five-man editorial board of the newspaper and the thirty-four full-time 'sellers'. Militant's response was to protest total and injured innocence, but they went a step further. Militant, the scourge of the establishment and unashamedly revolutionary in intent, had no compunction in threatening to use the 'bourgeois' courts to argue that what the Labour Party was proposing was against natural justice.

John Smith the Shadow trade spokesman, and prominent member of the right-wing Solidarity Group (which felt that if the mainstream left had recognised the problem earlier then there wouldn't have been this struggle now) was so alarmed by Militant's response that he persuaded Labour to seek the advice of a leading counsel. Smith contacted his best friend from Glasgow University days, Derry Irvine. The two had remained extremely close friends ever since. Irvine took on the brief and brought with him a young rising star in his chambers, Anthony Blair. Their initial advice was that Militant had a good case. Irvine and Blair argued that if the Party pursued selective expulsions, it would be skating on thin ice and that Militant would be able to mount a credible case that Labour's actions were against natural justice. Their advice was that the NEC was 'Obliged to expel all Militant Tendency members once the Militant Tendency had been declared ineligible to affiliate to the Party.'[13] In the end the NEC ignored the legal advice given by Irvine and Blair and pursued a policy of selective expulsions, although the Party leadership argued that they took action against anyone when the evidence was presented to them. But when Militant finally challenged the expulsions in the courts, it fell at the first hurdle. Mr Justice (now Lord) Nourse threw Militant's case out on the grounds that, if the Trotskyist organisation felt there had been a breach of natural justice, they needed to bring the case to court immediately, not wait for a year while they fought the decision within the Labour Party's constitutional structures.

But the episode had brought Blair into contact with some of the leading movers and shakers in the Labour Party of the time, and he had created a good impression. It was now time to be blooded in real political battle. Blair had done much of his preparation for this in Hackney Labour Party, where he and Cherie had set up home. The Queensbridge ward was stuffed full of people on their way up: as well as Tony and Cherie, there was Glenys Thornton, who went on to become chair of the Fabian Society; the Labour historian, Ben Pimlott, who was a prospective parliamentary candidate; and Charles Clarke, who was soon to become Neil Kinnock's aide-de-camp. Mike Davis, who was the ward secretary, remembers the somewhat ludicrous situation of having so many big names in such a tiny ward:

> We would be discussing some minor local matter like street cleaning, and up would pop each of these aspiring politicians, making ten-minute speeches which would fast become general critiques of what was wrong with Britain and why their faction of the Labour Party had the answer. I think some of them saw whichever classroom or church hall we were in as a rehearsal room for when they arrived in the Commons chamber.[14]

The Hackney Labour Party was not exactly fertile ground for a public school Oxbridge-educated barrister, but the minutes of the Queensbridge ward show that Blair was undeterred in his bid to climb the political ladder, and soon after arriving sought the local Party's nomination to stand as the local Labour candidate for Hackney Borough Council. But he was thwarted in his ambitions. Older members of the ward saw him as a bit of a Johnny-come-lately who hadn't served the requisite amount of time in the local Party to be given the nomination, while the activists regarded him as unforgivably right-wing, and little better than someone in the SDP. But Blair did not have to wait long before another – much more significant – opportunity opened up. Blair's break came in a completely hopeless parliamentary seat in the Home Counties.

Beaconsfield in Buckinghamshire is one of those seats where it is said they don't count the Conservative majority but weigh it. The by-election came during the Falklands War when Mrs Thatcher was at her most awesome and Labour at its most enfeebled. Blair sought the advice of Irvine about whether he should put in for the seat, and Irvine in turn put him back into contact with his old friend John Smith. It was to be the start of a close personal friendship with John Smith, even if they often made uncomfortable political bedfellows. Blair fought the seat, and, in the military metaphors that abounded in May 1982, duly went down in flames, coming a poor third behind the Liberal candidate and losing his deposit. Like any new candidate, Blair was taken to Walworth Road and briefed on all aspects of Labour Party policy. Unbeknown to Blair, the person who had been appointed chief economic adviser to the party was Adam Sharples, whom Blair had not seen since the pair were Ugly Rumours together at Oxford. And Sharples, having initially hired Blair as a singer, was now tutoring him in the finer points of Labour economic policy, having been the author of much of the Alternative Economic Strategy which a year later would play such an important part in undermining Labour's general election prospects.

Blair's election address was straight down the line in its adherence to party policy. On Europe it advocated withdrawal from the Common Market.

> Labour is not anti-European. But the EEC has pushed up prices, especially for food . . . Above all, the EEC takes away Britain's freedom to follow the sort of economic policies we need. These are just two of the reasons for coming out. Only a Labour Government will do it.

On defence, with cruise missiles about to arrive in neighbouring Berkshire, Blair's election leaflets railed against the Government's defence policy. 'Labour is the only party pledged to end the nuclear madness. Nuclear weapons are not a deterrent, they are an encouragement to attack.' The leaflet also had the novel innovation of a letter from Cherie attached to it, explaining what a nice, caring man her husband was. Under the title, 'A message from Cherie Blair' (no insistence on her maiden name there), she says that only the Labour Party showed real concern for the welfare of women, and she went on to say that, 'I know Tony would do a good and caring job of work for this constituency.'

But what was interesting in Blair's position on both nuclear disarmament and Europe was that during the campaign he would qualify both. When the local newspaper, the *South Bucks Observer*, suggested that Blair was a Bennite, he wrote back to put the record straight:

> I support the Labour Party's present leadership; Labour's plan for jobs; withdrawal from the EEC (certainly unless the most fundamental changes are effected); and nuclear disarmament, unilaterally if necessary.

Like any by-election candidate, Blair played host in Beaconsfield to all the senior Labour politicians of his day, including the Labour leader Michael Foot, who commended the young not-so-hopeful on his performance. Foot gave the endorsement for the cameras, but he was also privately impressed, and wrote to Blair afterwards congratulating him on the fight that he had put up, and expressing the hope that it would not be long before he was fighting alongside Foot and the rest of the Labour Party in the Commons. A few months later that letter would turn out to be a highly significant document as Blair fought to find a seat in a constituency a little more Labour friendly than Beaconsfield.

CHAPTER 3

The Road to Westminster

'There is a tide in the affairs of men,
Which, taken at the flood, leads on to fortune;
Omitted, all the voyage of their life
is bound in shallows and in miseries.'

Julius Caesar, William Shakespeare

With Blair back in chambers he told Irvine that he had been asked – and was inclined to accept the invitation – to stay on and fight the general election in Beaconsfield. Irvine told Blair that he needed his head examining. 'I advised him that sometimes amazing things can happen in politics, and persuaded him to ride his luck, take a chance and say no to Beaconsfield Labour Party.' When Blair eventually won his selection battle in a safe Labour seat in the North East, with just three weeks to go to the general election, Blair rang Derry Irvine and his wife, Alison, from the hall where the local Party had just met. And with the cheering still going on in the background, he told his former head of chambers it had been the best advice he had ever been given.

The by-election in Beaconsfield had come at around the same time as a couple of others, and the NEC took the novel course of action of inviting the candidates who had stood for Labour to report back on each of their campaigns and how they felt Labour policies were being greeted on the doorsteps. Blair had been invited by Joyce Gould, the Labour Party's Director of Organisation, and he made an immediate impression:

I remember Tony coming along to that meeting and that was my first sight of this bright young man, who even then you knew was going places. You had that instinctive feel that he wasn't going to be one of those people who, having fought a hopeless seat, was going to fade into the background.'[1]

Blair remembers being 'cautiously candid' with the NEC, and Foot, in recognition of his talents, asked Blair to help out with some speech writing. But it hadn't been difficult for Blair to stand out as a beacon of hope and brilliance in view of the opposition. One of the by-elections that had taken place around the same time was in Bermondsey, where the gay rights activist Peter Tatchell handed to the Liberals one of Labour's most rock-solid inner city seats.

Blair turned down the invitation to fight Beaconsfield again, but the aftermath of fighting the seat left Blair desperate to find a safer constituency as it would surely not be long before Mrs Thatcher went to the country again to seek a renewed mandate. Blair was looking around, applying for all sorts of constituencies, but not getting very far. It was now two years since Tony and Cherie had got married and they decided in the autumn of 1982 to visit Australia, to catch up with his old university friends, Geoff Gallop and Peter Thomson. Gallop was now a senior academic teaching at Murdoch University in Perth, and he persuaded Blair to deliver a lecture on the state of the British Labour Party. It is a fascinating document: twenty-three pages of closely typed and tightly argued script, essentially setting out some of the strands of thought that would later become the modernisers' creed, ten years before the word 'Moderniser' became a significant label within the Labour Party, and a year before Neil Kinnock set about his reforms.

In his paper Blair addressed what he said was a central dilemma for the Labour Party: that the reforms of the left to make the party more democratic had, in fact, in the eyes of the electorate, left it looking intolerant and undemocratic; destructive rather than constructive. Blair argued that the left had lost touch with the *aspirations* (a word now central to the modernisers today) of ordinary voters. Drawing on his experience of fighting the Beaconsfield by-election, Blair noted that,

> There are growing numbers of young often socially upward moving people who are simply not prepared to accept our basic ideology just because their forefathers did. There are very few of the younger age group converted to our ideology and we rely to a dangerous degree on the loyalty vote among older citizens.[2]

But those younger people who did become involved tended to be university educated and drawn from white collar public sector jobs, where their political agenda was very much further to the left than either the leadership or the more moderate unions. So, when Blair was preparing this lecture, the 1982 conference had by a four-to-one majority approved the setting up of the register to weed out groups like Militant, but 90 per cent of the constituency parties had voted to reject the register. It was a far cry from the early 1960s when Gaitskell depended on the constituency parties to defeat unilateralism. He described the party as becoming dangerously schizophrenic, with the top and bottom at odds with one another. To bring the bottom of the Party – in other words, the grassroots activists – back into touch, Blair argued that 'a local Party should grow out of a local community – the party members having roots in that community. That is not only for reasons of political efficiency; it is because the party will then be more sensitive to the needs and wishes of the electorate.' As an example of this remoteness, Blair picked on that hottest potato of the period, the sale of council houses. 'Labour would ban the sale of council houses . . . yet there is something mildly distasteful about owner-occupier members preaching the virtues of public housing to council tenants.'[3]

Another burning issue of the day was that new concept that the Thatcher government introduced, 'privatisation'. Blair recognised that the proposal that Labour should re-nationalise without compensation to shareholders would have a gut appeal to many activists, but he warned:

> Such a policy would cause much more trouble for Labour – in terms of Labour being portrayed as an extremist, authoritarian party both at home and abroad – than it is worth. Ultimately it would be a demonstration of political virility, not a rational policy taking account of practical reality.[4]

But if much of the thinking was modern, there were bits that fitted in well with the Labour orthodoxy of the time. Unemployment, he argued, would not be solved by 'the mild economic tinkering proposed by the Social Democrats'. And he went on to make the case for 'enormous state guidance and intervention'. He went on: 'That in turn will bring any Labour government into sharp conflict with the power of capital, particularly multinational capital.' And then, in words that the modern media-conscious politician would never utter today, went on to say, 'The trouble with the right of the Party is that it has basked so long in the praise of the leader writers of the *Financial Times, Times* and *Guardian* that it is no longer accustomed to giving them offence. It will find the experience painful, but it is vital.'[5] No mention there of the 'dynamic market economy' that would later be central to his leadership bid.

He concluded his lecture by predicting correctly that the SDP, which had been formed a year earlier, would not make the big electoral breakthrough at the next election that had been forecast, but he nevertheless urged Labour to realise the reasons why the SDP had grown so popular. And he insisted that if Labour was to win again, then it must appeal to middle-ground voters, a cry that twelve years on would help propel Blair to the Labour Party leadership.

This lecture was the first time that Blair had painted his political 'credo' on such a wide canvas. A lot of time and thought had gone into preparing it, and, although there are parts of it that are far more left-wing than the views he would express today, there are threads in it that have formed the back-cloth of his politics. It showed him to be a politician ahead of his time. The sort of things he argued for in that Perth lecture would only later become associated with the soft-left position that Neil Kinnock would argue for when he became leader. So, while Hansard quote after Hansard quote could be found to demonstrate how the likes of Kinnock and Jack Straw had been forced to recant from their more orthodox left-wing positions, by the time Blair came into Parliament he had already trimmed his sails.

Blair left Australia that autumn invigorated by his visit, but he returned to England depressed at not having found a seat to fight. With his thirtieth birthday beckoning, Cherie threw a surprise party. It was on 6 May. By now nearly every constituency in the country had selected its candidate, and Blair recalls being extremely miserable. But he heard that there was a seat in the North East, just a few miles down the road from where he had been brought up, that had still to select a candidate. Sedgefield had no sitting MP, as it was a new seat carved out by the Boundary Commission. But first soundings were not good. The short list had been drawn up, and it was essentially a two-horse race between two well-known left-wingers, Les Huckfield and Reg Race. The next morning he rang Derry Irvine and said that he would be taking a few days off. He packed an overnight bag, and in Cherie's words 'never came back'.

Once again a mixture of extreme good luck and Blair's per-suasive charm came to the rescue, as it had done when he secured his pupillage. One of the local Labour Party branches in the pit village of Trimdon had not nominated anyone. He rang the local representative to the selection conference, John Burton, and Burton agreed that he could go round to his house. Burton is a thick-set man, with wiry hair, a thick mous-tache and bushy eyebrows not quite hiding his twinkly eyes. He was a local comprehensive school teacher and still sings in a folk band. He is also, as Blair was to discover to his immense good fortune, an immensely canny political operator. When Blair arrived at Burton's house, he and a number of other members of the Trimdon branch were there, but unavailable. They were engaged in the altogether more serious business of watching Aberdeen playing Real Madrid. Blair was told to sit down, shut up, and pour himself a drink. The match went into extra time. And so did the questioning of Blair, once those present turned their attention to this rather smartly turned out barrister.

The group had gathered to watch the football and celebrate Labour's showing in the local council elections that had just taken place. One of them, Peter Brookes, who has now become a close friend of the Blairs, remembers Blair making an immediate impression. 'I thought he was a bit posh, but, once we got talking, it was quite clear that here was someone of vision and enthusiasm. The feeling that he was somehow different came across quite quickly.' A left-winger present that evening, Terry Ward, pushed Blair to agree with him on a number of defining issues, but Blair stood his ground arguing for Europe, for expelling Militant and against Bennite changes in the party. The man disagreed with everything that Blair said, but decided to work for him because he said, 'Here was someone who knew his own mind and would never be a dilettante.'[6]

All present that evening vowed they would start working for Blair there and then.

Burton now set about getting Blair's name added to the short list. Officially it had closed, but Blair cobbled together a hastily typed curriculum vitae, uncharacteristically full of typing errors and spelling mistakes, setting out his credentials:

PREVIOUS PARLIAMENTARY EXPERIENCE

I stood, during the Falklands war, in the Beaconsfield by-election, a Tory seat with a majority of 93,000. I lost, (unsurprisingly) but gained valuable experience. Michael Foot speaking on BBC Newsnight on 26th May 1982 said,
    "In my view Tony Glair will make a major contribution to British Politics in the months and years ahead".

This CV is a remarkable document, not only as a reminder of those days before word processors and 'spell checkers', but also for what it says. There can't be many politicians who have found it necessary to mention the background of their in-laws, but when it is Tony Booth and Pat Phoenix, Blair was obviously prepared to unashamedly name-drop in his bid to curry favour. For many years it resulted in a number of profiles being written wrongly suggesting that Cherie was Pat Phoenix's daughter. Blair also promised that he and Cherie would set up home in the constituency and he asserts, in a very un-New Man way, that Cherie's work – then she specialised mainly in adoption and child care – could easily transfer to the North of England. It is unlikely that she was making similar offers to move to the North East as she stood for election in the South East!

This CV also nails another controversy surrounding Blair's past. After Blair became leader, as Tories scratched around for scraps of information from Blair's past to discredit him, Michael Heseltine went on to the *Today* programme and in characteristically swashbuckling style said, 'Why should you believe a man who has got all the major judgements wrong in the first half of his life, when he tells you he is going to get them all right in the second half of his life?'[7] The presenter, James Naughtie, then challenged Heseltine to list these misjudgements, and the President of the Board of Trade accused Blair of having been a member of CND. 'CND?' spluttered a disbelieving and incredulous-sounding Naughtie. And Michael Heseltine, perhaps unsure of his ground, didn't press the point. But with a deftness of touch that has always characterised Heseltine, he simply turned the attack, arguing that if Blair had been too young to commit any errors of political judgement then surely he was too inexperienced to seek the highest office.

Later that day senior Labour Party sources went out of their way to dismiss what they said was a lie. David Hill, the Party's Director of Communications, fulminated against smears from Conservative Central Office and told Westminster lobby journalists that Blair had never been a member of CND. This denial was faithfully reproduced in the following day's newspapers and a successful damage limitation operation had been carried out. But then the Tories produced evidence which showed that as late as 1986 Blair had been a member of parliamentary CND. Hill then pointed out that it was a quantum difference to join parliamentary CND, which most Labour MPs had joined, and CND itself, which the Labour Party still maintains Blair has never been a member of. But in his hastily cobbled together CV dating from May 1983, under the heading 'membership of other organisations', Blair quite clearly lists that he was a member of CND. The fact is that, while Blair's wardrobe may not rattle to the sound of skeletons bumping into each other, it isn't quite as bare as Labour Party spin doctors would like to suggest.

But in the Labour Party of 1983 membership of CND was part of the orthodoxy, unless you were a member of the right-wing Solidarity group – and even they sought to bury their public differences with the lifelong unilateralist leader of the Labour Party, Michael Foot. Certainly, when Blair's keenest backer, John Burton, went to a meeting of the executive of Sedgefield Labour Party on 18 May to push for the addition of Blair's name to the short list, his membership of CND would have been one of the few pluses that Burton could pull from his hat. The executive was dominated by left-wingers and the unions, and they refused to let Blair address them. At the first fence, Burton had fallen. He had one last chance. The following night was a meeting of the whole selection committee. At a tense and fraught meeting at Spennymoor Town Hall the argument went backwards and forwards about whether to add Blair's name. The Transport Union leadership in London, which, although officially sponsoring Huckfield, had no time for him, quietly provided ammunition to the Blair camp, giving detailed questions that would embarrass Huckfield. Blair's good fortune was to unwittingly be the recipient of an almost nationwide 'stop Huckfield' campaign, a man who had powerful enemies in Walworth Road and across the union movement.

Then came the *coup de théâtre* as Burton stood up and pulled from his pocket the letter that Michael Foot had sent Blair in the wake of his defeat at Beaconsfield. Burton was economical to the point of being downright stingy with the truth of its contents. Waving the letter from the Leader of the Opposition, he told the eighty-three-strong General Committee, that it was a letter endorsing Blair's candidature for Sedgefield, and that Foot personally wanted him in the Commons. The second part was just about true; the first part was testing the elasticity of truth to breaking point. But no-one other than Burton and Blair knew of its precise contents, and as no-one asked to see the letter, Burton didn't exactly offer to have photocopies made so that other members of the selection committee could inspect its contents. This apparent endorsement by the Labour Leader clearly swayed a number of delegates, and a vote was taken. There were three tellers – one of them Burton – but what has never been disclosed is that each of them came to a different total on whether Blair's name should be added to the short list. However, all recorded the vote going in Blair's favour. At this point the other two tellers suggested – correctly – that there should be a re-count, but Burton was having none of it. He bullied and cajoled as they stood in the corridor outside the chamber and eventually persuaded them to keep quiet. They went back and the vote was declared: by 42 votes to 41 Blair's name was added to the short list. Blair's prayers had been answered. The morning of the final meeting, as Burton went to his local church to make his own pleas to God, Blair, who had been staying with friends outside Durham, returned to the city's cathedral. The battle had now been effectively won. And that night, they returned to Spennymoor Town Hall with Blair's selection considered a mere formality. Huckfield knew he was defeated when he failed to keep Blair's name off the short list the night before. On 20 May Blair was duly nominated as the candidate for the new constituency of Sedgefield. Twenty days later Blair was an MP.

Blair had come to visit Sedgefield with barely a change of clothing. He didn't go back to London until he'd been elected an MP. Now that Blair was the parliamentary candidate, he moved in to live with the Burtons and every day John Burton's wife would wash Blair's shirts and underwear, while they went out campaigning. After his election, Blair stayed with the Burtons for over a year-and-a-half every weekend until he found his own house in the constituency.

Burton has become one of Blair's most important sounding boards. He has good political judgement and antennae that are digitally tuned to the local people. Burton tells the story of how on one occasion Blair phoned up from London exasperated at progress on the policy review's deliberations on what the replacement to the poll tax should be. Bryan Gould had come up with a 'roof' tax, but Burton said to Blair the people of Sedgefield would never accept that. 'What do you think we need to do?' enquired Blair. 'If you came out with a scheme called fair rates, I'm sure we could sell that.' That evening Burton turned on the television to hear Blair talking about a new proposal called 'fair rates'. Blair trusts few people's judgement more than Burton's.

Sedgefield is a constituency that had been predominantly a mining area, but even when Blair arrived it was an industry that had disappeared, even if the traditions of tightly-knit communities that symbolised areas with collieries in them, had not. Sedgefield has twenty-seven villages in the constituency, and no major town. Sandwiched between Darlington to the south and Durham to the north, there is little obvious great wealth, but there are few signs of poverty either. There are no high-rise tower blocks, and the rows of restrained and modest council houses have been tarted up as residents have taken advantage of the right to buy, and the right to make their mark by personalising their property with distinctively painted front doors, cladding, double glazing, and all those other DIY extras that, at once, say: *casa mia*. There are also neat rows of eighteenth- and nineteenth-century cottages standing side by side, with grassy banks going down to the road. Pockets of light industry are scattered around the constituency, which has helped it survive the worst ravages of the recession. But what marked Sedgefield out politically from many other constituencies was that it had never gone down the path of loony leftism. Militant never came to Sedgefield, and one gets the impression that, even if its supporters had, the likes of John Burton and his colleagues would have driven them out of town very quickly.

But for all that Blair told the General Committee that he was not entirely happy with Labour's defence policy and was pro-Europe, this could not have been detected easily from either his CV or, more importantly, from his election address. The leaflet that went out to thousands of homes in Sedgefield showed little sign of what he had been arguing a few months earlier at Murdoch University. It was extracted directly from the 1983 manifesto. What is perhaps most extraordinary about this is that, in the forum where he stood most to gain by slavish adherence to the Party line – the selection meeting – he set out his own distinctive, less left-wing position.

The 1983 election address to the voters of Sedgefield makes him wince today. It promises that a Labour Government would create two million jobs in five years, and that it would negotiate a withdrawal from the EC 'which has drained our natural resources and destroyed jobs'. There's a commitment to increase housebuilding by 50 per cent, and an immediate increase of £1.45 a week for a single pensioner and £2.25 for a pensioner couple. Health charges would be phased out and 'we'll give our low paid NHS staff a decent living wage'. On defence, cruise missiles and Trident would be scrapped. The list of promises goes on and on.

Blair is rather sheepish about explaining away this leaflet, particularly his support for withdrawal from the EEC, which is something he insists he has never believed in. The half plausible explanation that he gives is that, because he had been selected so late, one of the Party workers simply rifled the Party manifesto, and Blair did not see the galley proof before it went to the printers. But Blair's manifesto in Beaconsfield went into even greater detail about why it would be desirable for Britain to withdraw from the Common Market.

Irrespective of the contents of his leaflets, Blair won the seat comfortably on 9 June 1983 with a majority of 8,281, and so began what can only be described as a love affair between the MP and the people of Sedgefield. In his first *Who's Who* listing in 1984, under the section where MPs and establishment figures normally list their membership of the Garrick, Pratt's or the Reform, the new MP details Trimdon Village Working Men's and Fishburn Working Men's as his clubs. What was Trimdon Village Working Men's has now become a cavernous, refurbished Labour club decorated with a Liberty print wallpaper. It is where Blair can be found most Friday evenings enjoying a pint with a revolving cast of locals, all of whom seem to treat him as proud parents behave towards a much-loved son. It is also the venue that Blair chose to launch his bid for the Labour Party leadership. There is a lot of banter and ribbing with Blair raising a hand or calling out a name as each new face wanders into the bar.

The Blair family live in a plump Victorian villa called Myrobella in Trimdon village; it is also open house to the local Labour Party. The view from the kitchen, which is dominated by a large Aga and scrubbed pine table, is a good metaphor for Blair's new model Labour Party. The kitchen looks out over gently rolling hills which once upon a time were Trimdon colliery. But the whole area has been seeded: there is no sign of the pithead and what were once slag heaps have become gentle grass slopes, giving little clue to the area's industrial past.

The Blairs spend most weekends and holidays there, but for all that, the house has a slightly unlived-in feel. The *objets d'art* and porcelain figurines of questionable taste in the sitting room look like they are there because someone didn't know where else to put them, and the brown dralon three-piece suite looks as though it must have been a cast off from somewhere else. The house also bears the scars of having had three children growing up in it: when the Blairs are in residence, getting through the front door requires delicate footwork as you pick your way through the tangle of discarded bicycles, football boots and toys.

Hello magazine has made repeated requests to come and film the Blair family *in situ*; the Blairs have – probably wisely – turned them down. Their frantic and busy lifestyle does not lend itself to creating *Homes and Gardens* style accommodation, where colours match, flowers are neatly arranged and order reigns supreme.

One side of the house is more or less exclusively devoted to the Labour Party – although peeking out from the mounds of leaflets and posters in the office are Postman Pat floor puzzles and children's jigsaws. It is from there that Blair built for Sedgefield a mass-membership party that he used as the model for the Party nationally when he became Labour Leader; a party not run by a small group of unrepresentative activists, but a mass-membership organisation which gave a stake and a role to ordinary members. Walworth Road was initially extremely suspicious about Blair's plans to start this pilot scheme, believing that it was no more than a naked attempt by Blair to build up his own powerbase within the Party, and to replace committed activists with armchair semi-socialists. Further grounds for suspicion came in the manner in which Blair intended to lure these new recruits, because he proposed a revolutionary project where people paid what they could afford for membership, not the fifteen pounds laid down centrally. Eventually Blair and his researcher in the constituency, Phil Wilson, persuaded Walworth Road that, in return for the Sedgefield constituency party guaranteeing to pay the same amount into central funds, Walworth Road would allow a pilot scheme to get off the ground. At the beginning of 1993 the membership stood at around four hundred; within two years of launching the drive to recruit more members, they had five times that number. The question for Blair when he became Party Leader was how to replicate that nationally.

The first day back at the Commons after a general election is very much like the first day of a new school term. Old friends slap each other on the backs warmly, happy that the vagaries of the electorate have not cast them on to civvy street, while new boys wander around looking lost, anxiously watching for someone they recognise. One piece of important business had been transacted on Blair's behalf before he arrived. Derry Irvine had arranged a 'pair' for Blair. Pairing is that vital informal arrangement where an MP of one party is linked to another, so that, if one is going to be away from the chamber on the night of a vote, the pair won't vote either, so that no difference is made to the overall Government majority. Without a pair, you have to stay at the Commons until late every night, unless the Chief Whip gives you leave of absence. The first MP to approach Blair when he arrived in the House was a Conservative new boy and fellow barrister, Michael Howard. He wanted to pair with Blair, but Irvine had already fixed him up with the wealthy and jolly MP Alastair Goodlad. (Later, when Goodlad became Deputy Chief Whip, a role which forbids pairing, Goodlad lent Blair out to other Tory MPs who did not have a pair on condition that Blair went back to Goodlad when he left the Whips' Office.)

Blair was also given a hearty welcome by another Conservative. As he wandered around and stood in the Members Lobby, soaking up the atmosphere, he was slapped warmly on the back by Sir Edward du Cann, the chairman of the Conservative backbench 1922 Committee, who thought here was one of the many Tory new boys thrown up by the landslide victory. But Blair was part of the Labour failure in 1983, not the Conservative success. In every sense, it was a dismal Parliamentary Labour Party that Blair joined when he arrived at Westminster. The country had returned just 209 Labour MPs, the lowest since 1935, and the Party's share of the vote was a lamentable 27.6 per cent, the smallest share ever won by a principal opposition party. It was Labour's worst result since the post-First World War election in 1918. And some of the Labour MPs elected in 1983 were suffering from a political form of shell shock that those who stumbled out of the trenches would have recognised. Labour as a party was dazed and demoralised. And still in the grip of the left.

The intolerant face of the Labour Party that the voters had decisively shunned at the ballot boxes Blair would soon encounter in his own backyard in Sedgefield. A rally had been organised in the constituency at which Blair was to share a platform with the long-time darling of the left, Dennis Skinner, the unyielding left-winger and MP for Bolsover. Blair spoke first, delivering a similar message to the one he had rehearsed with that group of Australian undergraduates a year earlier. Labour could not stand still; it had to learn the tough lessons of defeat. The Party had lost touch with its traditional supporters, he maintained, and salvation would only come when the Party had reconnected with the people it had left behind. It was a speech that did not conform to the orthodoxy of the time. Class based politics, rooted in old fashioned 'Labourism', were dominant. And it was a political outlook allied to the fallacious nostrum that perched above the playing field of British politics like a kindly giant pendulum which moved backwards and forwards every five years ensuring that the chance to govern was shared out evenly between the two main parties irrespective of policies and record in government. Blair thought that a chimera and took this opportunity to say so.

Indeed, in his challenging of conventional orthodoxies, Blair marked himself as one of that awkward band of believers in the disciplined environment of British politics: one who questioned and doubted. He thought it the mark of cowardice to accept 'my party right or wrong'. But it gave him a quality that many in the Labour movement time and time again would find unsettling, because in conversation Blair would often not sound like a politician. He would metamorphose from Member of Parliament and party activist to an ordinary voter, unable to understand why this or that policy was being held up as a sacred artefact if, in his mind, it had grown outdated. That night in Sedgefield, it made him a sitting target for the left.

Once Blair sat down, it was Skinner's turn to take to the rostrum. As he got up, Blair noticed the pin-striped suited figure of Les Huckfield walk in at the back of the hall. What happened next is now hotly disputed by the two central characters. According to Blair and his supporters, it was a crude piece of left-wing theatre. Skinner berated the new MP for his lack of socialist principles, and with his rhetoric running at full throttle, 'the beast of Bolsover' pointed to Huckfield at the back of the hall and said that was the man Sedgefield should have chosen. Blair, shocked at what had happened, turned to John Burton after the meeting to ask whether he had been wrong to say what he did. But Burton told him there was no need to worry: 'You must never stop saying those things. You mustn't move towards the Party; the Party must move towards you.'[8] Skinner, with an expression of injured innocence, has since denied adamantly that he behaved in this way. But Blair remembers the occasion as a small defining moment along his path from political boy to man. 'The scales dropped from my eyes that night,' he has since told friends. He came to recognise that for some on the left it wasn't just a question of taking a different political stance, it was also about intolerance and vindictiveness.

It must have been one of the Labour Whips' idea of a joke to lighten the gloom after the 1983 defeat to put Blair in an office with the newly elected MP for Coventry South East, Dave Nellist. Blair, who had been employed by the NEC to advise the Party on how to rid itself of Militant, was now sharing a glorified broom cupboard with an MP who was widely suspected of having more than a nodding acquaintance with the Trotskyist organisation. Kindred spirits they were not, and Blair would have probably found more in common with one of Sir Edward du Cann's new boys. Nellist, a perfectly charming and engaging man, was nevertheless happy to see the back of Blair and the Coventry MP moved out to share with Terry Fields, a Merseyside MP who had also just arrived at Westminster and had the same political inclinations. He would later be jailed for refusing to pay his poll tax, in defiance of Labour Party policy.

But in the rubble of 1983, Blair did meet someone with whom he was to build an extraordinary political friendship. Gordon Brown at the age of thirty-two when he entered Parliament, had already had a distinguished career as an academic, television producer and current affairs editor, and in between time had managed to become a prominent voice in Scottish Labour politics. Brown until his election had been Chairman of the Scottish Labour Party, and on the Party's Executive in Scotland. He had also been a candidate since 1976, so by the time he arrived at Westminster as a new boy, he was already a considerable player in Labour politics. They were also the two youngest Labour MPs in Parliament. Brown had been returned as the MP for Dunfermline East when he met Blair at the Commons, and Blair was immediately captivated by Brown's breadth of knowledge and his insight into the workings of the Party. Within six months they were sharing an airless office off the main committee corridor in the House that Nellist had moved out of. Where Blair trod tentatively, Brown seemed immediately sure of his footing, displaying a general *savoir faire* that would lead immediately to him being tipped for high, if not the highest office. Brown knew about the mysteries of television and the newspapers, and what you needed to do to get your name in print. He taught Blair how to draft a news release: how the most important fact had to go in the top line; what the 'bullet' points were; and how important it was to ensure that lazy journalists who might be writing up the press release with no further check calls had the who, what, where, when, why questions answered for them. 'My press releases used to read like essays before Gordon showed me how to write them,'[9] Blair would later tell the *Sunday Times*. And while Blair had been a considerable wordsmith as a barrister, he had little experience in speech writing and here again Brown showed Blair the way, advising him on how to make the phrases sing and how to structure the message. While Blair composed speeches that would have played well in the Chancery Division of the High Court, Brown knew how to rabble-rouse.

In the 1983 intake, Brown, with the exception of Blair, stood out head and shoulders above anyone else. The two men struck up a rare political friendship; but, most significantly, it was a relationship built on a common outlook about what was wrong with the Labour Party. From their first conversations they found they were of like mind about what had gone wrong and were of a similar outlook on what needed to be done to make Labour electable again. They would stay up late into the night discussing the kind of reforms that were necessary, how to defeat the left and how to persuade the Labour right that the political solutions of the 1970s were not the right prescription for the 1980s.

Brown by common consent is the more intellectually gifted of the two. He went to Kirkcaldy Grammar School at ten and took his Scottish Highers at fifteen. By sixteen he was already a first-year undergraduate at Edinburgh University, where he took a first in history. There is a joke that when Gordon Brown goes on holiday he has to pay an excess baggage allowance for all the books and weighty tomes that he takes with him. The son of a church minister, Brown and his brothers quickly developed a taste for politics as his father took Gordon and his two brothers around the parish to see the hardship suffered by others. Brown describes the home he grew up in as never having really been their own. 'There was a constant stream of people passing our front door . . . lots of people came knocking, some begging for money or a cup of tea, others with psychological or social problems. All of them had been hit hard.'[10]

Political awareness was to turn into political ambition at university. The fierce intellect was turned to mastering the arts of political intrigue, organising a coup that ousted the Principal, Lord Swann, who was later to become the Chairman of the BBC. Brown himself became rector of the university at the age of twenty-one, an honour he shares with other past political notables such as Gladstone, Disraeli, Churchill, Lloyd George and Baldwin. Brown's first crack at a parliamentary seat came in 1979 when he fought Edinburgh South. He failed there, but won Dunfermline East four years later, which took in part of his father's parish.

In Parliament, Brown's intellectual grasp, wide reading and powerful oratory gave him an edge over Blair. It also helped that Brown's political roots were dug in much deeper soil than Blair's. The bloc of Scots Labour MPs is the most powerful in the Party, sending to Westminster around fifty MPs, and Brown was very well known to most of them by the time he arrived at Westminster. While Blair waited until after he had left university to commit himself to the Labour Party, Brown was a childhood recruit, and everything he had done seemed to be pointing in one direction: a career in politics. The Scots Labour 'mafia' has also provided Westminster with some of the most gifted parliamentarians.

Both men found their political home in the Tribune group, but they were very much from the 'soft' left, and had no hesitation in backing Neil Kinnock for the leadership when Michael Foot stood down after the calamity of the general election. The 'soft' left had played an undistinguished and uncertain role in the great ideological battle between Benn and Healey two years earlier, but now they had a candidate whom they could unite behind. The forty-one-year-old fiery Welshman had precious little Labour front-bench experience, and absolutely no knowledge of what the inside of a red despatch box looked like, but, after the failure of Michael Foot's brief tenure, Kinnock looked like a man who could chart a successful course for Labour. Kinnock was always going to do well in the constituency parties and the union section of the electoral college, but his support among MPs was more flaky. The left saw him as a traitor after his failure to back Benn, the right-wing Solidarity Group, on the other hand, still viewed him as being little better than Benn. But once it became established that Kinnock would run with the Solidarity Group's Roy Hattersley as a 'dream ticket', Kinnock started to win support among the MPs as well. Neil Kinnock won convincingly, but the Shadow Cabinet that he inherited was hostile territory for the new man. Not one of its members had backed Kinnock, which meant the new Leader lost no time in bringing fresh talent on to Labour's front bench, not only to bolster his own isolated position but as a way of shuffling off political 'has beens' from positions of power.

This would very quickly pay handsome dividends for the new boy, Tony Blair. He was staggered by the level of incompetence and lack of talent that he found around him on the Labour benches when he arrived at Westminster. Blair had been used to dealing with smart and clever lawyers; what he found in the Parliamentary Labour Party were a lot of union 'place-men', who had become MPs as a reward for serving time as union officials. Blair and Brown stood out, even winning the grudging approval of that conspicuous Commons player and observer, Alan Clark, whose hapless task it was to field questions from the 'two bright boys, Blair and Brown . . . I got into difficulties immediately. They were bobbing up all over the place, asking impossible, spastic, questions of detail – most of them as far as I could make out to do with the fucking *Rule Book*.'[11] What particularly shocked the new boy was the casual way many of his fellow MPs went about their work, simply standing up when called to ask a question without first having thought about what it was they wanted to say. Blair's maiden speech during the Finance Bill paid no heed to the tradition that an MP's first speech should seek to steer clear of party political controversy. He waded into the Government's handling of the economy, accusing it of being unfeeling to the plight of the unemployed, particularly in his beleaguered constituency. It had been well researched, carefully prepared and was effectively delivered, but perhaps the most interesting part of it was the final peroration. Having made his case against the Government he went on to explain what it was that had made him a socialist:

I am a socialist not through reading a textbook that has caught my intellectual fancy, nor through unthinking tradition, but because I believe that, at its best, socialism corresponds most closely to an existence that is both rational and moral. It stands for co-operation, not confrontation; for fellowship, not fear. It stands for equality, not because it wants people to be the same but because only through equality in our economic circumstances can our individuality develop properly. British democracy rests ultimately on the shared perception by all the people that they participate in the benefits of the common weal.[12]

It was a maiden that caught the eye, and earned him a congratulatory letter from the Speaker, Bernard Weatherill, in which he wrote that it had been an admirable speech of which he could be proud. He offered warm congratulations and finished with the words 'well done indeed'. Blair, ever the conscientious and diligent grafter, would spend literally hours preparing if he knew from the Commons order paper that he was likely to be called to ask the Prime Minister a question. He also knew that, if there was one guaranteed way of impressing his peers and his opponents, it was in that fifteen minute glamour showcase between 3.15 and 3.30 each Tuesday and Thursday afternoon when Mrs Thatcher would come to the House to take on all comers.

On one occasion, just after the Government had banned workers from belonging to unions at the Cheltenham listening post, GCHQ, Blair asked a well targeted question which he finished with, 'when will she learn . . . that the British people prefer democrats to autocrats.'[13] Mrs Thatcher, who was to later make a statement on the matter, sidestepped the question, but *The Times* the following morning judged that Blair had drawn blood.

Thatcher, a devastating Commons performer, was to have her revenge on Blair and in so doing brought a whole new verb to British politics. Nigel Lawson had a few days earlier made a speech declaring that unemployment was a social rather than an economic problem. Blair, having spent his usual amount of time preparing his question, challenged Thatcher to say whether she agreed, and he went on: 'If she does, how does she square that with her endorsement at her Party conference of the 1944 employment White Paper which puts the battle for jobs at the heart of economic policy?'[14] It was a well-prepared question, and as Blair sat slowly to cheers from his side, Mrs Thatcher rose with the merest hint of a grin and more than a suggestion of menace. While fixing Blair with a look of utter disdain, she reached down for her handbag. 'Unemployment is both an economic and social problem,' she said. 'One cannot possibly argue against that. If the Honourable Gentleman were fully familiar with the 1944 White Paper I am sure he would agree that it has a great deal in common with the policies that the Government are pursuing.'[15] And then came the *coup de grâce*: she opened the handbag and from it pulled out a heavily marked and annotated copy of the 1944 White Paper, and proceeded to quote from the relevant parts of it which supported her argument. Considering the Prime Minister has no way of knowing what questions are likely to be fired at her from opposition MPs, it was a remarkable victory for her, lapped up by the cheering mass of Tory MPs behind her. Blair had been handbagged. To handbag was to become part of everyday political parlance.

If asking a well targeted question is the best way to get noticed by your fellow MPs, the easiest way to secure publicity in your constituency is through a late-night adjournment debate. These take place each night, just before the close of business for the day, and the subject matter will be chosen by the backbencher, normally relating to a matter of controversy within his or her constituency. A minister always has to reply to the half hour debate, and, even though there are only normally a handful of MPs in the Chamber to listen, it is a sure-fire way of getting coverage in the local newspapers and on local radio. Blair asked for and was granted an adjournment debate on plans by a subsidiary of the British Coal Board to close the Fishburn coke works in his constituency. But, as he rose to speak, the Labour MP for neighbouring Durham, Mark Hughes, a little the worse for wear – or tired and emotional, to give it the *Private Eye* euphemism – made a lunge at Blair and tried to land a number of punches on him before other North Eastern MPs like Giles Radice and Stuart Bell pulled him off. Mr Hughes was unhappy about boundary changes to his own constituency which, for reasons coloured by alcoholic consumption, he blamed Blair. The boundary review that had carved out the Sedgefield constituency had given some of Mark Hughes's strongest Labour voting areas to Tony Blair. The adjournment debate certainly received local headlines, but they had little to do with the plight of the coke works.

Blair had been in the House barely seven months in January

1984 when he received a phone call from Charles Clarke, who had now become the Labour Leader's chief of staff. 'Neil wonders whether you would be free to drop round for a chat,' Clarke, the son of a former Whitehall mandarin, intoned. Blair walked along the narrow booklined corridor behind the Commons chamber, past the door to the left that leads to the Prime Minister's suite of Commons offices, and on to the Opposition Leader's rooms. When he arrived his hands were shaking. He thought he had done something amiss and was about to be on the receiving end of a Neil Kinnock tirade. Clarke, for protocol reasons, couldn't tell Blair why he had been called in, but he assured him there was nothing to worry about. As Blair sat down in one of the green armchairs in Kinnock's room that looked over New Palace Yard, Kinnock, puffing away on his pipe, offered him a job on Labour's front bench to look after Labour's relations with the City. No-one had been given a job on the front bench so soon after entering the Commons since a young West Country MP by the name of Dr David Owen.

CHAPTER 4

Rising Star

'The duty of an Opposition, if it has no ambition to be permanently on the left-hand side of the Speaker, is not just to oppose
for opposition's sake, but to oppose selectively.'

Sir Henry Campbell-Bannerman
(Liberal Prime Minister, 1905–1908)

Blair's rapid appointment as Treasury and economic affairs spokesman inevitably provoked envy and resentment among his colleagues. Gore Vidal's famous comment that every time he saw a contemporary succeed another little part of him died is how most MPs react to the advancement of their peers. But Blair wasn't fazed by the antagonism – and neither was Neil Kinnock. Of the many reforms that Neil Kinnock introduced and pursued to make Labour electable once again, the one that has been remarked upon least was his determined efforts to foster new talent within the Parliamentary Labour Party, and to get away from the left/right balancing act that had hitherto determined who made progress in the PLP. In the 1980s, elections to the Shadow Cabinet were dominated by the slates of the Solidarity Group on the right and the Tribune and Campaign Groups on the left. They would in turn be backed up by the big voting blocs in the Labour Party, like the group of Scots MPs or Northern MPs. While Neil Kinnock was more or less impotent to influence how the PLP cast its votes for the annual elections to the Shadow Cabinet, the one power of patronage in the gift of the Leader was to promote people to key junior posts, and it was here that he was able to ignore left/right balancing, and put in position those whom he wanted in the Shadow Cabinet. And Kinnock recognised the need to promote both Blair and Gordon Brown as quickly as possible:

> I knew Tony was smart and he was one of half a dozen people that I thought, OK, the faster we get them on the front bench the better. All of them were set demanding tasks; all of them performed well. Both he and Gordon particularly shone. Gordon I knew much better before he came into Parliament. I got on particularly well with both of them. Not in any clubby sort of kitchen-cabinet way, but simply because they were friendly, lively younger members who were serious about the job they were doing, and virtue has its own rewards.[1]

The Treasury job also required someone who could deal with highly complex pieces of technical information. The Shadow Chancellor at this stage was the Deputy Leader, Roy Hattersley, who, while a considerable political thinker, brilliant essayist and man of many talents and much hinterland, was not one of life's natural economists. He was more of the Sir Alec Douglas-Home school, who famously remarked of his own approach: 'When I read economic documents I have to have a box of matches and start moving them into position, to illustrate and simplify the points to myself.' Hattersley wasn't as much at sea as that, but it was recognised that he needed people around him who could grasp the finer points of economic management, and Blair fitted the bill. His training as a barrister meant he was quick to take a brief, and Archie Kirkwood, now the Liberal Democrat Chief Whip, said he used to turn up at sittings of the Finance Bill, and would wait for Blair to speak so that he could have explained to him what was going on. Indeed, after the long-drawn-out proceedings of the committee stage of the Finance Bill, the Financial Secretary to the Treasury, Peter Brooke, congratulated the Opposition, which was led by Blair, on a well fought battle. According to the *Scotsman* newspaper, Blair was 'notable among the Labour team, suddenly drawing on the advice from within the City and taking the battle on to the Conservatives' own ground with tough, highly technical debate over tax and VAT issues.'[2]

The Treasury brief had a particular importance and difficulty for the Labour Party. With the advent of Big Bang in 1986, which deregulated financial dealings in stocks, gilts and bonds and put an end to restrictive practices on the Stock Exchange, Labour needed a spokesman who was forensically sharp and legally watertight to deal with the complex changes and regulatory questions that were coming to the fore in the worlds of banking and equities. The City has always been enemy territory for the Labour Party, even though paradoxically the stock market has made some of its greatest gains under Labour administrations, and it had grown doubly hostile during the 1983 general election campaign, because it seemed that the Conservative Party was offering so much, and Labour so little. A call to nationalise one or more of the main clearing banks and to introduce protectionism in the financial markets, with restrictions on the buying and selling of shares to stop speculative dealing, was hardly likely to bring the city slicker into the Labour camp. It all contributed to a general perception that the Labour Party, as well as being inherently hostile, didn't really understand what the City did.

But all those questions about whether there was sufficient regulation over the City were to be drawn into sharp focus in the autumn of 1984, when a merchant bank nearly collapsed. Johnson Mathey Bank (JMB) was not in itself a big player in the City, but if it had gone under it would have had a devastating effect on confidence because its parent company was one of the leading bullion dealers. On 1 October, as the Labour Party was gathering for its annual conference, the Chancellor Nigel Lawson was telephoned by his Permanent Secretary, Sir Peter Middleton, with news that the Governor and Deputy Governor of the Bank of England were seeking an urgent meeting with the Chancellor before the markets opened. The Bank were of the view that JMB had to be rescued – interestingly not out of concern for the bank's depositors, but because of the potential damage it would do to the London bullion market. Strictly speaking this was not within the ambit of banking supervision.

Although the Bank of England did not require the Chancellor's authority for the planned rescue, it was known that a very large sum of money was at stake. There was a real danger that the Bank, which proposed to acquire JMB for the token payment of £1, could be facing losses of up to £100 million. There were concerns that the Bank's own free reserves, which it held for this sort of rescue, might fall short of the amount needed for the rescue. The Bank of England was asking the Chancellor to give an open-ended guarantee of taxpayers' money in support of a rescue plan about whose wisdom, as he admitted himself, he was not entirely certain. Lawson decided to rely upon the Bank's judgement, deliberately leaving his position ambiguous. He did not provide the required guarantee but neither did he state that under no circumstances would the Treasury make public funds available if and when necessary. With that in mind he advised the Bank to do what it felt best. Not surprisingly the Bank went ahead with the rescue confident that the Treasury would provide funding if necessary.

Fortunately for Lawson, this episode began during the summer recess, giving him three weeks to prepare for the anticipated Opposition onslaught when the House of Commons re-assembled. Bank regulation fell very much into Blair's ambit of responsibility but, to the Chancellor's amazement, by the time he delivered his statement to Parliament on 17 December 1984 (almost two months into the new session), which announced the setting up of a committee to look into banking supervision, the official Labour Opposition had never once raised the matter.

The only remotely serious probing had come from the Opposition back benches, in the person of the austere left-wing xenophobe and conspiracy theorist, Denis Skinner, the maverick Member for the mining constituency of

Bolsover – an accomplished parliamentarian with the best and quickest repartee in the House, and a better sense of where the Government was vulnerable than the whole of his Party's front bench put together.[3]

A further potential embarrassment to Lawson came when the chairman of the Public Accounts Committee, Bob Sheldon, enquired as to what the Bank's liability was in respect of JMB. The Chancellor replied in good faith that, other than the £1 spent on the acquisition of JMB, he had been informed of a £75 million indemnity, but it was too early to gauge how much of that would be required. However, it subsequently became apparent that, unbeknown to Lawson, the Bank had in fact deposited a further £100 million in JMB. Lawson had therefore inadvertently misled the House in his response to Sheldon's question. Luckily for Lawson the Opposition never seemed to pick up on his misdeed, and it wasn't until the Chancellor made a detailed statement on what had happened to JMB some months later that Blair really took up the case.

The internal inquiry into what had happened was chaired by the Governor of the Bank, Robin Leigh-Pemberton. The further the investigation went the less surprising it became that Johnson Mathey had collapsed, but the more embarrassing it became for the Bank of England, and indirectly for the Government. The Bank had clearly failed in its regulatory function, and fuelled Labour demands for better safeguards and guarantees to prevent the same happening again. Lawson's statement to the Commons in July 1985 pinned the blame firstly on the Bank for failing to pick up all the obvious danger signals, and, secondly, on the auditors, Arthur Young. But the candour of the statement only came after some aggressive parliamentary questioning by Blair, who harried the Government with a series of probing interventions on why the Bank had failed to detect what was going on. He also alleged that the Treasury had attempted to withdraw a number of parliamentary answers which confirmed that there had been a departure from normal banking practices during the collapse. Blair described the affair as the 'first steps in a financial Watergate'.[4]

Kinnock watched Blair with quiet satisfaction as he scurried around fulfilling what was expected of him as Labour's most junior member of the front bench. But Kinnock was more concerned about the 'big picture' for Labour and his overriding concern was knocking the Party into shape for the next general election. After his election as Leader he vowed that the Party would never again go through the trauma of the 1983 election defeat. Saying that unity was the price of victory, Kinnock declared that, 'Anyone who becomes tempted to go back to the old ways should remember one thing. Think to yourself: June 9 1983. Never again will we experience that.'[5] Kinnock, having started life as a Leader isolated by the Labour establishment, was forging an alliance with the centre left and the right to build up a formidable degree of control over the Party – whether in the Shadow Cabinet, the NEC or in humbler surroundings of a local constituency general committee.

By the time the autumn conference came in 1985, the miners' strike had ended and Militant had at last been marginalised, some five years after Anthony Blair, the barrister, had given the Party legal advice. Kinnock's excoriating attack on Militant in Bournemouth still ranks as one of the Welshman's finest moments. It symbolised graphically a part of Labour's unhappy past that had finally been dealt with and Kinnock won warm plaudits for the courage of his stance and determined way in which he pursued it. Emboldened and encouraged by his reception, Kinnock was now convinced it was time to re-launch Labour as a party fit for government. To do this, Kinnock took on a young television producer, who had once been politically active, but who had drifted off into the more rewarding world of the media during Labour's dog days at the end of the 1970s. Peter Mandelson, who had been a contemporary of Tony Blair at Oxford, although the two men's paths never crossed there, was appointed Director of Communications. (When Mandelson was recently asked had he known Blair at Oxford he quipped: 'No, why should I have done? I was interested in politics!')

The grandson of one of Labour's most distinguished politicians, Herbert Morrison, Mandelson was brought up in prosperous Hampstead Garden Suburb. During the 1964 election, Mandelson toured the local polling stations on his bicycle, and afterwards was invited to have tea with his parents at Number 10 when his former neighbour had won the 1964 general election. From an early age the glamour and intrigue of politics have coursed round Mandelson's bloodstream, as they do so today. Mandelson runs on high octane nervous energy. He is a political obsessive who seldom relaxes, but who has a wicked sense of humour and fun. Tall and slim with a rather delicately featured face, he can be charming to the point of unctuousness, and at other times he can lash with the sharpest of tongues if he feels the occasion demands it.

Peter Mandelson is fascinated as much by the process of politics as he is by the policy. Now an MP, as he stalks around a conference hall, it is not fellow politicians that he seeks out, but the journalists and image makers. Mandelson made it his business to find out early on in his career as Communications Director the detailed mechanics of what puts a story on the front page; how editorials could be influenced; what pictures the television producers would be looking for. And most importantly of all, he made it his business to get to know all the key senior figures in a newspaper or broadcasting organisation so that he had a direct line to the opinion formers. On a daily basis he would seek to find out what every newspaper would be running on their front pages before the paper was put to bed. He would patrol the corridors of the press gallery, poking his head round doors, finding out how lobby journalists were treating a particular story. Often reporters would be sitting at their terminal filing a report only to find Mandelson peering over their shoulder, with suggestions on how the story might be improved, or exploding with indignation if it did Labour down.

There was no-one in the Conservative Party to touch him.

While Central Office was filled with charming young men and women who were polite and attentive but would never dare tell a journalist what to write, Mandelson and the press team that he assembled were forever interfering, bullying and trying to shape the political coverage of either the newspaper or the broadcaster. Often Mandelson would in no uncertain terms be told where to go. But more remarkable was the number of occasions on which his view or 'spin' on a story prevailed. Part of it was because younger members of the lobby were slightly scared of him. If, for example, he took against a particular story that a reporter had filed, Mandelson would think nothing of going right to the top of either the newspaper or broadcasting organisation to complain in the most frank terms about the professionalism of this or that reporter. But the main lever that he had was that he knew where all the bodies were buried in Walworth Road and in the Labour Party, and his thirst for gossip made his private briefings always worth listening to. On the principle that journalists rarely bite the hand that feeds them, Mandelson was someone who for personal and professional reasons it was imperative not to be on the wrong side of. He was invaluable to the journalists because he was able to paint seemingly dreary Labour events in glorious, vivid Technicolor. But the reporter would only be given this kind of invaluable information if he or she could be trusted to put the correct gloss on the story.

From the politician's viewpoint, Mandelson was an even more awesome figure. Kinnock had entrusted him with the job of improving Labour's image in the media, and Mandelson ruthlessly set about doing just that. There can be little doubt about the power he wielded. He realised that young up-and-coming politicians would do nearly anything to get on television, and Mandelson seemed to hold the keys to the TV Studios. He would occasionally joke that these people were his 'puppets'. Blair was one of those. Mandelson insisted that all bids for a front-bench spokesman to appear on radio or television programmes had to go through his office. In the name of Party discipline, Kinnock backed Mandelson on this, but in doing so gave the Communications Director enormous power. He would take in a bid from, say, *Breakfast News* for this or that spokesman, and if he thought someone would be reliable and was a good television performer, Mandelson would sanction the interview; if he did not, then he would put someone else's name forward. In the name of professionalism, Mandelson was able to wield huge influence over the development of a politician's career. Not surprisingly, he made many more enemies than he did friends.

Mandelson once joked to his colleague John Denham (the MP for Southampton Test), with whom he shared an office when both men arrived at Westminster as new boys in 1992, that only 50 per cent of what was written about him was true. But if it is as much as 50 per cent, that still leaves an exceptionally deep font of stories that must be authentic. There are the funny stories like when Mandelson and Kinnock were campaigning in a by-election and they had stopped off for some fish and chips. Kinnock ordered some plaice, and Mandelson in the middle of a northern town asked for what he thought was guacamole. The man behind the counter looked bewildered. 'The mashed avocado,' Mandelson persisted. At which point everyone in the chippie erupted into laughter. What the urbane North Londoner had thought was guacamole was in fact mushy peas.

But Mandelson will be judged in his period as Communications Director for the revolution that he brought to the way that Labour approached the business of communicating. The emphasis would move dramatically to the mass media, instead of supplying endless briefs to local party organisations. Under Mandelson's predecessor, the accent had been on knocking on doors and leafletting, but this was seen as dated and irrelevant. So the purpose of campaigning became not to reinforce the views of the believer but to win over new converts. It is such a commonplace now for all political parties to follow this approach that it is easy to forget what a radical shift in direction and professionalism Mandelson had effected.

Philip Gould, who had spent ten years at the top of the advertising industry, was brought in to conduct detailed polling on targeted groups of voters. He in turn recruited a diverse range of talents from the advertising and marketing industries and moulded what much later became known as the Shadow Communications Agency. While the Conservative Party had the funds to keep one agency on the case permanently – Saatchi and Saatchi – Labour had to eke out their more limited resources. The ad hoc group gave Saatchi's a good run for their money. Within two months of their starting work under Mandelson's guidance, the Labour image was thoroughly reworked and red rose designer socialism was born. Kinnock had for some time believed that the 'red flag' image had become dated and was in need of a thorough overhaul. Labour's sister parties on the Continent had used a red rose clasped by a burly fist. Kinnock wanted the rose, and one of the designers from the Shadow Communications Agency was set to work. After two hundred drawings of roses of different size, shape and stem length, the one that still adorns all campaign literature and headed notepaper was selected.

It was a National Executive meeting in February 1986 that finally gave birth to the Shadow Communications Agency. It was to be chaired by Chris Powell, the managing director of one of the leading advertising companies in the country (ironically, his brother was Charles Powell, Mrs Thatcher's hugely influential Private Secretary. And now the youngest Powell brother, Jonathan, who was a high flying diplomat serving in the Washington embassy, has given up the Diplomatic Service to become Blair's overarching head of the Leader's office), but the most important relationship was between Philip Gould and Peter Mandelson. In their book, *Labour Rebuilt,* Colin Hughes and Patrick Wintour chart the course of their work:

> He [Gould] was commissioned by Mandelson and reported to Mandelson. They spoke to each other every day, and so fused their operations that they often found it hard to distinguish who proposed what. But their division of responsibility was clear: Gould diagnosed and evaluated,

Mandelson carried out the surgery . . . often taking enormous political risks with his own position in order to do so.[6]

Mandelson was the driving force, the nervous energy and the brain behind a whole series of changes that came together in the 1987 general election campaign. With the support of Neil Kinnock, Mandelson had amassed considerable power. Mandelson, an unelected official from Walworth Road, seemed able to make or break the career of an elected member of the Shadow Cabinet. He marginalised John Prescott, sat upon Michael Meacher and ensured that some others never came face to face with a television camera. But for all the legend and mythology, there was no sorcery or magic – well, not that much – in what Mandelson did. It came down to sheer force of personality. He worked, bullied and cajoled non-stop. A certain mythology has grown up about Mandelson's powers. When Shaun Woodward became the Conservative Party's equivalent in the run up to the 1992 general election, he told people that the professional he most admired and would seek to emulate was Mandelson. Kinnock, though, who saw him at close quarters, is rather more measured about his influences and achievements. His line on Mandelson is that he was neither as good as some have made out, nor was he as bad.

Blair and Brown in 1987 were still comparative unknowns outside the Westminster greenhouse, but Mandelson, who had a keen sense of who was in and who was out as well as who was moving up and who down, had recognised their worth. They joined the team that Mandelson called the 'grenade-lobbers'. It was their job to appear at news conferences with the sole purpose of 'mixing it' with the enemy. Gerald Kaufman, a man who could start a fight in an empty room, was put in charge of the unit. Blair and Brown were his deputies. But on one of Blair's first outings in this role, the grenade-lobber found that he had thrown the pin while the explosive was about to blow up in his face. The subject under discussion was housing policy, and Blair, in response to a question, accused Margaret Thatcher of being unhinged. Michael Brunson, ITN's sharp political editor, pounced. 'Are you really saying that Mrs Thatcher is mad?' enquired Brunson. Blair, blushing slightly and sounding nervous, felt the ground falling away beneath him. He dissembled and retreated. Mandelson, meanwhile, made straight for Brunson to play down (in spin-doctor parlance, 'downspin') what Blair had said. Blair's first sortie had not been wreathed in glory, but Mandelson saw in Blair someone who was anxious to learn and keen to please. The 1987 election campaign saw the blossoming of two critical friendships. The first between Mandelson and Blair; the second between Mandelson and Brown.

If Blair was one of those who prospered under Mandelson's patronage, John Prescott was one of the losers. The former National Union of Seamen official had a profound antipathy to the Oxford-educated élite (even though Prescott had spent a brief amount of time as a mature student at Ruskin College, Oxford, where he took a diploma before gaining a degree at Hull University) that Kinnock had surrounded himself with, and an even greater hostility to the way Roy Hattersley was carrying out the job of deputy leader. It was an antagonism that was hand-somely reciprocated. In the run up to the 1987 general election campaign, Prescott was the Party's employment spokesman, and had been due to play a key role in a jobs campaign that Labour were launching in March 1987. But the day before he got into a famous quarrel with the former Labour Prime Minister Jim Callaghan over defence policy in the Commons tea-room, dur-ing the course of which Prescott accused Callaghan of snookering Labour's election chances. Mandelson as a result tried to have Prescott excluded from the news conference which was due to launch the jobs package. Prescott was eventually allowed to be there, but he said nothing and left by a back door.

After the election, Prescott's challenge for the deputy leader-ship against Neil Kinnock's wishes led to an even greater deterioration in Prescott's relationship with Mandelson. And when, after Blair had been elected leader in 1994, Mandelson was spotted in a first class compartment on a train travelling down to London chatting to Prescott, the incident was considered significant enough to appear in a newspaper diary. In fact it was the first proper conversation the two men had had in six years.

The presentation of the 1987 election campaign was for Labour – and Peter Mandelson in particular – an extraordinary success. The problem was the result was another humiliating defeat. The Tories still had a hundred-seat-plus majority, and Labour had once again unravelled over taxation and defence. The crumb of comfort for Labour politicians was that the Party looked like a serious player again on the political stage. But the harsh reality that Neil Kinnock had to face was that it was a defeat without excuses – the message had been put across as effectively as it had ever been but the voters were still holding their noses. The campaign turned Mandelson into the stuff of legend. His fans thought him a genius; detractors like John Prescott and those who had been cast into outer darkness thought him an almost sinister, malevolent influence who should carry the can for Labour's failure. Blair believes that in fact Mandelson, and Mandelson almost alone, saved Labour from even greater humiliation at that election.

But Kinnock was on Mandelson's side, and, if anything, his influence grew as the Labour Leader pondered the lessons of the 1987 election defeat. Under Mandelson's guidance, in November 1987 the Shadow Communications Agency presented a three-and-half-hour-long lecture to a joint meeting of the Shadow Cabinet and the National Executive on what had gone wrong and what was needed to make it right. The detailed polling evidence and market sampling made the case for a thorough overhaul of Labour Party policy, so that it could be presented to the electors at the next election as a cohesive whole. There is a joke in the Labour Party that MPs write press releases while press officers make the policy. It was a gag written for Peter Mandelson as he knew more clearly than many the direction in which he wanted to take Labour Party policy. And on more than one occasion, members of the Shadow Cabinet complained to Neil Kinnock directly that Mandelson was subverting their work, by giving separate briefings to the press contradicting what the Shadow Cabinet member had said.

The left were deeply suspicious of what Kinnock's hidden agenda was in launching the policy review. Bryan Gould, who had been campaign manager during the 1987 election campaign, and had grown very close to Kinnock, had already argued that policy making must pay greater heed to what people wanted: 'What we ought to be doing is looking at where policies ought to come from, what the demand is, what interests we ought to be serving. In that way we can make sure that the policy includes its popular appeal from the outset.'[7] To the left it looked like the most blatant attempt to water down Labour's commitment to socialism, as it had been understood over the past twenty-five years. That the views had been expressed by someone so close to Kinnock was interpreted as being the Leader's view spoken through a convenient cipher. But it wasn't just the left who were panicked by what was seen as a headlong rush into opportunism and populism in the search for lost voters. One of the fiercest broadsides was fired by the deputy leader and leading right-wing Labour politician, Roy Hattersley. A week after Gould's comments on the radio, Hattersley went on television with an outspoken counter-attack. His words still echo, as Tony Blair continues the modernisation process that Neil Kinnock embarked upon:

> The idea that six weeks after an election defeat, somebody can come along and say: 'These are all the things we do; we change this policy, we have a new defence policy, we abandon nationalisation, we give up our view of equality. What we do, we send out a lot of marketing men into the country, just as the Democrats in America did twenty years ago and say "what are the policies people want?" and then when we find out what they'll vote for we'll write it into our manifesto' – that is not the sort of politics I want to be

involved in . . . I've not gone through the last six years –
the defeat of '79 as well as the humiliation of '83 – to
make the Labour Party into a new sort of Social
Democratic Party.[8]

The 1987 Labour Party conference in Brighton where the idea
of the policy review was presented was a sullen affair. Numbed
and mesmerised by yet another defeat, left-wing delegates who
felt this was nothing more than revisionism and an attempt to rip
the socialist heart out of Labour had neither the energy nor the
ammunition to mount a serious challenge to the leadership. The
proposal to set up a policy review was passed with next-to-no
serious blood-letting. Blair saw it as a vital path that had to be
travelled to make Labour electable again. 'No ditching of basic
principle is needed,' he wrote in *The Times*. 'The dichotomy
between "principles" and "power," has always been false.'
    Blair then went on to set out the case for change within the
Labour Party.

Any political party that, like Labour, aspires to govern
must show that it is fit to manage the economy, responsible in its presentation of itself and listens to the people.
That much is obvious, a necessary but not sufficient
condition for success. But to win Labour must fashion an
agenda of its own. The 1980s may have seen the triumph
of 'the market'. The '90s will be about how to deal with
its failures. The Tories are wholly ill equipped for such a
task. Labour is the party of social action, socialism is the
creed of the community, the belief that we are more than
just a group of individuals competing against each other.[9]

And he said that with society undergoing a period of radical
change,

the policy review should not dwell over-long on how
Labour grapples with the issues of the past. These should

be dealt with flexibly, realistically but also sharply. Our energy and sense of purpose should be directed to the challenges of the future.[10]

This was one of Blair's first forays out of the confines of his narrow front-bench role and into the wider area of the intellectual debate going on about the future of socialism. It was a mark of Blair's growing self-confidence as a politician that he felt able to do this, but what he was saying was very much in tune with Neil Kinnock, which made it a less risky undertaking. But Blair developed a taste for writing on subjects beyond his front-bench responsibilities, and was soon using the Commentary column of *The Times* as a sounding board for his wider political views. For about a year, Blair wrote a piece every two or three weeks. He ranged freely, commenting on televising parliament, abortion, fire safety, law and order and Gorbachov's *perestroika*. Blair's frustration at being a bit part player in opposition politics at least found an outlet in writing.

After the 1987 election defeat, Kinnock made Blair the Party's City spokesman, the number two job in the Trade and Industry team under Bryan Gould. Soon after he started the job came Black Monday, the stock market crash when billions were wiped off the value of shares in a day of frenzied selling. Blair immediately courted controversy with the left of the Party by setting up a committee to look at how such volatility could be avoided in future. Membership of the committee remained secret out of deference to the Labour sympathising City figures who wanted their Labour colours to remain hidden under their pin-striped suits. But it set tongues wagging that Blair was selling out to the enemy, the City of London. Blair, however, was clear in his political purpose:

There are real problems in the way the City works, but I think Labour should be attacking on a credible long-term basis, rather than concentrating on gossip about scandals . . . we will continue to raise scandals when they occur, but I am not a scandal monger. I am more interested in ensuring the Labour Party knows how the City works and can provide proposals for reform that will have a direct benefit for the economy.[11]

But if part of Blair's job was to court the City and make others in his Party less intemperate of what happened a couple of miles down the river from Westminster, then his other task was to reposition Labour in terms of the small investor. Part of the Conservatives' success was in attracting small investors into the stock market – the Tories' favourite phrase was of creating a 'share owning democracy'. Gould and Blair recognised that these small investors needed to be given good reason to come back to Labour, so Blair set about conducting some original research into the sort of service given by the Stock Exchange to small investors. He contacted 151 broking firms with a view to selling 200 British Telecom shares. A third said they would not deal in such small quantities, while a further third wanted to charge such high commission rates that any profits gained from increases in the share price would have been wiped out. The publication of his findings at a Westminster news conference allowed Blair to paint Labour as on the side of the minnows in a pool of financial sharks.

That concern for the small investor came to the fore when Blair harried the Government over the collapse of the Barlow Clowes investment empire. News of the collapse came as Blair had just returned from the Far East. He had gone with John Smith, who was then Shadow Chancellor, on a fact-finding tour at the invitation of the Chinese Communist Party. The two already knew each other extremely well, but this was the most prolonged period they spent in each other's company. The Communists believed that Labour would soon be in power again, and treated the delegation like visiting heads of state. In Shanghai, there was a memorable evening when the head of the region's Communist Party challenged the leader of the British delegation, John Smith, to a drinking competition. Unbeknown to the Chinese, Smith had a near legendary capacity for alcohol. Blair tells the story that, by the end of the evening, the local commissar was on the floor while the rest of the Chinese officials, after a brief period of instruction from Smith, were linking arms and singing 'Auld Lang Syne'.

Blair returned to England via Tokyo and came back to the Barlow Clowes affair. Others in his team, like the Cardiff South MP Alun Michael, were astonished that, despite being completely jet-lagged, Blair called a meeting immediately, pinpointing what needed to be done, and identifying a strategy to help the eleven thousand small investors who had had their fingers badly burnt by Barlow Clowes. Blair's insistence that there ought to be a lifeboat fund was initially rejected by the Government, but when the cry was taken up by the Parliamentary Commissioner, the call was eventually heeded.

With work on the policy review now well underway in November 1988, the Labour Leader appointed a new, more 'youthful' front-bench team cast much more in Neil Kinnock's image. Of the twelve new appointments to the front bench, eleven had only come into the Commons at the general election a year earlier. But what gave Kinnock most satisfaction was seeing Blair win a place on the fifteen-strong Shadow Cabinet. Blair was rewarded for his highly effective attacks on the Government by winning a place on the influential Tribune slate for the forthcoming Shadow Cabinet elections (although the facional slates have diminished in importance over the years, the biggest single grouping in the PLP is the Tribune Group, and securing their support for the Shadow Cabinet elections will give a fillip to a candidate's chances); it meant his election was a betting certainty. He was offered what Kinnock thought would be a key post with electricity privatisation beckoning: the post of Shadow Energy Secretary. Electricity privatisation was the most complex undertaken by the government at that stage, as it involved a separation of the generating companies from the distributors of electricity. It also involved – at that stage – plans to privatise the nuclear industry, with the massive, but unknown, costs of decommissioning the ageing Magnox stations. But from Neil Kinnock's viewpoint, essential as it was to have someone able to grasp complex detail quickly – Blair's strongest suit – it was also a handy way of punishing John Prescott for his decision to challenge Roy Hattersley for the deputy leadership a few months earlier, very much against Neil Kinnock's wishes. Kinnock pushed Prescott into what had always been a political siding, namely transport (ironically it turned out to be one of the most high profile jobs in the Shadow Cabinet as his appointment was marked by a succession of transport tragedies with planes falling out of the sky, trains crashing and boats sinking, which resulted in Prescott's face being seen endlessly on the television, hugely bolstering his position in the Party, completely contrary to what Neil Kinnock had intended). Here in the Shadow Cabinet Blair joined his friend Gordon Brown, who had earned his appointment as Shadow Chief Secretary to the Treasury the previous year.

It was in this post that Blair was first given the opportunity to prove his political acumen, taking charge of Labour's opposition to a central plank of the Government's legislative programme. In Westminster politics opposition is easy; it is effective opposition, the sort of opposition that makes the Government sweat a little, that is difficult. With a Commons majority of 101, no amount of blocking on the floor of the House by Labour will stop the Government getting its business passed, but in the Committee stage of a bill, when a smaller group of MPs spend hours poring over the finer detail, well thought out and constructive opposition can halt even the most determined Government in its tracks. With Kinnock's backing and encouragement, Blair fought a clever tactical game, targeting only those parts of the bill that were vulnerable to sustained attack rather than offering the more usual blanket opposition.

The Barnsley Central MP, Eric Illsley, served on the Standing Committee with Blair and remembers that he would call his team together every Tuesday and Thursday that the Standing Committee was in session to work out fresh lines of attack, and angles that would keep the Government's accident prone piece of legislation on the front pages. Illsley was deeply impressed: 'He's a very strong minded character and I think much more strong minded than a lot of people have given him credit for. He imposed his will on how the committee would operate. It ended up being a very high profile bill which it might not have been had someone else dealt with it or dealt with it in a different manner.'[12]

Blair dispensed with the political blunderbuss in favour of the sniper's rifle. The trouble is, for a politician who wants to be noticed, the committee process is long, interminable and complex, and is routinely shunned by Westminster journalists unless they know something exciting is likely to emerge. Blair learnt quickly that, with advance briefing, it was possible to give the reporters a story and keep the most controversial issues concerning electricity privatisation bubbling in the public consciousness. His tactics were to allow huge chunks of the legislation to go unchallenged. So MPs in the morning would turn up, and the Labour side would then surprise the Tories and Cecil Parkinson, the Secretary of State for Energy, by letting a certain number of clauses go by, before hitting one particular section of the bill very hard. When they got to that Clause, Blair would make his speech, knowing that the press were in attendance and already briefed on the significance of the point he was making, and it would be left to the hapless Parkinson to try to respond.

Throughout the Committee stage of the bill there were several 'leaks' of private internal documents which mysteriously found their way into Blair's pigeon hole. Parkinson, looking back, believes there was a mole inside his office briefing Blair. One such document which arrived in a plain brown manila envelope at the office of the Shadow Energy Secretary was an internal CEGB memorandum revealing that the hidden costs of privatisation amounted to a substantial 76 million pounds. It was estimated that every householder would have to pay a £2 supplement on their bills to cover the cost of advertising, legal and financial advice and other costs incurred during the preparatory period for the flotation. For a Government that was promising a cheaper and more efficient industry, which in turn would give savings to the consumers by removing the 'dead' hand of the state from the affairs of the electricity business, this was a highly damaging piece of information. Blair accused the Government of burying such additional costs in the general price of electricity.

It is one thing to be the recipient of a damning leaked document; it is another to know what to do with it. Timing was clearly of the essence, and Blair had to decide what would be the best moment to play his trump card, ensuring maximum media interest and the highest degree of embarrassment possible for ministers. Blair chose his moment. Late one night during the Committee stage of the bill, he was engaged in highly detailed argument over some minor clauses. As the night wore on Blair suggested they draw the debate to a close and re-convene in the morning. The following morning Blair unusually was not in his seat at the appointed time for the resumption of discussion and other members of the committee decided to go on without him. Eventually Blair turned up, but he was not alone. He had brought with him a posse of lobby journalists. Parkinson spotted them instantly and guessed correctly – that a trap was being laid for him. A number of them were television and radio journalists, and, with the lunchtime news approaching, Parkinson realised what he had to do. He launched headlong into a monologue that lasted for the best part of an hour, and didn't stop talking until he knew it would be too late for Blair to get anything on the lunchtime bulletins. The Energy Secretary was well judged in his caution. Blair's intention had been to floor Parkinson and the other Tories on the committee by using the leaked memorandum on the cost of electricity privatisation as a hand grenade, simply tossing it into the proceedings, without giving the Secretary of State any prior warning. Blair later that day certainly did get huge coverage for the leaked memorandum, even if Parkinson slipped the net that lunchtime. Interestingly, Parkinson believes that Blair missed a golden opportunity to embarrass the Government even more, in view of the potency of the document that he had received. Parkinson believes that while Blair showed that he was calculating, he didn't try hard enough to maximise the Government's discomfort, showing a readiness to move on too quickly to the next item of business. But it taught the senior and experienced minister to tread cautiously in his dealings with Blair and to never underestimate him as a political operator. Parkinson rated him highly:

> I think he's very shrewd. One of the things I noticed during the passage of the Electricity Bill was that, for a newly appointed leading spokesman, he used his effort sparingly. He had a big point he wanted to make each day and he clearly put a lot of effort into that, and that was clever. He would then let the others follow up on the point he had made, which I thought was a grown-up thing to do.[13]

Parkinson, who by common consent came off worse from the exchanges, would nevertheless tease Blair that he was a 'single-barrelled shotgun', only able to fire one shot a day.

Blair's success proved to be a combination of skill and good fortune. The good fortune was that civil servants were prepared to take huge risks in leaking information to him which was highly damaging to the Government. But such are the dangers involved in running off a photocopy of a classified document, that it is also true that those who are doing the leaking are highly selective in whom they leak to. To be the person on the receiving end of a civil servant's leaked documents is a sure sign of a politician on the inside track. The various stages of this bill were littered with such episodes, bringing the Government many headaches and putting a nail in the coffin of Cecil Parkinson's already faltering comeback whilst enhancing Blair's reputation as a force to be reckoned with within the new Shadow Cabinet.

The Electricity Privatisation Bill was doomed to be difficult for the Government. Indeed, by the following September, in what Blair described as a 'monumental shambles', the Government decided to put plans off to privatise electricity for at least a year. At the Labour Party conference that autumn Blair called for electricity privatisation to be abandoned altogether. 'Born out of dogma, reared on deceit, this privatisation is now exposed for what it is and always has been, private prejudice masquerading as public policy.'

Kinnock would have kept Blair where he was for a little bit longer had he not been confronted by a bigger, far more sensitive problem that required someone who could be trusted absolutely to do what was required for the leader.

CHAPTER 5

The Closed Shop Opened

'Despite all the rhetoric, the Labour Party remains a wholly-owned subsidiary of the trade union movement.'
Conservative Party Campaign Guide, 1994

The polls told them reform was needed; Labour leaders knew in their hearts that the relationship needed an overhaul; the newspapers screamed for change; and Conservative politicians made hay. Labour's links with the unions were the source of the Party's greatest strength – and weakness. The Labour Party, conceived and born as the political wing of the trade union movement, had ever since the Winter of Discontent been dragged down by the unions, even though the unions bankrolled the Party. Legislation to curb the powers of the unions had proved highly popular with the electorate. Now Neil Kinnock decreed it was time to grasp the nettle of Labour's policy towards union reform. It was one of the most sensitive areas of the policy review. A mixture of Neil Kinnock's grinding determination and Mandelson's presentational *élan* kept the process driving on as shibboleth after shibboleth was thrown from the policy window. Out went the anti-European baggage, ditto the Party's unilateral disarmament policies. There would be no more penal tax rates, and the Party would accept some of the Government's trade union reforms. But it was on the endlessly prickly question of Labour's relations with the unions that the policy review was getting bogged down. The Shadow Employment Secretary, Michael Meacher, had given the Labour Leader's office a number of problems with his determination to be his own man on the question of union reform. So in the wake of the Shadow Cabinet elections in the autumn of 1989, Kinnock summoned Blair to take over.

What made this challenge so different from anything he had done in his political career to date was that it would be his first proper gladiatorial contest, and with some of the Labour movement's most wily battle-hardened streetfighters – the union general secretaries. Kinnock knew that the classic compromise which kept the Party together but did not convince the electorate would be torn apart by the Tories and the press. Into this testing arena Blair was tossed.

The challenge to Blair was multi-layered. Clearly the worst outcome was that he would fail. But for him personally even a simple victory was not enough. He could win the day for Kinnock but make so many enemies among trade unionists and Party activists, who would forever cast him as the hard man of the right, that he would become a marginal figure in Labour politics. So a complete victory involved not only changing the policy but also winning the argument in the minds of most union and Party members, avoiding the perpetuation of the image of the Party as split and fractious, while impressing the electorate at large.

Kinnock, Mandelson and other key strategists were firmly of the view that Labour's ability to sell its 'new look' policies on the unions was of paramount importance if success was to come at the next election. Under Labour, 'popular' elements of Tory employment law would remain intact, such as pre-strike ballots. But before Blair took over, Michael Meacher, who was chairing that section of the policy review committee, was wandering in a direction that caused fury in the Leader's office. The battle between Kinnock and Meacher was fought with varying degrees of intensity. Mostly it was behind the scenes, as draft proposals were batted from one to the other; occasionally the hostility found its way onto the front pages.

When Meacher defied the leader's wishes by discussing the draft policy review on the BBC's *On the Record* – something Kinnock had specifically requested that none of the convenors do while the policy review was going on – the heavens opened.

Despite a curt reminder from Mandelson, Meacher appeared on the programme, discussing secondary picketing and secondary action. When Jonathan Dimbleby asked him, 'Does that mean that you would restore that kind of action to the point at which it existed before 1979?' Meacher's response, 'That is indeed along the lines that we would be thinking,'[1] clearly indicated that he had no intention of shedding the uncomfortable vote-losing legacy of mass picketing prevalent during the strikes of the 1970s. His effective call for an abandonment of the Conservatives' trade union laws indicated to Kinnock that either Meacher hadn't grasped what the leadership wanted to do or that he was flouting the wishes of the leader. Kinnock spoke to Charles Clarke; Clarke spoke to Mandelson; and Mandelson finally got his deputy Colin Byrne to do the dirty deed.

Within hours of the broadcast, Byrne, who with his slicked back hair looked like a gangster's 'knuckles', was on the phone to selected members of the lobby. He was telling newspaper journalists that the interview was unauthorised and did not represent Party policy. Byrne did for Meacher what Bernard Ingham had done for John Biffen a couple of years earlier when he described him as being semi-detached. Further discomfiture for Meacher came in the following weekend's *Sunday Telegraph*. There appeared an article outlining Labour's new tough policy on trade unions – quite clearly not the Meacher line. Meacher suspected this was planted by Mandelson to entice the policy review committee into accepting an interpretation of the draft document that the employment spokesman so overtly opposed.

Meacher, who has an academic's thirst for detail, but has often lacked the politician's touch, was now being increasingly seen by the leadership as 'not on board', and never likely to be. His policy review group had not delivered the report that the Leader's office had wanted. One month after the 1989 Labour Party conference Kinnock replaced Meacher with the committed Moderniser, Tony Blair. In this most sensitive of posts Kinnock had to have someone he could trust explicitly to reflect the new *zeitgeist*, especially important in the run up to the next general election. The one thing that was almost more important than the policy itself to Kinnock, though, was that it should not come unstitched in the three weeks of an election campaign, as Labour's tax plans and defence policy had at the last election.

Although Kinnock had great faith in Blair's ability to carry out the task at hand he was aware of the obstacles which loomed. Firstly, Kinnock was aware that the industrial policies Blair was inheriting were incomplete, ambiguous and philosophically incoherent. Meacher still saw the Labour Party as the political arm of the union movement, rather than as a free-standing party of the centre left dedicated to a respect for individual rights. And many thought he was unable to stand up to the collectivist aspirations of the trade union movement and instead merely dressed up his proposals in the language of individual liberties. Blair had quite a task ahead of him – to clarify and cement Labour's policy on industrial relations. His job was to get the message across to the unions: 'you get fairness not favours' – a message that he has repeated to the unions since becoming leader. He had the full support of Neil Kinnock in this delicate task:

I said to Tony this is what we've got to do, we've got to finalise it. Have a look at it, get on with it and I will back you 150 per cent, and if you ever need to refer back to me at any time of the day or night, do it. If anybody challenges you whether it's my view tell them – yes it is, don't even bother to call.[2]

Another possible hurdle which seemed to concern them both was Blair's background. How would an Oxford-educated public school boy be received by the rank and file brothers of the trade unions? Kinnock allayed his fears,

Well, I said to him if anybody says that to you, you tell them to bugger off. He smiled one of his smiles and I said – I'll tell you what, if they say that to you, and you don't want to tell them to bugger off, you tell me and I'll tell them to bugger off.[3]

But the Kinnock strong-arm tactics weren't required. The union barons, impressed at the speed with which Blair put himself around, had already been over the course with Meacher, and knew what was coming. They also knew Blair spoke with the authority of the Leader's office, and were strangely flattered that one of Labour's rising stars had been put in charge of a brief that had often been used as a political dumping ground. Also, word had gone out from the unions involved in the electricity industry that here was someone who could fight his corner. Blair would be available and visible. He would pop in to Congress House, next to the British Museum, to see Norman Willis, the General Secretary of the TUC, and his deputy, John Monks (who went on to succeed Willis), for breakfast on his way from Islington to the Commons. He made a point of dropping in on all the senior union leaders, and they found him intelligent, friendly, keen, ambitious but absolutely determined about exactly where he wanted to take the Labour Party. The creases that Meacher had failed to iron out were dealt with in no time.

Relations with the unions had grown fraught as Neil Kinnock sought to restructure the Party's relationship with them. And there was some suspicion that Blair was being sent in as the hatchet man. But John Monks says that Blair brought a delicate political touch to an extremely difficult area for the Labour Party:

Under Kinnock there were times when the unions were made to feel like an ugly Siamese twin brother, whom the Labour Party would dearly like to get rid of, but couldn't. It was a mark of Blair's success that he foresaw problems early, and manoeuvred skilfully to avoid them becoming a flashpoint.[4]

Blair's style was to keep an open-door policy so that, any time a union leader wanted to get hold of him, he would be readily available. He would see people quickly and regularly.

Blair's confidence and determination to 'deal' with the unions became immediately apparent when he told them that the closed shop, an arrangement which gave them monopoly bargaining power in a factory or workplace by forcing every employee to be a member of a given union, was over. This was the stuff of the political highwire. He had to confront the unions with a message that many did not want to hear and would generate furious opposition from General Secretary down to shopfloor worker. In the past some of the classic showdowns between union leaders and Labour Leaders have focused on issues about which the union grassroots member has cared little. But for around half a dozen unions the closed shop was the pinnacle of a hundred years of struggle. And for the ordinary union member it seemed that Blair was attacking their very way of life. But, in an extraordinary sequence of events, Blair, through a mixture of opportunism and skill, persuaded the unions in a matter of days to agree to give up something they had fought for over decades. But for such an historic U turn there were no fanfares or banging of gongs. Blair simply slipped out a statement, one Sunday while he was at home in Sedgefield, announcing a 'policy clarification'. In it he stated that Labour's new approach to industrial relations would 'start with the rights of the individual and recognise that the proper role of the collective is an instrument for the advancement of the individual', and he said the practical consequence of that would be 'in accordance with Article 11 of the Social Charter a right to join or not to join a trade union'.

A year before Blair became employment spokesman, the trade union movement went through its greatest policy U turn ever, when it was overnight converted to the cause of Europe and the Common Market. As Jacques Delors, the President of the EEC, addressed '*les frères*' in Bournemouth at their annual conference, he offered a vision in which British workers would find protection and security in the Social Charter. Not surprisingly after the raft of Conservative legislation that had clipped their wings and neutered their power, they were queuing to sign up to this offering from Brussels with all the enthusiasm that children wait for party bags. But in their haste, there was one small thing they had overlooked. The Social Charter put a strong accent on individual rights of trade union members. So just as the Social Charter would allow any worker to join a union, the concomitant was that it would be up to any worker to decide whether he or she *didn't* want to join, and that in turn called into question the whole basis of the existence of the closed shop. John Monks says that it hadn't really dawned on any of them. 'We'd bought the whole lot that Jacques Delors was offering and had never really grasped that it had a lot of implications for the closed shop.'[5]

But the Tories had picked up on this and, at one session of employment questions, they repeatedly challenged Blair to reconcile his support for the Social Charter with his approval of the closed shop. Blair dissembled, but with the Government's Employment Bill being published the following week, which was to render unlawful the pre-entry closed shop, Blair felt that, as long as Labour was clinging to the closed shop, his position was intellectually unsustainable. There would have been many Labour politicians who would have sought to fudge the issue with weasel words, but Blair went straight in to see Kinnock and said there was a need to move immediately. Kinnock gave his backing – with some hesitation – and Blair started to move with lightning speed.

Blair went straight round to TUC headquarters to explain to Willis and Monks what needed to be done. Monks's advice was that the print unions and entertainment unions would resist it bitterly, and that perhaps the Transport Union would, too, because of the closed shop they ran in the ports through the National Dock Labour scheme. But Blair won Ron Todd round even though the union felt uncomfortable about it. He saw the GMB and AEEU, both of which had several closed shop agreements in certain factories and companies, and brought them on board. The one real contretemps that Blair had in this period was with Tony Dubbins, the General Secretary of the print union, the National Graphical Association (now the GPMU). It was a union that had traditionally enjoyed the benefits that closed shop agreements conferred, and its leaders were horrified to read of its demise without warning.

Blair prepared meticulously and consulted widely, but the one union that he never saw was the NGA, although there are conflicting reports about who was to blame for this – Blair says he tried repeatedly to speak to Dubbins; Dubbins insists there was no contact from the Shadow Employment Secretary. The day after Blair had issued his statement about the abandonment of the closed shop, Blair received a furious call from Dubbins insisting that he come straight to the union's headquarters in Bedford. Blair agreed, and while he was there he was subjected to extreme verbal abuse as they ranted and raved at him. Dubbins recalls:

> People expressed their views in the strongest possible language. We had a very fierce bust up because we'd only found out about this unilateral change in Labour Party policy when we read about it in the papers. It was policy making on the hoof, and decisions like that should be made by the Party conference. But what made us even angrier was that, no matter how much we protested, he just didn't seem to understand or appreciate what impact the ending of the closed shop was going to have on our 260 thousand members' jobs and conditions.[6]

The hostility felt by the union towards Blair has not dimmed with time: in the 1994 leadership contest, they were the only affiliated union whose members did not back Blair for the Labour leadership.

But Blair's approach was not just to say what the unions could no longer have – i.e. the closed shop – but what they would have in future. He offered a positive agenda with the focus on rights of recognition and individual rights, and rights to bargain. He saw nearly every union leader at least once and many more often than that as he embarked on a dizzying round of meetings. So a few days after having lost the argument in the Commons to the Tories, Blair had executed a significant change in Labour's policy towards the unions.

> If as a country we are to obtain a settlement in industrial relations law that endures, we must demonstrate – in contrast to the Tories – that industrial relations are not merely about the balance of power between employers and unions, but are rooted in the rights of individual people at work. The criticism of the Tory industrial-relations laws is not that they gave certain rights to union members exercisable against their unions, but that they failed, in addition, to give fair rights exercisable against their employers and refused to recognise in part at least that individual rights of employees will depend on their ability to function collectively as well as individually.[7]

The speech – like so many politicians' Sunday speeches it was never actually delivered, but it was given to the newspapers through a press release, a handy way of putting something into the public domain – served two purposes as far as Blair was concerned: It established publicly that Blair was capable of doing things that did not meet with the unions' favour; but it also gave him a more credible defence to Michael Howard, the Employment Secretary's charge that Labour was dining à la carte on the Social Chapter, only selecting the bits that suited Labour. The unions eventually gave Blair their backing for the revised industrial relations package at the TUC conference in September 1990.

There was a lot of concern in the GPMU, but from other unions there were no censure motions, no moves to oust him and no accusations that Blair had been a class traitor. He had pulled it off. Charles Clarke looks back on it as a turning point in the way other politicians and members of the Labour movement looked at Blair:

He showed in that whole process an ability to decide where he was going. Was he going to that window or that filing cabinet? And having decided where he was going he would set a course and move towards the target clearly, manoeuvring round the various obstacles, walking round the chair rather than tripping over it. Now a lot of politicians faced with those issues firstly don't identify where they're going, and, even if they do identify where they're heading, they have no idea how to get there. Blair both knew where he was going and how to get there by displaying a mixture of intelligence and opportunism.[8]

Blair's next campaign was to make it clear that Labour would not repeal all the anti-trade union laws. There would be some new Labour statutes, but he was absolutely clear that pre-strike ballots were here to stay. It became Blair's political hallmark that he would always try to find something positive to say to sell something which might at first glance appear unpalatable. So he went round the union leaders and said to them, 'Obviously we could go into the next election with a message that we're going to scrap the need for ballots, and then there could be the slogan "vote for Labour and you'll get less democracy". Alternatively we could put forward constructive proposals that will protect the rights of individual members.'

Labour's changing policy on relations with the unions gathered momentum in the first half of 1990, culminating in the policy document *Looking to the Future* in which Blair put his signature to Labour's industrial relations policy review, bringing an end to the uncertainties and omissions left behind by Meacher. Where Meacher's review had been confused on the issue of picketing, Blair's new approach insisted on laying down official guidelines under which there would be 'a right to picket peacefully, in limited numbers, in accordance with a statutory code of practice, secondary picketing being permitted only where the second employer is directly assisting the first employer to frustrate the dispute.'[9]

Blair also clarified the new approach on sympathy action. Where Meacher had somewhat ambiguously said that secondary action would be permitted as long as workers had a 'genuine interest' in the outcome of the dispute, Blair offered an unequivocal elucidation of the policy. Sympathy action would be lawful

> where there is a direct interest between the two groups, of an occupational or professional nature. This would cover, for example, situations where the employer is doing the work of the primary employer or is otherwise an immediate customer or supplier; where the outcome of the primary dispute will necessarily or probably affect the terms and conditions of the other employer's employees; and where corporate legal identity is used artificially to make sympathy action unlawful.[10]

A further aspect of Blair's review was the confirmation that strike action could only take place if the members had been balloted.

> . . . in order to qualify for legal protection, industrial action requires the support of a properly conducted ballot. Where action is lawful, however, individual employees should have the right, as in other European countries, not to be dismissed for that action. This would end the anomaly which gives the union immunity for lawful strike action, but the individual none.[11]

Blair explained that under this proviso union members would be effectively represented whilst being accountable under law. 'You acknowledge the right to ballot and the duty to ballot, but you also place on people a right that they can exercise so that they are not dismissed when lawfully on strike.'[12]

Blair suggested a shopping basket of measures that would extend the role of the law in industrial relations. Gone was the notion that the unions were immune from court action as Blair expressed Labour's commitment to the introduction of a specialist Industrial Court established to regulate and resolve industrial conflict. 'The issue today is not "law or no law," but "fair or unfair law." '[13] In the immediate aftermath of the publication of the policy review document, Blair's media appearances were kept to a minimum, and it was a period in which Peter Mandelson almost became his personal press officer. For months Mandelson never seemed to leave his side when he was giving interviews on the closed shop or Labour's acceptance of some of the Government's trade union legislation.

Under Mandelson's tutelage they devised a media strategy that was as daring as it was cynical. In essence, they were determined to control the media agenda and not allow the media to push them around. With appearances strictly rationed, Blair would only give interviews if he knew precisely what the journalist wanted to discuss. He would then seek to find out whether the television or radio interview was going to be broadcast as a complete interview or whether a 'clip' would be taken from it to be used in a news bulletin, or in a compiled report on a programme like *The World at One* or *PM*. If it was to be a clip, no matter how many questions you asked Blair, the answer would be the same. Mandelson from his time working for the TUC was much more aware than Blair of just what a minefield relations with the unions could be, and so they decided in advance what they wanted to say, said it, and that way ensured they gave no unwitting hostages to fortune. During this period every answer ended with Blair enthusing about how Labour's policy on training would bring about a skills revolution. All this was done with a smile, good humour and no latitude.

Blair was beating the media at its own game. He was absolutely correct in his surmise that journalists would carry on a lengthy trawling exercise just to see what could be caught on film, even though the intention was probably to use only fifteen or twenty seconds of it. That mastery of the media was in marked contrast to Gordon Brown who would later come unstuck trying the same tactics, but failing to recognise the need to ration appearances. It is one thing to say the same thing whatever the question when appearances on screen are limited; it is quite another when day after day, week after week, you are saying the same thing, as Gordon Brown seemed to be doing when he was Shadow Chancellor.

One of the most frequent tributes paid to Tony Blair throughout his career has been for his skill at absorbing complex issues quickly. One contemporary described him as 'very efficient and very quick; he certainly worsted Parkinson over electricity privatisation: Parkinson is hopeless at detail, whereas Tony is very good. You can bet he worked out very carefully what he was going to do and say about dropping the closed shop: he always would.'[14] But Tories say all that Blair had proved in his career to that point was that he was a good barrister, able to take a brief – no more no less. And, like a barrister, he argued the case – whatever case – with complete thoroughness and zero commitment.

It is here where Blair stands open to attack. For example, the arguments he was putting forward during the debates on the 1984 Trade Union Act were very different from the case he was making out when he was Shadow Employment Secretary between 1989 and 1992. During the second reading of the Bill on 8 Novemher 1983, Blair particularly objected to the notion of pre-strike ballots, arguing that the Government was trying to weaken the power of the unions. He criticised the Secretary of State's motives in introducing this aspect of the Bill

> . . . the purpose of part two of the Bill is to allow union members rights over their union. This is the stated purpose of the Bill but its actual purpose is different. The actual purpose of the Bill is to alter the industrial balance of power and to tilt it definitely and calculatedly in favour of the employer.'[15]

While his concluding remarks echoed the heretical thoughts for which Meacher was later sacked from the Employment portfolio.

It is a disgrace that we should be debating today the taking away of fundamental freedoms for which British trade unionists have fought for a long time. Having fought long and hard for them, they will not give them up lightly. We shall oppose the Bill, which is a scandalous and undemocratic measure against the trade union movement for partisan reasons.[16]

Michael Howard sparred with Blair from when they were new boys in the 1983 intake. They were also pitted against one another when Howard was Employment Secretary and Blair was his opposite number, and the double act came together again when Howard was appointed Home Secretary and Blair his shadow. Both men have the highest personal regard for each other, Blair regarding his opposite as quite the toughest opponent that he has had. But Howard scorns the view that Blair was always a moderniser:

He may well have wanted to change the Labour Party in 1984, but he was accusing the Government then of behaving in an absolutely outrageous way for giving union members the right to vote before being called out on strike. So the gulf between what he now says were his private thoughts and what he said in public is actually rather significant and important.[17]

But the speech that Blair made to the 1990 Labour conference in Blackpool demonstrated to many in the Labour movement (who privately shared some of Howard's concerns) that the man was bright, and that he believed in something: that there was fire in his belly as well as a cool head on his young shoulders. He spoke passionately about the denial of union recognition to North Sea oil workers and civil servants employed at GCHQ. He denounced the exploitation of part-time women workers. And he rounded on shady right-wing groups like the Economic League, which kept a blacklist of union activists. His speech won plaudits, particularly for his passionate commitment to invest massively in training. The *New Statesman* even went as far as to suggest that the speech marked Blair out as a future leader.[18] What he did in the speech was achieve that rare double of winning the gut support of the conference, while impressing the intellectuals and the commentators with his analysis and vision.

The 1990 Labour Party conference also saw the bowing out of Peter Mandelson as Labour's Communications Director. Having spent six years as a political fixer, he now wanted to become a politician. Mandelson had targeted a seat in the North East, but Kinnock had warned Mandelson that Hartlepool would never adopt him: 'Kid, for your own sake I hope you don't get hurt. I know that party. They are not going to take someone like you.' They would go for someone with local connections, or at the very least someone with greater connections to the working class, and who did not come to the constituency with such a mystique attached to him.

Mandelson was hurt by Kinnock's response, but Blair was supportive. 'What Tony gave me was the confidence. He was the role model and never flagged in giving me encouragement because there were others who didn't want me to come to the northern region.[19] Blair's constituency neighbours Hartlepool, and throughout the period Mandelson was trying to secure the nomination he stayed at the Blairs' house in Trimdon. Mandelson shared a room with the Blairs' youngest daughter, Kathryn, who was at that stage still in nappies. And he remembers waking up each morning to find Kathryn standing up in her cot beaming down at him. Blair also lent Mandelson the formidable John Burton, who smoothed the path for the aspiring MP.

The Howard/Blair clashes became one of the regular events in the political calendar. If they weren't tearing into one another across the despatch box, they were at it in the television and radio studios, or across *The Times*' letters page. But their spats were just a warm up for the big fight which took place during the 1992 general election campaign. In one corner stood Howard seeking to gloss over the Government's record on unemployment, but hitting out at Labour's support for a minimum wage; and in the other was Blair, trying to keep the spotlight on the jobless figures while defensive over Labour's plan to make £3.40 an hour a job market minimum. The minimum wage was the jewel in the crown of the package of rights that Blair offered to trade unionists when he was trying to persuade them to accept some of the Conservatives' trade union legislation and of the need to accept the end of the closed shop. It was a policy that soon after he became Party Leader he sought to rewrite to such an extent that union leaders saw it as a U turn.

Perhaps it was a recognition of the effectiveness of the onslaught mounted by the Conservatives in the 1992 general election campaign, in which they repeatedly argued that a minimum wage pitched at £3.40 an hour would destroy jobs by the thousand, that led Blair only three years later to back away from such a clear cut commitment. In the election the Tories were almost in danger, though, of overplaying their hand, arguing that up to two million jobs would be swept away by Labour's plans. If that figure was dreamed up on the wilder shores of political fantasy, the concerted way in which Howard and Conservative Central Office attacked the policy threw Blair very much on to the defensive. In the run-up to the election, Blair had to issue a news release under the heading LABOUR REFUTES TORY FABRICATION OVER MINIMUM WAGE.[20] It went on to detail ten points where, in Blair's view, Howard had either used statistics mendaciously or had invented figures. But there were two points worth noting about this: firstly, it did show the extent to which the Tories were putting Labour, and particularly Blair, on the rack over this policy; but, secondly, even though the Conservatives did seem to be winning the argument, Blair held the line, even if there were occasions when he didn't seem particularly comfortable with or convinced by his own policy.

Nowhere was that more vividly demonstrated than on the phone-in programme *Election Call*. Politicians can go through gruelling hour-long sessions at the wicket with the best inquisitors in the business, playing a dead bat to the most difficult questions, picking up the odd run here and there with a push or a leg-glance down to the boundary ropes, and occasionally crashing the ball out of the ground when an interviewer asks an ill-conceived question. But nothing in the politician's armoury can prepare them properly for a really determined member of the public pursuing a point where they know their subject, because all the blocking techniques suddenly make the politician look shifty. Blair underwent such an experience at the outset of the election campaign.

In the space of five minutes, a Mrs Joyce Elliott from Hereford, who ran a day-care nursery with twelve staff, did more to expose the weakness of Labour's case on the minimum wage than any professional interviewer or journalist in the election campaign. She ran the centre for low-paid working mothers who, if they had to pay any more to leave their children there, would have been better off staying at home on benefit. She paid herself nothing, and said all she could afford to pay her staff was £2.00 an hour, not the £3.40 that Labour was advocating. Reducing the number of employees she had was not an option, because the Children Act laid down precisely child/supervisor ratios. Blair talked about how other European countries managed with some form of minimum pay provision and how the rules would apply equally to other employers. But Mrs Elliott kept on coming back saying that Blair was failing to answer the details of her case. And the bald truth was, he had no answer. He sat on his chair in the television studio as though the cushion were full of protruding razor blades.

Blair did everything and more that was asked of him in his own employment brief, but a battle was raging at the top of the Labour Party in the run-up to the 1992 election about economic policy, and, according to Charles Clarke, Neil Kinnock felt disappointed in Tony Blair. The simmering disagreement between the Shadow Chancellor, John Smith, and Neil Kinnock came to the boil at a dinner that Kinnock hosted at Luigi's in Covent Garden for half a dozen members of the lobby. Labour's policy was to abolish the National Insurance ceiling. As things stood, anyone earning below £20,000 paid 9 per cent of their earnings in National Insurance; but anyone earning more than that only paid NI contributions on the first £20,000. Labour wanted to end that anomaly, meaning that if someone earned £30,000, they would pay 9 per cent on all that amount, not just the first £20,000. In other words, they would pay an extra nine pence on every pound they earned above £20,000. The policy had been agreed by the Shadow Cabinet, but Kinnock had grown increasingly worried that this policy would hit the very people that Labour had been trying to attract. It seemed to carry the message that, if you earned less than £20,000, then you were someone that Labour wanted to help; if you earned more than that, then you were someone to be punished with heavier taxation.

During the course of the dinner Kinnock floated the idea that the policy need not be brought in overnight but could be phased in gradually. This remark might have passed unnoticed, but what alerted the journalists present was that Kinnock was unusually precise both about how it could be done and – more significantly – where a precedent could be found in an earlier policy document, *Looking to the Future*. Kinnock quoted chapter and verse. But Smith had not been consulted, and blew a gasket when he found out. He made it clear in private that this was intolerable and must not be allowed to happen again.

Kinnock had become increasingly isolated in the run-up to the 1992 general election. Charles Clarke had to handle Kinnock's violent swings of mood from great highs to volatile lows. But, according to Clarke, even though Blair, and to a lesser extent Gordon Brown, shared many of Kinnock's reservations about the direction in which Smith was taking Labour's economic policy, they failed to speak up. As Clarke says:

Neil wanted and would have liked Tony and Gordon to be more active than they were in marking out what they thought was necessary. He thought they were too loyal to John. And, yes, there were a number of occasions around then when Tony and Gordon agreed with Neil, but wouldn't say so . . . Tony more so than Gordon, didn't participate enough in the collective leadership of the Party and the Shadow Cabinet. They often didn't come to meetings. I used to go and say to Tony 'Look, it's five o'clock on Wednesday; you've got to be there.' But they were very very dilatory, and Tony was worse than Gordon. And Neil was frustrated at that.[21]

As the election campaign wore on, and Smith presented his Shadow Budget, it began to seem that Kinnock's wariness was right, as the Conservatives seized not so much on Labour's figures but on the fears among the electorate about what Labour might do over taxation. 'Labour's Tax Bombshell' screamed Tory posters across the country, claiming that every family would be £1,250 a year worse off under Labour's plans.

It was a figure calculated in the highly partisan and distorting atmosphere of an election campaign, with some fairly wild assumptions about Labour's tax and spending plans used to arrive at the figure. But as a piece of propaganda it was brilliant. It played on the deepest fears of the electorate about what a Labour government would do. And despite all the pre-planning and war-gaming and efforts made to ensure that Labour would not unravel again over tax and spending, Labour unravelled. John Major, if not the rest of Tory High Command, could scent the sweet smell of blood.

If the 1987 election campaign sought to portray Kinnock as a somewhat presidential figure in that now famous Party election broadcast made by Hugh Hudson (the director of *Chariots of Fire*), then, in view of Kinnock's poor standing in the polls, Labour strategists probably correctly played on the strengths of the 'team' in 1992. And that meant a starring role for Tony Blair in much of the Party's campaigning. He was a regular in Party election broadcasts. But Blair, according to friends who were with him throughout the campaign, never had any real doubts that Labour would lose once again. The only occasion when he thought Labour might actually deprive the Tories of an overall majority was on the night of the famous Sheffield rally, when three polls suggested that Labour could be heading for victory.

Much time has been spent assessing the various twists and turns of the 1992 general election campaign in an effort to identify the reasons why Labour lost again. Was it the shambles over Jennifer's ear, Labour's highly emotive election broadcast about a two-tier health service and one girl's wait for an operation, while another jumped the queue? That piece of 'faction' unravelled when the mother of the dramatised girl revealed herself to be a Conservative supporter. Then there was that Sheffield rally when Kinnock, in a moment of complete indiscipline that he now bitterly regrets, started bellowing into the microphone at the ten thousand present, 'Are you all right . . . are you all right?' It sounded awful and probably focused the minds of many electors on the fact that, within a week, Neil Kinnock could be Prime Minister. Then there was the final week of the campaign when John Major shrewdly played on the importance of the Union with Scotland, and the threat to it posed by Labour, while Labour started to talk about constitutional reform. Neil Kinnock was left floundering by a television interview before a studio audience when he was pressed by Sue Lawley to say whether he was in favour of electoral reform – he was, but it wasn't Labour policy and he seemed to freeze on screen.

The Labour Party had been through exhausting upheaval, with Neil Kinnock both the driving force and the engine of change. Blair had been at his side throughout, playing a prominent role in the election campaign itself. But it had not been enough. And yet, as the campaign started, while no-one thought it was going to be easy, the omens looked favourable for Labour. The economy was mired in recession – Michael Heseltine in a memorable phrase said bad economic news was pouring down 'like bricks from heaven' upon the Conservative Party's head – and the Government had to defend a record that included such abject policy failures as the poll tax. There was also deep mistrust about the reforms to the Health Service that had set up Trust hospitals and fund-holding GP practices. Labour for its part had shed more of its old baggage in its attempt to look modern and in touch with what people wanted. The polls at no stage suggested that a fourth successive election defeat was looming.

That defeat came so unexpectedly suggests that the reason for failure was more fundamental than the sum total of individual gaffes: Labour had not sufficiently regained the trust of the electorate, and even if Jennifer's ear, the Sheffield rally or John Major's soapbox had not happened, the result would have been the same. The overwhelming impression left by the 1992 general election campaign was that voters were looking for excuses to return to the Tory fold, and nothing in that election campaign could have altered that. As has been often observed, elections are won in the three years before polling day, not in the three weeks of the campaign.

CHAPTER 6

To Modernise – To Clintonise

'Young man, there is America – which at this day serves for little more than to amuse you with stories of savage men and uncouth manners; yet shall, before you taste of death, show itself equal to the whole of that commerce which now attracts the envy of the world.'

Edmund Burke, 23 March, 1775

The Labour Party has never been short of factions and labels to identify this or that school of thought. There have been left and right, Bevanites versus Gaitskellites, anti-marketeers versus pro-marketeers, and myriad sub-organisations in between. There are the different party blocs which in today's Labour Party are the Campaign Group, which represents the Bennite left, the Tribune Group, which is more mainstream left, but also includes people who would be seen as right wingers, like Tony Blair and Gordon Brown. And then there is the Solidarity Group, a right-wing grouping born out of the divisions created by the departure of prominent Labour MPs to form the SDP. The Solidarity Group (of which John Smith was a leading member) was made up of those who had decided to stay and fight for the soul of the Labour Party from within. And throughout the 1980s they saw it as their job to fight the Bennite left for every inch of political soil. But, in the dismal hangover of the 1992 general election, came a fresh set of labels – two new groupings to behold. These were the Modernisers and the Traditionalists. And Tony Blair was as modern as they came.

There was no hard and fast dividing line between Modernisers and Traditionalists, but everyone in the Labour Party seemed to know on which side of the line most of the key players fell. The problem for conventional Labour watchers was that here were groupings that didn't conform to any of the normal types of behaviour. It was not a left/right split. It was more a distinction between those who felt that Labour had changed enough and that it had to stay true to its traditional, enduring values and policies to secure victory; and those, like Tony Blair, who passionately believed that Labour still had a long way to travel.

Election night 1992 provoked a number of different responses. Most Labour MPs just wanted to go back to their homes, crawl into bed, pull the duvet up tight over their heads and disappear for as long as possible. But, as Tony Blair stood amid the empty beer glasses, trestle tables and discarded rosettes at Spennymoor Town Hall in his constituency, having increased his own majority to nearly fifteen thousand, a different emotion swept over him. He told John Burton, his agent, in no uncertain terms that he felt angry, and, far from wanting to go to bed, he rang the Labour Party press office in London to say that, if any of his colleagues had pulled out of slots on the *Today* programme, or *Breakfast News* – or anywhere else, for that matter – he would take their place. He had a simple message that he wanted to get across: it was not that Labour had changed that explained this latest defeat; it was that Labour had not changed enough. That bald, uncomfortable message was to become a rallying cry for those who were soon to be dubbed 'the Modernisers'.

The Tony Blair who had kept quiet during Shadow Cabinet meetings (and who had from time to time stayed away), and who refused to discuss areas beyond his immediate concern, had gone. It was a tougher, more determined politician who emerged from the ashes of defeat. John Monks, who had worked closely with Blair during the trade union policy review, said it was like coming across a different man when the two of them shared a platform together at a seminar soon after the election: 'He was impatient, not with anyone personally, but with the Labour Party in general. It was as though he wanted to pick the Party up and shake it by the scruff of the neck. He was angry. Angry with the small c conservatism of the Labour Party. Angry at its resistance to change.'[1]

In the cold light of Sedgefield day on 10 April, as Tony Blair ruminated on the depressing prospect of more years of fiddling on the sidelines while the Conservatives played on the pitch, he was aghast that some people were arguing that Labour's result had not been that bad, pointing to the fact that the Party had gained forty-two seats, its best performance since 1966, and anyway it was a huge electoral mountain that Labour had to climb.

It is a plausible case. In fact, the number of seats that Labour picked up was a huge victory for the tacticians at Walworth Road. They had decided to devote all attention to the key marginals, where Labour did achieve disproportionate swings that were not repeated in the rest of the country. If Labour had been able to do nationally what it had done in London – where the Party gained ten seats from the Tories and the two remaining SDP constituencies – and in the East Midlands then election night would have been a very different story. Those gains, though, serve to mask just how badly the Party performed when the votes cast are put in a national context. Looking at the other end of the telescope, Labour's share of the vote was only 34.5 per cent – its lowest since 1931, taking the disasters of 1983 and 1987 out of the equation – and was way off the 38 per cent the Party received in 1979 when it lost power to the Conservatives. But the bald figure, from which there was no hiding place for even the most complacent Labour politician, was that in 1992 2.5 million more people voted for the Conservative Party than they did for Labour. The Tory vote of 14.1 million was the highest number of votes ever received by a British political party.

How Labour politicians reacted to these results was a rough and ready means of determining whether someone was a Moderniser or a Traditionalist. The Traditionalist, or 'one more heaver', took the same approach as the First World War general: with each push they would move ever closer to overrunning the enemy position. So by this reckoning Labour might achieve a

Hung Parliament by 1996/97, and, come the new millennium, there would at last be a Labour Government with an overall majority. For Blair, not only was the logic of this approach completely flawed, he also thought it was a dangerous excuse for total inaction.

For the man who had led his troops into battle, and once again failed, it was time to hand over the Field Marshal's baton. It is undoubtedly true that, while Neil Kinnock had done more than anyone to make Labour electable again, he was part of the problem too. Canvassers for all the parties found that more or less wherever they went in England – and it was an English rather than a British phenomenon – the reaction on the doorstep to Neil Kinnock was negative, and so trying to sell him as a future Prime Minister was always an uphill struggle for Labour. An adviser to Chris Patten, the Conservative Party Chairman, said at the time that 'the Kinnock factor' was crucial in all those marginal constituencies in the South East. 'We were finding that the reaction against Mr Kinnock was stronger the further South you got.'[2] And one area where the polls were getting it about right was on approval ratings for Neil Kinnock. The final Harris poll of the campaign showed John Major with a two to one lead over Neil Kinnock when voters were asked which of them would make the best leader.

For those who had the stomach, at 5.30 a.m. on 10 April, as the champagne bottles were being cleared away at Central office, across the river in Walworth Road a devastated Neil Kinnock emerged at the top of the steps of Labour Party headquarters to deliver a speech of valediction. His face etched with sadness, his normally deep resonant voice cracking with emotion, as he clung tightly to Glenys he looked to the future. There was dignity in defeat: 'I naturally feel a strong sense of disappointment, not for myself for I am fortunate in my personal life. But I feel dismay and sorrow for so many people in our country who do not share this personal good fortune. They deserve better than they got in this election.' He did not say so then, but it was clear to all that it would only be a matter of time – and a very short space of time – before

Neil Kinnock announced that, having spent longer as Leader of the Opposition than anyone this century, he was going to resign.

That announcement came three days later, on 13 April, and that of course meant another leadership contest. There were some, like John Prescott, who wanted Neil Kinnock to stay on for a bit so there could be a seemly post-mortem about what went wrong, before the Party plunged itself into hustings. But Neil Kinnock, sickened by failure, didn't want to stay on for a minute longer than he had to. 'I will be proposing to the National Executive Committee that the elections be held as quickly as proper organisation allows. The elections will therefore take place in the second half of June.' And that was that. In a shade under two months, Labour would have a new leader. There were some cries of 'what's the rush?', and the NEC were mindful of this when they defied Kinnock's wishes by voting to put off the contest by a further three weeks. But even before Kinnock had made his announcement from the Shadow Cabinet room, the jockeying had started and the union barons were wheeling their guns into position.

There was only one interesting question in all of this: who was going to be deputy leader: it was such a foregone conclusion that the leader's crown would pass to John Smith. Smith's biographer, Andy McSmith, estimated that Smith already had 10 per cent of the electoral college votes tied up the weekend *before* the Party even knew there was to be a contest. And by the time they had lined up on the starting grid, John Smith's position was even more emphatic, making it impossible for the would-be challenger, Bryan Gould, to overhaul him. By the time the election was announced, the main concern of his backers was that the contest should not look too much like a stitch up.

The weekend after the general election, a council of war was called at Blair's house in Trimdon for the three leading Modernisers in the Labour Party. Peter Mandelson, newly elected MP for Hartlepool, came over from his neighbouring constituency, while Gordon Brown came down from Edinburgh. Their overriding concern was to resist, in the wake of a fourth election defeat, the headlong rush to push proportional representation up the agenda. Kinnock had come unstuck on this during the election and all three knew from private conversations with Kinnock that he felt it was now time to embrace electoral reform. Robin Cook had never made any secret of his support for reform of the voting system either, and Blair and Brown were worried that, in the despondent mood that had settled on the Labour Party, there would be others who would see PR as a panacea for their problems. The other concern was to hammer home the message that the programme of reform for the Labour Party had barely begun. While Brown and Blair issued press releases to that effect, Mandelson was busy briefing the Sunday papers on what needed to happen. There was one other item on their agenda, and that concerned the vexed and hitherto out-of-bounds question of whether the Labour Party's constitution needed rewriting: should a modern Labour Party that believed in the market economy still have a clause in its constitution that committed it to massive nationalisation? There was agreement that Clause IV was dated, but they recognised this might be opening up one too many fronts on which to fight. But the campaign to modernise the Labour Party had started.

The other big question that needed to be resolved in Trimdon that weekend was whether Blair should challenge for the deputy leadership. Blair at this time was weighing up the options. Certainly, if those in the media had had votes, he would have cruised into the deputy's job. There was a daily procession of calls enquiring what he had decided to do. Blair thought long and hard about it, and, although he has since said that the reason he didn't go for it was out of concern for his children, that is the most opaque of explanations. In fact, as Blair, Brown and Mandelson sat in the sitting room of Myrobella overlooking the pretty garden, Blair's instincts were to run for the deputy leadership. But others were less than encouraging: Kinnock rang and counselled Blair that it would ruin his family life (part of Kinnock's reasoning could be explained by his desire to see Bryan Gould succeed to the deputy leadership); Brown worried that he did not have a sufficient base of support in the Labour Party (Brown was more or less precluded from running as it would have been unacceptable to have two Scots as leader and deputy, but his advice was a foretaste of the frictions that would lie ahead); Blair rang Margaret Beckett who was being tipped as a likely deputy but she said she had not made up her mind. It seemed likely at that stage that Blair might still run, but the decisive moment came when Smith announced that he wanted a woman as his number two, and Beckett made it clear that she would oblige.

Close friends of Blair describe this as a watershed in his political development. He had not backed his own judgement and instincts and had listened too attentively and deferentially to the advice of those around him. He was more cross with himself than with any of those who had sought to dissuade him, but he resolved that history would not repeat itself. And that explains why when John Smith died, two years later there was not even a flicker of hesitation from Blair that he would run for the leadership. Mandelson, who was with him that crucial weekend after the 1992 general election, says now: 'Never underestimate the determination and steel behind the charming and diffident manner. His resolve is tangible.'

But Blair and Brown were desperately needed by the Smith team, even though Smith's victory was destined to be measured by miles rather than inches. The launch of the Smith campaign had been marked by a rare uncertainty from the Scottish advocate as he hesitantly parried a series of questions about where he stood on key issues like electoral reform, the position of the unions and constitutional reform. Solid, wise owl, bank manager lookalike he might have been, but Smith suddenly looked terribly weak and unconvincing on 'the vision thing'. Smith received an unusually bad press for this lacklustre start and his campaign manager, Robin Cook, who had always had a rather prickly relationship with Peter Mandelson, rang Mandelson at home – the first time he had ever done so – to seek advice on how to handle the press. But Cook got more than he bargained for when

Mandelson suggested that Smith should bring in some of the young Turks, like Brown and Blair, to assist.

The result of the deliberations of Brown and Blair was *New Paths to Victory,* John Smith's six thousand word policy statement. But their recruitment by the Smith campaign did not pass without a typically Mandelsonian flourish. He rang selected Sunday newspaper journalists to tell them that Blair and Brown were being called in to bolster Smith's faltering campaign, and the stories printed the next day duly painted the two as the cavalry riding to the rescue. Cook was irritated but not surprised to see Mandelson's handiwork.

From a moderniser's viewpoint the manifesto fairly echoed to the rafters with right-sounding phrases: no policy can be viewed as 'out of bounds'; a 'radical response' was required from the electorate. The central plank of the document was the creation of a Commission on Social Justice to review distribution of wealth, welfare policy and taxation. But as time went on Smith seemed more interested in bolstering his position with more traditional sections of opinion within the Party than he was in pleasing those clamouring for change.

The centrepiece of the leadership campaign was the debate over reform of the Party's relationship with the unions. Most vociferous in his calls for fundamental change was John Smith's opponent in the contest, Bryan Gould. He wanted a system of one member one vote – OMOV – for future leadership contests, while union members paying the political levy would be able to convert to become full members of the Labour Party. This was very much what Neil Kinnock had been pushing for, and certainly would have carried through had he stayed on as leader after a victorious election. It is also what Blair would later argue for when he arrived on the National Executive, but Smith was wobbling. After some hesitation, he sought to steer a middle course through this minefield that had suddenly been laid by Bryan Gould's enthusiastic advocacy of radical reform. Smith said:

1. Tony Blair, aged 5, the smile already in place.

2. (*Top left*) The past Blair had hidden from him: his 'Vaudeville' grandparents, Charles Parsons and Cecilia Ridgeway.

3. (*Top right*) Blair's christening in 1953 with mother, Hazel.

4. (*Middle left*) Blair at Fettes College, Edinburgh.

5. (*Middle right*) Tony with older brother Bill in the foreground.

6. (*Left*) Blair with spiritual mentor, Peter Thomson, on a visit to John Macmurray, Scotland, 1974.

7. (*Left*) John Smith helping Blair in hopeless Beaconsfield By-election, May 1982.

General Election
Thursday, 9th June 1983

SEDGEFIELD
THE NEW CONSTITUENCY

VOTE LABOUR

TONY BLAIR

YOUR
LABOUR CANDIDATE

Published by George Ferguson, 99 Wood Vue, Spennymoor.
Printed by Macdonald Press Ltd., Tudhoe, Spennymoor.

8. (*Right*) Leaflet etched in green, not red, to maximise Irish Catholic vote.

9. The new MP and his family on 9 June 1983; sister Sarah, father Leo, step-mother Olwen, and older brother, Bill.

10. (*Left*) High tension and deep mourning: Tony Blair and Gordon Brown at John Smith's funeral.

11. (*Left*) Deep in conversation, Tony Blair and Peter Mandelson – trusted adviser and architect of Labour's modernisation.

13. Jubilant in victory. A proud father; a proud wife. Leo Blair and Cherie Booth celebrate as Tony Blair is made Leader of the Labour Party.

12. The start of a beautiful friendship? Blair and Prescott, leader and deputy on 21 July 1994.

14. Blair's first tussle with John Major at Prime Minister's Questions on 18 October 1994.

" We have grown apart and there is little of common interest between us.... we have therefore decided to seek divorce.... "

15. Peter Brookes' clever cartoon perfectly captures two major headlines in one as Camilla Parker Bowles announces the end of her marriage and Tony Blair begins his move to break with the 'old' style Labour Party.

Draft: version, eighty-four

By the strength of our
common endeavour
to (achieve what we cannot do alone
   over come the limitations of

to grant each of us the power to realise
our full potential,

and all of us the means to create,

for this & future generations,

a community,

in which power, wealth and opportunity
are in the hands of the many not the few,

where the rights we receive reflect

the duties we owe,

do that, freed from the tyranny of
poverty, ignorance & fear,

we may live together in a spirit of
solidarity, tolerance and respect.

+ economy
+ society
+ international

16. A work in progress. With the leadership battle over, Blair
embarked on something no other Labour Leader had dared do in 35
years: rewrite Clause IV of Labour's constitution.

17. As one political journey begins another ends. Tony Blair joins the ranks of mourners at the funeral of Lord Wilson, the last Labour Leader to win a general election.

We will have one member one vote for all our key decisions, but we have to find a way in which OMOV is consistent with organisations being in the Labour Party . . . If radical change involves the Labour Party subverting its principles and aborting its mission, then I'm conservative in that very narrow sense – I don't want to abort our mission.[3]

This debate caused greatest offence to the union leaders, who felt that once again they were being made a scapegoat for Labour's failure at the polls, even though they had remained hidden from view throughout the campaign. But they were to stay silent no longer. Tom Sawyer, one of the most progressive of the union leaders and who would later become Blair's appointee as General Secretary, warned the then leadership what the consequences would be of reducing the unions' power in the Labour movement with a phrase, 'No say, no pay'. It would be a phrase that Conservative Central Office would use again and again to show that the unions were still in control. And Sawyer's message was one that Labour Party apparatchiks had to take seriously as three quarters of the Party's funding still came from the unions. The anger of the unions over this latest attempt by the Party to distance itself added to what was a bad tempered leadership campaign. Gould was seen as the principal villain of the piece, even though many of the arguments that he made were to frame Labour's post election debate on the way forward. Smith won the leadership spectacularly, taking 91 per cent of the vote. His result, not surprisingly, was even more emphatic in the union's electoral college. Their 40 per cent vote split 38.5 to Smith with just 1.5 per cent going to Gould.

That weekend, as the *Sunday Times* thudded on to the Smiths' doorstep in Cluny Drive, Edinburgh, instead of an encomium on Smith's achievements at becoming leader a day earlier, its magazine devoted several pages to an article entitled 'Labour's Leader in Waiting'; the strap beneath it read, 'Yesterday Labour elected a new leader. Some feel the Party should have skipped a generation and gone for Tony Blair.' And this was no 'scissors and paste' job. No, the Blairs had allowed into their home Barbara Amiel, wife of the newspaper magnate and owner of the less than Labour loving *Daily Telegraph,* Conrad Black, and had apparently given her free rein in the house. It was a piece that had taken much negotiating; the timing of its publication was deliberate. Peter Mandelson was closely involved in the project from beginning to end. So too was the *Sunday Times'* editor, Andrew Neil, whose admiration for Blair was matched by his ambivalence towards John Smith, whom he saw as something of a political dinosaur. When Roy Hattersley was later asked whether in view of Blair's decision not to contest the deputy leadership he thought Blair lacked ambition, his reply was to the point: 'You don't have Barbara Amiel come to stay for the weekend without being fairly driven by ambition!'[4]

Blair, for all his media friendliness, is deeply protective of his family, and his friends are immensely protective of him. But Amiel was given access to those 'close friends' who are normally out of bounds to interviewers, and Blair's wife, Cherie, spoke publicly for the first time – an experience she either found so awful or unhelpful that it was not to be repeated until her husband became a candidate for the leadership two years later. Not that it was exactly a kiss-and-tell story that Amiel dragged out of her. What she did say, though, lent credence to the idea that it was for family reasons that he had not entered the race:

When it came to whether or not he was going to run for the deputy leader's job, Euan said he was glad that Daddy has chosen to spend more time at home. I think Tony is incredibly talented and I want him to succeed – he's got an incredible amount to offer – but we've got young children and they need to be protected.[5]

She also referred in passing to the problems she faced in her childhood when her errant father was starring in *Till Death Us*

Do Part: 'Life when my father was at the height of his fame had its problems for me. I understand it.'[6]

This was a forceful piece in Britain's bestselling quality newspaper; it was the manifesto for the man who had decided to stay at home. It was a 'hey, don't forget me next time' interview. Indeed, to Smith's annoyance, the impression that Labour had picked the wrong man was evident in a mischievous question that Sir David Frost put to Jack Cunningham on his *Frost on Sunday* programme just after the leadership contest. With a twinkle in his eye Frost asked Cunningham who he thought would be the next Labour Prime Minister – John Smith or Tony Blair? On another occasion, Paddy Ashdown in a brilliant quip said that in the 1970s Labour had the right leader for the 1960s; in the 1980s the right leader for the 1970s. Now that it was the 1990s, Labour had picked the right person for the 1980s. It hit the target. No sooner had Smith been elected than the talk was of how the Party should have skipped a generation in the same way as the Conservatives had done when they chose John Major to replace Margaret Thatcher.

But Smith had won by a huge majority and he was a big man, not consumed by petty jealousies. More important to him was to learn the lessons of the 1992 election defeat. A paper prepared for the National Executive by the Party's General Secretary, Larry Whitty, and the Communications Director, David Hill, seemed to get to the heart of it: 'The Labour Party is seen as a Party of the past, as one which holds back aspirations and tends to turn the clock back.'[7] Many others made similar points. Gerald Kaufman put it slightly differently. It wasn't so much that Labour was a Party of the past; it was that people remembered what Labour had *done* in the past that mattered: 'Labour was swamped in the 1983 election because it was profoundly mistrusted by a large portion of the electorate, and was defeated in 1987 by a further landslide because the mistrust remained. I fear that the Party's defeat last month was due to too much of that mistrust lingering on.'[8] David Hill in a separate piece noted that: 'Our major long-term problem appears to be the fact that we carry too much baggage from the late 1970s and early 1980s to persuade people that they can fully trust us.'[9]

Blair made a similar point in an essay that he wrote on why Labour had lost the 1992 election:

> The last election should have been won and was lost by seven-and-a-half points, a larger margin than 1979 . . . we cannot minimise the need to build our support . . . The worry of the electorate in 1992 was not that Labour had changed, but the concern was that the change was superficial . . . The reason Labour lost in 1992, as for the previous three elections, is not complex, it is simple: society had changed and we did not change sufficiently with it . . . Labour does need a clear identity based on principle, not a series of adjustments with each successive electoral defeat.[10]

This piece was the Moderniser's credo. Many in the Party, particularly those who were part of the Blair generation at Westminster, supported the project.

The Traditionalists on the other side of the debate would not necessarily seek to divorce themselves from everything that Blair said about why Labour lost. It was common ground after the 1987 election that Labour had to appeal to the upwardly mobile working class, who had bought their council houses and purchased BT shares. But in their analysis of the 1992 election the Traditionalists felt that not enough had been done to harness the votes of traditional supporters. That was often a euphemism for saying that Labour's tax plans had been too cautious and insufficiently redistributive. And when John Smith set up the Social Justice Commission, a foretaste of the rows that were ahead came over whether benefits such as child benefit should continue to be universal (i.e. available to everyone) or whether the Party should consider 'targeting' as a way of ensuring that those in most need received the greatest help. Blair was extremely hostile at this time to those who argued that what lost the Labour Party the last election was that there hadn't been enough socialism. 'Have these people forgotten what happened in 1983,' he told friends. 'No-one could accuse us then of not having enough socialist policies. And look what happened. We were hammered.'

On a more trivial – though no less passionate – level, another distinguishing feature of the Traditionalists was a profound antipathy to the way the Party had sold itself. Prescott made his point when, during the Sheffield Rally, he alone walked down the central aisle without a red rose pinned to his lapel. He would later slam the 'beautiful people' and the 'spin doctors'. The former union official and now Labour MP for Pontypridd, Kim Howells, condemned 'the clique of spin doctors and Party managers who foisted on us the anodyne policy statements and gut churning embarrassment of the Sheffield rally . . . all of which contributed so much to the decline in Labour's electoral appeal.'[11] The targets of Howells's ire were people like Patricia Hewitt (she had been Kinnock's press officer, and had gone off to start the left-wing think-tank, the Institute of Public Policy Research), who was brought back by Kinnock during the 1992 election as an unofficial campaign manager; Peter Mandelson who, although long departed having secured a safe seat at Hartlepool, was blamed as the originator of 'glitznost'; and Philip Gould of the Shadow Communications Agency who presented all the Party's private polling to the leadership, and was seen as having a disproportionate influence (he would later play a key role in advising Blair during his bid for leadership, and was brought in from the cold). Interestingly, both Hewitt and Gould disappeared from the scene under Smith's leadership. Of course, without an election to fight it might simply have been unnecessary to keep these people on. But more likely it was a recognition by Smith that, in the name of Party unity, their presence would have been an unhelpful reminder of the *ancien régime,* and Neil Kinnock's more aggressive leadership style.

When John Smith set about the task of fashioning his Shadow Cabinet, balancing the various factions was central to his calculations. He offered Blair the job of Shadow Home Secretary. It has traditionally been one of those no-win jobs for Labour politicians; just like being a Conservative Health Secretary, where, no matter how many hospitals you build, what proportion of the waiting list you clear and how much in extra resources you devote to the provision of primary health care, the opinion polls stubbornly show that voters think Labour would have done even better. So it has been with the Conservatives' lead over Labour on law and order. If Blair had been hoping for a job that would have acted as an obvious springboard for the leadership of the Party, this was not it. Traditionally it was a job where it had been remarkably easy to offend; incredibly difficult to make headway. But it was a job that Blair had long thought should be a 'Labour' issue, and it was the job that he had wanted. What Blair hadn't worked out was the political strategy to turn the issue of crime into a vote winner. And, in truth, during the summer of 1992, he was not devoting that much of his time to finding an answer. The preoccupation of Tony Blair was the internal Party battle that needed to be fought, and how to secure a position on the Party's ruling National Executive.

That listlessness from Blair was picked up by the Conservatives, with the Home Secretary, Kenneth Clarke, using his speech at the Conservative Party Conference to engage in some sharp and well targeted political knockabout. And to crow a little, too. Clarke proclaimed that he was looking forward to Parliament's return, 'if only so that I can remind myself what Tony Blair looks like.' And Clarke, now warming to his theme went on, 'Tony Blair is Shadow Home Secretary but he's so shadowy it's ridiculous. I know he is out there somewhere lurking. It reminds me of the poem:

> As I was going up the stair
> I met a man who wasn't there
> He wasn't there again today
> I wish to God he'd go away.'[12]

It was rhetoric that played well with Clarke's partisan audience. The Home Secretary went on to insist that 'we are the party of law and order and the Labour Party know it – and the general public know it.'[13] But the Conservative case was not a strong one. The Conservatives had spent 50 per cent more on the police in real terms since they came to power in 1979, yet, in the same period, recorded crime had more than doubled. When Kenneth Clarke made his speech it was a year in which there had been 5.6 million recorded offences. If it had been a Labour Government, the Conservatives would no doubt have accused Labour of throwing money at the problem to no useful purpose; the difficulty for a Labour Party in opposition was how to attack a Party that, despite the spiralling crime rate, was still perceived as the Party of law and order. One of Blair's closest advisers at that time recalls that, while Blair worried about finding an answer to that tactical dilemma, he was at a low ebb.

The prospect of another four or five years in opposition filled him with horror. What compounded Blair's sense of frustration was that he began to believe that many of his colleagues actually rather enjoyed opposition. It did not require making hard choices; it was a pleasant enough life with sufficient intrigue over who would get elected to the Shadow Cabinet or NEC to keep the average MP contented, and that, combined with the modest privileges of being at Westminster, led Blair to the conclusion that many Labour MPs had become so institutionalised by electoral defeat that opposition was the sum of their ambitions. They could envisage no other life.

Blair, along with other Modernisers, spent much time navel gazing, picking at the bits of fluff that might help explain why Labour had lost four elections on the trot. But they also lifted their eyes to a wider horizon, to look at how political parties abroad with similar ideas and ambitions had turned defeat into victory. And that inevitably meant looking across the water to the United States and the victory of the Democrats, whose period in the political wilderness ran through roughly the same period as Labour's dog days. After the failure of Labour in

Britain, socialists looked across 'the pond' to what happened there with wide-eyed wonderment.

Blair visited the United States on a number of occasions during the first couple of years of Bill Clinton's presidency, but the traffic in ideas was even busier. In that period the Labour Party built up an extensive network of contacts with the Democrats as the Modernisers sought to establish a direct line to the key people at the heart of the Clinton Administration. The links were at all levels: researcher to researcher, press officer to press officer, and needless to say politician to politician. Not since the Kennedy era had there been such a cross fertilisation of ideas. Where once Labour looked to the European socialist parties or the Scandinavian social democrats, the Modernisers were looking to America. Inevitably it was dubbed the 'Clintonisation of Labour'.

The help given by senior Conservative Central Office staff to George Bush and the Republicans in the 1992 US presidential election rankled with the Democrats. The Clinton administration were in little mood to forgive or forget what the Conservatives had done. By coincidence the British diplomat charged with smoothing Anglo/US relations with the new Clinton administration was the First Secretary at the Washington Embassy who would later go on to run Blair's private office, much to the shock of the Foreign Office. Having been assigned to stick closely to the Democrats during the election, Jonathan Powell was seen as the perfectly placed person to help the Government get relations back on an even keel. What had irked the White House most was the disclosure that the Home Office had acceded to requests from the Bush camp to look through files to see if there was anything on Clinton during his period at Oxford as a Rhodes scholar. In the immediate aftermath of the American election when bad feeling still festered, there was an open door for senior Labour politicians to walk through, which MPs like Brown and Blair gladly did.

The lessons of Clinton's victory were studied closely by Blair and those of like mind. One of the most profound lessons was that putting together a rainbow coalition of disparate interest groups would never be enough on its own to win an election. Just as Labour policies had been variously targeted at women, the unemployed, the disabled and the ethnic minorities, so Democrat policies would traditionally be aimed at gays, Jews, blacks, Hispanic Americans, etc. But in the 1992 US Presidential election, those policies were abandoned. Clinton's advisers calculated there were simply not enough votes in the traditional rust-belt states topped up by rainbow alliance support to secure the White House. This message was spelt out to Labour in no uncertain terms when Stanley Greenberg, the Democrats' opinion pollster, came to London in January 1992 to lecture the Labour Party on what it needed to do. He told his audience that the Democrats had won because they had convinced the middle classes that they wanted to enlarge opportunity in society, not close off avenues to advancement.

Another prominent figure from the Clinton inner circle who came over to advise Labour was Paul Begala, Clinton's speech writer. To the embarrassment of the Labour leader, John Smith, in a meeting with Tony Blair and Gordon Brown he told them: 'Tactics and strategy matter in an election, but are strictly secondary to the necessity for a good candidate. I had the candidate of a lifetime in Bill Clinton and I made that clear.' Comparisons in the charisma stakes were inevitably made between Clinton, before he had run for the presidency, and Blair. One middle-ranking Tory minister commented ruefully soon after Blair took over the Labour leadership that, 'The trouble with Tony Blair is that he is Bill Clinton with his flies done up!'

This cross-fertilisation of ideas between Washington and London produced some strikingly similar phrase-making. Not so much two peoples divided by a common language, as united by it. *Newsnight* cleverly pulled together chunks of Clinton and put them next to bits of Blair. Viewers were invited to spot the difference. So, while Blair said, 'The theme that I would put forward is the theme of national renewal and change,' Bill Clinton had said, 'My fellow citizens, today we celebrate the mystery of American renewal.' And on responsibility, the Blair version is, 'Where people are given chances and opportunities then it's important that we understand they owe a responsibility to other people,' while Clinton said, 'We must do what America does best, offer more opportunity to all and demand more responsibility from all.'[14]

Soon after Clinton had been installed in the White House, Brown and Blair travelled together to Washington to meet some of the key people who had delivered an improbable Democrat victory. Gordon Brown had for a long time been a close watcher and student of the American scene. He met Bill Clinton in Berlin some time before he became the Democrat nominee. Brown was also present in New York when Clinton won the nomination. While they were in the United States they met up with Paul Begala and spent a lot of time with Elaine Kamark, another close adviser of Clinton, who wrote the family policy section of the book-cum-manifesto, *Mandate for Change*. Many of the ideas expressed there have found an echo in the policies that Blair outlined during his subsequent election campaign. Kamark herself was influenced by another guru of the Clinton administration, a sociology professor from George Washington University, Amitai Etzioni. His 'communitarianism' had won admiring glances from many in the White House. He argued that the West has become so hooked on individual rights that people had lost sight of their obligations towards each other. And he insisted the only way that a sense of community could be restored was through the restoration of mutual responsibility. Society had to move from concerns about 'me' to concerns about 'we'. Although Etzioni's work, *The Moral Dimension*, is contemporary, its message was not so very different from that of the Scottish philosopher John Macmurray, whom Blair was so influenced by when he was an undergraduate at Oxford.

Greenberg also made clear that the Democrats had used the British Labour Party as an example of how not to do it. He said the Democrats had fallen into the same trap in previous presidential races: 'The Democrats simply ratified a collection of interest group demands and called it its "Governing Agenda". The problem was, as our base shrunk, the agenda was no longer broad enough to meet the demands of the middle class in this country which determines who wins and loses presidential elections.'[15] Two of Neil Kinnock's key advisers during the 1992 election, Patricia Hewitt and Philip Gould, Labour's advertising supremo, had come to similar conclusions. They argued that the Party should emulate Clinton's success in discarding the Democrats' image 'as the Party of the poor and of the past' by forging 'a populism of the centre rather than the left.'[16]

The admiring glances that Modernisers kept throwing their American counterparts was clearly antagonising the Labour Traditionalists who saw this as yet further confirmation of their worst suspicions that no socialist policy was sacred in the search for power. An editorial in *Tribune* warned:

> Everyone involved in the argument knows that Mr Clinton won a particular election in a particular place at a particular time and there is no way that his campaign can simply be copied in Britain. We do not have Presidential elections, there is no British equivalent of Ross Perot and our political culture is radically different from America's . . . The self styled modernisers having nothing more substantial to offer than making Labour even more bland in pursuit of elusive affluent working-class and centrist middle-class voters . . . They have failed to see that the main reason for 'lack of trust' in Labour is that people can see through politicians who appear to be all packaging and no substance.[17]

And one of those who was most critical was the person who coined the phrase 'Clintonisation' as an insult – Labour's transport spokesman, John Prescott. Prescott saw the process as nothing less than a battle for 'the heart and soul of the Labour Party'.[18] He later argued: 'The same people who are advocating this Clintonisation, or many of them anyway, are people who have been very much identified with the kind of hidden agenda going on at present that Labour should break its links with the trades unions, or at least weaken them.'[19] That was a less than coded swipe at Blair, but, in the raging debate over how to make Labour electable again, Bill Clinton inadvertently had become a surrogate for the factional row taking place in Britain.

Clintonisation was a convenient shorthand phrase, but it told only part of the story of why it was happening in the Labour Party. Blair and Brown were not seeking to ship – lock, stock and barrel – the Democratic Party across the Atlantic to then try to graft its methods and philosophy (or lack of it) on to the British body politic. The political culture in the United States is very different, but Blair and Brown were convinced that, for all the differences, there were points of similarity. Not only in how to win, but what to do once you have won. Long before the Democrats were trounced in the mid-term elections, Blair was aware of the mistakes that Clinton and his advisers had made. While they had devoted huge amounts of brain-power working out how to win, what they had not done was devote enough attention to detailing a policy strategy for when they were in power. Blair would later declare, 'We are not being Clintonised but there are similar strands.' The political seed had been planted in Brown's and Blair's minds about what needed to be done three thousand miles away. If the reason that Labour had lost was that the Party seemed only interested in blocking people's progress then they had to learn the lesson from the Democrats and turn Labour into the Party of aspiration. The two returned from the States reinvigorated, and determined to start applying the lessons learnt.

CHAPTER 7

Growing Disaffection

'Death is unexpected. It doesn't come neatly at the end of a paragraph, but often cuts short a life in mid sentence. At least John Smith had completed the work of readying his party and himself for power, so his death at least came at the end of a chapter.'

Tribute to John Smith at his funeral

The relationship between Tony Blair and John Smith went back to before Blair had even entered Parliament. They had holidayed together at Derry Irvine's holiday home in Mull. Blair, at Irvine's suggestion before he came into Parliament, wrote a detailed paper for Smith on the legal mechanisms the Government might use in pursuit of its privatisation plans; Smith was so impressed he circulated it to the rest of the Shadow Cabinet. Smith advised Blair to run for Beaconsfield in 1982, and came and canvassed for him. They had travelled around China together. They had got drunk together. Their families knew each other. They were both active Christian socialists. They were personally close. But politically relations were becoming ever more strained, as Blair sought to push forward the process of modernisation and Smith insisted on proceeding at his own pace.

The focus of this antagonism was over Labour's relations with the unions, and the proposals to alter fundamentally the role the unions should play in electing the leader and deputy leader of the Labour Party. Doubts about Smith's credentials as a Moderniser arose even before he had become leader. After the general election there was to be one final meeting of the National Executive with Neil Kinnock as leader. It fell on 24 June, midway through the leadership contest. Smith then was not a member of the NEC, but Robin Cook, his campaign manager and cipher during that period, was. Before the general election Kinnock believed a move to pure one member one vote was a mere formality. A key paper that he had prepared supporting the principle was passed overwhelmingly by the executive, with only Tony Benn and Dennis Skinner opposing it.

The outgoing leader recognised that it would be a battle to get the policy through Conference, but Kinnock had calculated that it would only take the movement of a medium sized union to win the day. But in his last NEC as leader, Kinnock suffered a rare defeat. Smith had indicated a certain sympathy with the unions who wanted the whole question looked at in the context of a wider review of the Party's relationship with the unions, and so as the Executive gathered it was agreed that no decision would be taken until the 1993 Party conference. Significantly, the proposal was put forward by Robin Cook, Smith's campaign manager. It was backed by Traditionalists like John Prescott and Clare Short, and union bosses like John Edmonds of the GMB.

It looked to Kinnock as though Smith had missed a golden opportunity to assert his leadership over the Party. 'I thought, OK, the game's up – in a couple of weeks' time there'll be a new leader – get on with it. It's not my position to try and run things from the political grave.' But Kinnock believed it was more than just a lost opportunity, he felt it had been a foolish tactical blunder:

> By the time '93 came round a mythology had been built about severing connections with the unions, denying them a legitimate role in the Party and all that – absolute bloody nonsense. But of course mythology's almost always more difficult to fight than real dragons and that was why John Smith was confronted by such an unnecessary drama last year [1993].[1]

Smith's views on Party management were unsophisticated – Blair told friends they were twenty-five years out of date. Smith, like many of his generation, followed that famous description – and prescription – made by the late Ian Mikardo of the Labour Party: he said the Party was like a bird – it needed a left wing balanced by a right wing to make sure it could fly. Smith had never been overly concerned by the internal machinations of the Party. It was remarkable that, despite having been a cabinet minister and a leading figure in the Party for many years, he had never served, nor sought to serve, on the National Executive. And, significantly, when he became leader – and therefore an ex officio member of the NEC – he handed over nearly all of the responsibility for relations between the leader's office and the wider Labour movement to Margaret Beckett. To Blair and other Modernisers it seemed exasperatingly as though Smith had simply abdicated responsibility for Party management. One said, 'Smith thought all you had to do was balance out the traditional right with the traditional left, and there you had good Party management. What he didn't seem to realise was that those divisions had become almost meaningless.'[2] Another said that Smith simply thought that as long as the left- and right-wing factions of the Party were kept happy, then Labour would win the next election because through unity they would regain the trust of the electorate.

But such debate as there was on the future direction for Labour came to a grinding and shuddering halt on 16 September 1992. The centrepiece of the Government's economic strategy, Britain's membership of the Exchange Rate Mechanism, had been blown to smithereens in an extraordinary thirty-six hours on the world's currency markets. Suddenly and quite unexpectedly the whole political climate had been transformed. From heroic victors only months earlier, John Major and his Chancellor, Norman Lamont, suddenly looked beleaguered, crestfallen and vulnerable. The Government was without an economic policy, and John Smith was looking at a sitting target. The Prime Minister had little choice but to recall the Commons for an emergency debate. It also helped transform the standing of John Smith. Whatever internal problems the Labour Party had were put on a back-burner as John Smith prepared to mount his assault on the Government. He mercilessly picked apart John Major's record, throwing back in his face taunts about which Party was now the Party of devaluation (an accusation that had been thrown at Labour since the devaluation of 1967). He mauled the Government, while reducing those sitting behind the front bench to helpless laughter as he cracked cruel jokes at Major's and Lamont's expense.

Happy as the Modernisers were to see the Government in disarray, it had a quite unexpected spin-off which gave them less cause for satisfaction. The 1992 Party conference in Blackpool, far from resembling the wake that everyone had been expecting after the fourth successive election defeat, looked almost celebratory as John Smith basked in the warm congratulations from those who had witnessed on television his demolition of the Government. And as ministers stumbled and tripped from disaster to catastrophe, Smith the witty prosecuting counsel, was always on hand to deliver a hefty push or kick along the way. But all talk of fresh policy initiatives for Labour seemed to disappear from the Labour leader's mind. His friends have always asserted that Smith had his game plan worked out, and it had never been part of his strategy to reveal his hand early on in the life of the Parliament. Modernisers scoffed at that.

Neil Kinnock through this period was a model of discretion and restraint. He harboured deep reservations about John Smith's leadership but was determined to do nothing that could either be interpreted as disloyal or which would have the effect of undermining his successor. All he allowed himself to say was that the sooner the Party's policies were in place the better, as it would give MPs plenty of time to campaign on them and for the public to understand them. But when this was put to Smith he was having none of it:

> I don't believe that you should rush forward and put everything in your shop window for next Wednesday. I think you've got to do the patient and careful work, taking some

original thoughts, working them through in practical ways, and, when you're ready to do so, presenting them to the public in a way which commands and maximises not only the support for the policies but for the Party.[3]

And so the strategy of 'the long game' was born.

When a friend once asked Blair whether he thought that John Smith was a Moderniser like him, Blair shrugged: 'I just wish I knew.' There were definitely two sides to John Smith. He could be the life and soul of the party, telling witty and indiscreet stories about friends and colleagues. He was capable of great warmth and charm. But he was intellectually stubborn, to the point of arrogance, and he was rarely prone to self doubt. Roy Hattersley was once asked how easy was it to get John Smith to change his mind. He simply laughed, saying, 'John Smith hasn't changed his mind on anything since he was seven years old.'[4] One very senior Labour politician gave a shrewd appraisal of Smith, saying:

The good news about Smith is that, because of his noted abilities and his reputation, he actually didn't need to do very much, but he thought he had to do even less than he had to do. Not only on constitutional change and sustaining the momentum, but also on policy change. This theory of 'the long game' was invented in panic by David Hill [Labour Party Communications Director]. It provided an apparent rationale for 'steady as she goes'.[5]

But as 1993 began, so the 'steady as she goes' approach to policy came under closer and closer scrutiny. It is probably true to say that Smith would have been under even greater pressure from the media to come forward with ideas and initiatives were it not for the fact that the newspapers were obsessed with the travails afflicting the Conservative Party. In that sense John Smith had an easier time of it than might otherwise have been the case. But warning shots were being fired from both the left and the right of the Party. Bryan Gould, who had resigned from the

Shadow Cabinet after his failed leadership bid, was the most outspoken, keeping up a barrage of criticism against his former Shadow Cabinet colleague. Blair, privately, was also growing restless.

But in public, Blair was starting the fightback on his law and order brief. Labour's traditional concern for the underdog had led, in his view, to the mistaken impression that all Labour cared about was a neat sociological explanation of why the criminal had committed his crime. But in explaining Labour looked as though it was excusing, and Blair wanted a radical shift in thinking. With his number two, Alun Michael, and researcher, Tim Allan, Blair told them that 'our starting point has to be what is right, not what has been our traditional position'. It might have seemed no more than ordinary common sense, but it did mark something of a break from conventional thinking. Labour wouldn't abandon its traditional belief that it was impossible to disentangle rates of crime from social factors like levels of unemployment, education and housing conditions, but what Labour spokesmen would now do more pugnaciously would be to attack the criminals. It was also time to pay much more attention to the needs of the victims of crime. When Tony Blair went to talk to the Parliamentary Labour Party early in 1993 to sketch his new thinking with particular reference to juvenile crime, he went expecting to be mauled. Instead there were some minor protests from the civil libertarian wing of the Party and grumbles from more authoritarian members that he wasn't being anything like hard enough, but overall the Party gave him a big thumbs up. The fact was that the single issue that filled constituency mail bags was crime and the fear of it, and now they could go back to their constituencies and say to the police and the victims of crime 'look, we're on your side, too'.

Blair's approach may have been decided in the desiccated atmosphere of his air conditioned office, but his awareness of what a potent electoral issue this was came from the heated discussion meetings with local constituents in his Sedgefield constituency where feelings about crime and vandalism were inflamed. Blair recognised that, awful as the crime figures were, the fear of crime was even greater. And the testimony of the older people at these meetings made Blair realise what an explosive issue this had become. Many were frightened to walk the streets at night; pensioners felt like prisoners in their own homes. And each Friday and Saturday when Blair went back to Sedgefield to hold his weekly surgery there would be a regular flow of local people coming in to complain that their lives were being turned into a living hell by hooligans. 'I can't tell them,' he said, 'we are going to have to wait until we can have a better society to be protected.'

They found Blair a receptive listener. It is largely generational. Blair wasn't a politician of the 1960s; he was never a part of the 'liberal' consensus, so he shared the gut instincts of many of his constituents; not the received wisdom of what the next Home Secretary, Michael Howard, disparagingly referred to later on as the 'do-gooders' who ran the criminal justice system. Blair saw the 1960s as a morally lapsed time when the distinctions between right and wrong had become blurred.

There was perhaps a feeling that if there was an absence of guidance for people they would naturally come to the right conclusion – and at times a feeling that the only problem that existed for people was the problem that society had given to them.

And he went on to express despair at the simple polarity of the argument over this issue:

The two great fundamentalist views of this century were either that everything can be encapsulated in society or within the state; or the view of the Conservatives, certainly the Conservative right, that everything is down to the individual and you do whatever you do on your own.[6]

But Blair was clear that, if ever anything illustrated the extraordinary sterility of the standard of political dialogue on an issue that affected millions, it was a speech by John Major at the end of January in which he sought to pin some of the blame on urban Labour councils for the rising tide of crime. A few days later Blair took the opportunity to counter this, giving a clear guide to his new thinking on the subject. 'We need to get away from the approach that says it's either all society's fault or it's all a matter of individual responsibility.'[7] Blair was in debate on this programme with the Home Secretary, Kenneth Clarke. Not for the first time, it seemed that the Home Secretary's position was a good deal closer to Tony Blair's than it was to the Prime Minister. Clarke said with his usual engaging frankness, 'We are in danger of agreeing on the analysis.'

There was something else, though, gnawing away at Blair that he only confided to a select few around him at this time. It was well known to those close to him that his Christianity underpinned many of his beliefs, but he had always made a point of resisting the temptation to become a pulpit politician. Christianity he had always sought to maintain as something that was very private to him and no part of his public persona. He was all too aware of the whiff of hypocrisy that often stuck to politicians when they started jabbing fingers at other people's moral fibre. There was a conventional wisdom that this was something to be avoided at all costs. Opinions are divided about how strong a selling point it is for an ambitious politician to proclaim loudly 'I am a Christian socialist'. As Conor Cruise O'Brien observed: 'Does a nation that is mostly neither Christian nor socialist want a Christian socialist as its Prime Minister?' Blair's friend, neighbouring MP, and fellow Christian socialist, Hilary Armstrong, put it slightly differently: 'Most Christians would not call themselves socialists, and in Britain most socialists are not Christians.' But one event, one crime among the millions, a murder statistic that stood head and shoulders above all others, sent the nation into a state of profound shock that February in 1993. It made Blair abandon some of his usual caution.

Poignant, grainy photographs taken from a security video of

two older boys leading a toddler out of a Liverpool shopping centre, were to spark a huge search for a two-year-old boy, Jamie Bulger. The details of the case were almost too grotesque for anyone to comprehend. It brought out feelings of guilt and shame. Was there such a thing as 'pure evil', people were asking; what sort of sickness and disease was running through the body of society. The nation was doing some profound soul searching, and reaching no particular conclusion. But it had focused debate on what was wrong in a way that no single crime had done since the Moors murders. It was an event that had left an indelible mark.

As Blair travelled the familiar journey back to Islington that week to put his own young children to bed he resolved to tackle these moral issues. Blair some months earlier had accepted an invitation to speak to Wellingborough Labour club the following Friday evening. It is one of those routine engagements that fill an MP's diary, but, after long and hard thought, Blair told his researcher, Tim Allan, that now was the time to speak out. He was going to abandon traditional caution and tackle questions of right and wrong, of moral descent, of society's decline. His only gesture towards playing safe was to not mention the Bulger case by name. But he didn't need to; it was the vivid backcloth to his speech-cum-sermon:

The news bulletins of the last week have been like hammer blows struck against the sleeping conscience of the country, urging us to wake up and look unflinchingly at what we see. We hear of crimes so horrific they provoke anger and disbelief in equal proportions . . . These are the ugly manifestations of a society that is becoming unworthy of that name. A solution to this disintegration doesn't simply lie in legislation. It must come from the rediscovery of a sense of direction as a country and most of all from being unafraid to start talking again about the values and principles we believe in and what they mean for us, not just as individuals but as a community. We cannot exist in a moral vacuum. If we do not learn and then teach the value of what is right and what is wrong, then the result is simply moral chaos which engulfs us all.[8]

Blair then went on to argue the case for the sort of beliefs and values that he had started to think about when he was an Oxford undergraduate. Britain had to be rebuilt as a community, he said, in which a new relationship is established between society and individual based on rights and duties that go together. On the Sunday, Blair was invited to come together once again with the Home Secretary to take part in a live debate on *The World This Weekend*. It was during the course of these exchanges that Blair suddenly crystallised what Labour's approach would be: 'we need to be tough on crime and tough on the causes of crime.'[9] It was a memorable phrase that stuck in the mind, and although it sounded off the cuff it had been well rehearsed, even if its parentage has sometimes been argued over. It was designed to encapsulate a new approach, and although Tories admired it as a phrase they insisted it was no more than empty rhetoric.

Blair tackled the subject of his own Christianity in the foreword to a book on the subject of Christian socialism. In his short essay, Blair eschewed the kind of dogmatism that many have found repellent. He didn't seek to argue that if Jesus were alive today he'd definitely be in the Labour Party. But what he sought to do was 're-unite the ethical code of Christianity with the basic values of democratic socialism.'[10] Much of what he has had to say about the importance of community and an individual's rights and responsibilities within it can be seen in this context. He says that Christian socialism is the belief that people

are not stranded in helpless isolation, but owe a duty to others and to ourselves and are, in a profound sense, dependent on each other. In reality the Christian message is that self is best realised through communion with others. The act of Holy Communion is symbolic of this message.[11]

What is much more striking in his contribution is what can be called his hard-headed Christianity. It may not be the hell, fire and brimstone of a Free Presbyterian like Ian Paisley, but it certainly isn't hand-wringing liberalism either. 'Christianity is a very tough religion. It is judgemental. There is right and wrong. There is good and bad. We all know this, of course, but it has become fashionable to be uncomfortable about such language.'[12] And, although he chooses not to say so, the political party that has felt most uncomfortable with this approach has been the Labour Party. But Blair has always maintained that his brand of modernisation was not about sweeping away the past, but putting Labour back in touch with its traditional values, where Labour could talk about right and wrong.

Indeed, the more Blair read his way into the subject of law and order, the more convinced he became of, not so much the newness of his approach, but the tradition in which it was steeped. He studied the works of the Labour historian and Christian socialist R. H. Tawney and the speeches made by ministers in the post-war Attlee Government and found they were every bit as clear about the difference between right and wrong and the need for a strong sense of civic responsibility. Tony Blair had no regrets about making his Wellingborough speech, but he was nervous about how it would be received; after all, this had strayed a long way off the politician's normal Friday evening text.

He needn't have worried. The trickle of letters that arrived on Monday and Tuesday at his office had become a flood by the end of the week. When MPs speak about their 'postbag' as if a few letters gave them a higher insight into the heartbeat of the nation, they normally amount to no more than a couple of dozen pieces of correspondence. But that week Blair's office was to receive nearly a thousand letters as a direct result of the speech. From Gloucester a woman wrote:

I'm just a member of the usual silent majority and a mum and like millions of others am sickened by our society today. Having heard you talk about the subject of young offenders, although I'm a lifelong Tory I feel you have the right ideas.

There were hundreds of others in similar vein. Blair had reached out to the normally silent parts of middle England. Many around him, soothsayers of doom, warned that there could only be a downside for Labour to talk about crime. It was a 'no-hope' issue as far as they were concerned. And John Major certainly tried to turn up the heat in a bid to restore the Conservatives' long-standing credentials as the party of law and order. In an interview in the *Mail on Sunday,* following his attack on immoral Labour councils as a lush seed-bed for juvenile delinquency, Major returned to the traditional right-wing philosophy: 'I feel strongly . . . that society needs to condemn a little more and understand a little less.'[13] They were remarks which seemed strangely out of tune with the mood of the country as it grappled to comprehend how a civilised society had seen two ten-year-olds commit one of the most horrific crimes in memory. Major repeated the phrase a week later at the Conservative Central Council, but this time added a gloss: 'This was not a simple cry for retribution. My point was this. Unless society sets rules and standards and enforces them, we cannot be surprised if others flout them.'[14]

But now Blair was warming to his theme. The moral compass he brought to bear was not only distinct from the Conservatives, it was fundamentally different, too, from what Labour politicians had been pushing for the previous thirty years. In May of that year, Blair went to speak to the Police Federation's annual conference. His speech was peppered with references for the need to both understand and condemn. 'We do not excuse and we do not ignore,' he told his audience of rank and file coppers: 'If we dare not speak the language of punishment then we deny the real world. If we do not understand the need for social action then we deny the possibility of changing it.'[15]

While Blair made the running, the Government were stumbling. The Sheehy report, which recommended a radical shake-up in the police service, had sent the normally quiescent and Tory-supporting policemen, from constable all the way up, into paroxysms of rage. Group IV, which had taken over some prison escort service work, had got off to an inauspicious start, with a number of prisoners escaping, leaving Blair to crack the joke, 'Now we know what Margaret Thatcher meant when she said that privatisation would set the people free!' John Major in the late spring of 1993 also intervened to free two West Midlands girls from a Thai prison after they'd been convicted of drugs smuggling, which in turn brought a menacing snarl from Norman Tebbit, who remarked, 'Labour's Tony Blair is tough on crime. John Major secures the release of convicted drugs smugglers.'[16] John Major had said before the leadership contest which elected John Smith that the person he most feared on Labour's front bench was Tony Blair; now a number of other Conservative MPs were beginning to see why. Blair was winning the argument.

But he was having a harder time winning the argument with his 'comrades' on the National Executive about the way forward on union reform. Blair found himself on a steep learning curve. As a newcomer to the National Executive, he found its hidebound traditions a culture shock. Baroness Gould, who as Joyce Gould was the Labour Party's Director of Organisation, remembers him as being somewhat naïve on the Trade Union Review Group:

> He flew a number of kites which didn't fly. There was the whole question raised of how to extend OMOV, to which he was as firmly committed as to the rest of Labour Party policy. So he had a vision of referenda and postal ballots on every issue. It was seen as an anti trades union thing, as it was an attempt to take the unions away from policy making, but at the end of the day Tony had to concede it was a non-starter.[17]

It seemed Blair had not really thought through the proposal

159

of permanent referenda as a means of making policy. As the three-million-pound cost of the leadership contest itself proved, participatory democracy for the whole Labour movement might be a wonderful thing, but it is extremely costly. If the same process were followed for every policy, the Labour Party would be bankrupt before it reached the next election. One of his fellow members of the review group, Clare Short, was more blunt: 'He was being downright silly. I think he showed himself up.'

He also made himself the *bête noire* of the trade union conference season by being the most outspoken senior politician supporting reform. The form of pure OMOV that Blair had wanted had been abandoned, largely because Smith saw no merit in pushing a case that he felt certain he would lose. There was an argument that to lose at the Party conference in 1993, but refuse to budge and take the proposal back the following year and win, would actually strengthen Smith's position, but it was a piece of brinkmanship that was not the leader's style. The problem for Blair and his friends was to find a way through this maze. The war of words between the unions and the Modernisers was intensifying, and in the spring of 1993 some of those who, in private, were most passionate in advocating OMOV were strangely silent in public. On one weekend after the leader of the Transport Union, Bill Morris, had launched a ferocious broadside, Blair was at home in Islington. He agreed to put the other side of the argument but expressed exasperation to the film crew which turned up to interview him that it now seemed that he was the only person who would speak out against the unions. 'Why can't you get Gordon [Brown] or any of the others to do this?' he protested. Gordon Brown, whose willingness to go into a television studio knew no bounds, was strangely unavailable through this period. The episode showed a significant difference between Blair and Brown. Brown's silence could be explained by the fact that elections for the NEC were around the corner, and to have gone out on a limb risked alienating support from the unions; Blair was also standing for the NEC, but he figured that the argument over OMOV was more important than how he fared in the NEC elections.

Until June 1993, Blair was arguing that only union members who joined the Labour Party should be able to vote in the Party's elections. His point was a simple one: around 90 per cent of union members paid into the political fund held by their union; but statistics showed that only about 50 per cent of them actually voted for Labour.

> Simply allowing any Trade Union levy payer to have voting rights in the Labour Party leads to the quite eccentric situation that those who don't even vote Labour but may vote Tory should have the right to decide who the Labour candidate is. This cannot be sensible or democratic.[18]

But a month later John Smith was to signal a further compromise towards meeting the unions' concerns:

> There would be a case for individual trade unionists taking part in the election of the leader and deputy leader of the Labour Party provided we can get certain principles established. That is we get an end to block voting, and also that I know that the people taking part in that are Labour supporters.[19]

In other words John Smith was prepared to drop the requirement that anyone participating had to be a Labour Party member. Instead, the Smith compromise foresaw a register being established of trade unionists who, so long as they said they supported Labour, would be able to vote in the leadership contest, even though they had not gone the extra step of becoming Party members.

In one of his few shrewd moves that summer, Smith surprised the review group at its final meeting in a committee room adjacent to the House of Commons by turning up himself to sell the revised proposals for electing the leader and deputy: An electoral college splitting the votes, with a third going to the constituency parties, a third to the unions, but voting as individuals not in a block, and a third to MPs and MEPs. For the selection of parliamentary candidates one member one vote would apply in its pure form, with union members paying a nominal extra sum to join the Labour Party if they wanted to vote. This became the package that the Modernisers had to accept and it became the deal that John Smith tried to sell to a still sceptical union movement.

Part of that selling job took Smith down to Brighton for the annual TUC conference. By the time he had read through the thirteen pages of text, the union members were on their feet. Smith had delivered a speech that had been music to their ears. To those watching it looked suspiciously like payola; to the Modernisers it smelt like a sell-out to save John Smith's skin. He once again raised the banner of full employment, something that Labour leaders had studiously avoided doing for many years for fear of giving rise to policy pledges that were unattainable; he promised a national minimum wage and called for a new charter of rights putting part-time and full-time workers on the same legal footing. It gave those who were seeking to promote a more traditional Labour message a whole new lease of life.

Blair was furious. The speech seemed to him a hostage to fortune that would saddle Labour with policies it could never realistically sell to the electorate. It also confirmed his view that it was only because Smith was so poor at Party management that he had got himself into a position where his TUC speech took on the character of a Dutch auction. Kinnock was aghast too. Smith had done little advanced selling of what he wanted. He had not taken senior union officials into his confidence early on to tell them how important it was for them to deliver for him. Key players like the GMB leader, John Edmonds, were kept out in the cold by Smith; but it wasn't that they were outside an inner circle – there was no inner circle. While Smith's aloofness had a certain charm for purists, it was no way to play the Labour Party.

Even as the Labour Party conference drew near, it seemed that defeat was looming. David Hill, the inventor of the phrase 'the long game', found himself once again having to come to Smith's rescue to prevent a PR disaster. Hill told anyone who would listen that the outcome would not be a question of arithmetic but chemistry. The phrase was nearly as enticing as it was ludicrous. Of course it came down to arithmetic, but Smith until the final day did not have the numbers. In the end the arithmetic did add up, following some fancy footwork by Smith's Parliamentary Private Secretary, Hilary Armstrong, to persuade the white collar union, MSF, to switch their block vote at a lunchtime delegation meeting. On the grounds that the OMOV composite they were voting on had a commitment to women-only short lists, Armstrong managed to persuade the union to change sides. It was that, plus the most remarkable speech heard at a Labour Party conference for many years made by the quintessential traditionalist, John Prescott, which finally won the day for the Labour Leader. But the whole experience of that conference shook Smith. He had survived, but by a squeak, in a tense and exhilarating day that few who were there will forget in a hurry. Victory, *The Times* noted the following day, had been bought at the TUC conference three weeks earlier. It was clear to all around him that John Smith now wanted to paddle his canoe in calmer waters. Further reform was put on hold.

Blair's frustration at the pace of reform and the torpor that had set in shone through in an angry piece he wrote for the *Fabian Review* which came out during the Party conference. He said after each election the Party went through a curious pattern of behaviour.

The defeat is like being caught in a shower of cold rain. The Party is shocked, depressed, but determined. It is honest and blunt with itself. It is going to provide against the next cold shower and move to more clement territory. But it dries out terribly quickly. The sun of opinion polls comes out and warms its back. The sky looks cloudless. The breeze of public hostility is now gentle. So it puts its feet up and relaxes. And it waits. Until the next shower. It was his determination to break this pattern that led Neil Kinnock to push through party reform. It is the determination of the present leadership under John Smith to continue that process and end the pattern for good.[20]

For reasons of tact and necessity, the article presented John Smith as part of the solution, but it was clear that Blair thought the leader was part of the problem. Indeed, close friends had to spend their time in Brighton trying to play down the strength of the attack.

On the law and order front, Blair was on altogether safer ground. Without any hint of embarrassment he stood at the rostrum in the Brighton conference centre and declared:

> Fourteen years of Tory government and crime has doubled; fourteen years of destroying the criminal justice system, and now their Home Secretary last week confesses he has no confidence in it. Fourteen years of the Tory lie that they are the Party of law and order. Let us tell them: those days are over . . . Labour is the Party of law and order in Britain today. Tough on crime and tough on the causes of crime.[21]

It was a remarkable turn around from a year before when Kenneth Clarke had stood before his Party and taunted Blair as the 'nowhere' man.

In Michael Howard's set piece speech a week later in Blackpool there was a marked change of emphasis. Gone were the easy jokes about how little Blair had done. Instead all Howard sought to do was impugn Blair's motives in changing tack, but it was a clear recognition of how Labour policy had changed:

> Throughout the 1980s, Labour were the Party against law and order. They set their face – both their faces – against

getting tough on criminals . . . But now they are pretending to change course. Not out of conviction, but out of convenience. They have just worked out there are no votes in being soft on crime.[22]

To that particular charge, Blair would probably happily enter a plea of *mea culpa*. And there was no doubt how much concern it was causing Conservatives that Blair had made so much running with this issue. Polls too bore witness to the advances Labour had made, suggesting for the first time that Labour was now more trusted to deal with law and order than the Conservatives: just before the 1992 general election when Gallup asked which Party would best handle the problem of law and order, the Tories had a huge lead with 46 per cent while only 25 per cent of voters thought Labour would do a better job. A year later the Parties were at roughly level pegging. By the spring of 1994, it was Labour who were seen as the best Party to deal with law and order, opening up a five point lead over the Conservatives.[23] A good deal of this can be explained by the relative changes in the standing of each of the Parties overall, but not all of it. And for many Conservatives this opened a whole new source of anxiety.

It was in a bid to deal with the Government's standing on law and order that Michael Howard embarked on two weighty and controversial pieces of legislation when the Commons returned to work in the autumn. There was the Police and Magistrates Courts Bill, which sought to implement bits of Sheehy that the Government had agreed to and some of the recommendations that Kenneth Clarke had made in his Police White Paper. It took an absolute mauling, not in the Commons, where the Government's majority was sufficient to drive it through, but in the Lords, where former Tory Home Secretaries led by Lord Whitelaw lined up like a row of guns on one of Whitelaw's beloved grouse moors to take pot shots at the legislation.

The other piece of legislation was the Criminal Justice Bill that

Howard had promised at the Party conference to implement his twenty-seven new announcements. This was also enacting recommendations of the Royal Commission enquiry, and it too ran into political turbulence before it found its way on to the statute book. One Tory minister confided that it had also been designed to be so unpalatable to Labour that it would force Blair to oppose the Bill at the very time he was trying to convince people that Labour were now tougher on law and order than the Conservatives. The minister said: 'If we don't force Blair to vote against these proposals, then we'll come up with another twenty-seven that he'll have to oppose.'[24] The Conservative strategy could not have been clearer, but Blair did not buckle and he stopped Labour from moving into a position of outright opposition to the Bill.

This may have been clever tactically, but it did not play well with those working in the Criminal Justice system who were looking to Labour for a more robust stance against what were widely seen as pieces of legislation driven by dogma and ideological imperative. Blair held regular meetings with groups like the National Association for the Care and Resettlement of Offenders and the Prison Reform Trust, and, while personal relations were good, they made no attempt to hide their opposition to Labour's new stance on law and order. This unease culminated in a sulphurous attack on Blair in the *Guardian* from the leading civil rights barrister, Michael Mansfield QC. Mounting the prosecution case against Blair, Mansfield accused the Shadow Home Secretary of equivocating on plans to build new secure units for twelve- to fourteen-year-olds which would be run by the private sector, even though both the Bar Council and the Law Society had opposed the move. On the question of judges being able to draw conclusions if a defendant chose to exercise his right to silence, Blair was accused of being 'all mouth and no trousers'. And then, most damning in their eyes, was Blair's reasoning.

We need a vociferous campaign to galvanise opposition;

what we have had from the Opposition is – abstention. Yes, led by Tony Blair, the Labour Party's position on this draconian attempt to emasculate civil liberties has been to abstain. We have the unedifying spectacle of Tory and Cross-bench Lords bitterly opposing the Government while Blair pretends he's pulled off a clever stroke. He thought Howard was going to lead the debate with a 'Labour is soft on crime' rhetorical onslaught. Blair's decision to abstain is an attempt to wrong foot Howard.[25]

Blair the following day sought to defend his tactics, saying there were key passages of the Bill where Labour opposition was vociferous. But, interestingly, nowhere did he seek to deny the central charge of Mansfield: that this was ultimately a piece of positioning by Labour to show that Her Majesty's Opposition was as tough on crime as the Conservatives. The civil liberties lobby and a good many Labour MPs saw Blair's approach as cynical and politically bankrupt. But if Blair's prime concern was to deny Michael Howard and his colleagues the opportunity to drive a wedge between Labour rhetoric and voting practice, then, tactically at least, Blair was probably correct to surmise that blanket opposition was courting trouble. And so Blair forced his party to abstain even though the gut instincts of many of his colleagues was to do otherwise.

One interesting question is how much John Smith went along with what Blair was trying to do. Certainly he recognised the success he'd had in radically overhauling Labour's profile in an area where there had only been negatives in terms of the electorate. And in speeches Smith did echo some of what Blair had been saying. But Blair himself always suspected that Smith had been wary of his approach. Smith, of course, was also a part of the legal establishment, and it seems the Labour leader was concerned that old friends felt they were being 'done over' by an ambitious politician on the make.

In the early part of 1994, Labour seemed to be drifting aimlessly. There was still enough Government misfortune to keep the focus of the media fixed firmly on the travails of the Conservative Party, but within Labour it seemed that the Modernisers' ambitions had been thwarted. Those going 'public' with their criticisms of Smith were still a tiny minority. But one senior Labour politician said that in the early part of 1994 Smith's troubles were growing: 'Unease had started to run through the ranks, people were saying "What the hell are we doing?"' Blair was one of those whose anxiety levels were increasing. Blair had a high regard for Smith; but not as high as Smith had of himself. Blair's worry was that Smith thought he could win an election, almost single-handed, without having to do very much.

At the end of April an article appeared in the *Spectator* written by Alastair Campbell, the former Political Editor of the *Daily Mirror* and former Associate Editor of *Today*. In it he berated the lack of purpose and ambition shown by the leadership:

> Labour are so used to enjoying the Tories' troubles that they have stopped thinking about their own. The Government's incompetence is a huge help but not, on its own, enough. The public are tired not just of the Government, but of politicians generally, and Labour are not exempt. If the current line is held to the election, the ducking and diving of Labour will become as big a turn off as the deceit and dissembling of Conservative ministers. When he was Shadow Chancellor, John Smith was convinced that Oppositions didn't win elections, Governments lost them. He may be right. But the Government he faces at the next election may bear little relation . . . to the one he faces now. The Labour Party, on the other hand, may look suspiciously like the one that lost the last election.[26]

What made this much more significant than an ordinary piece of Labour bashing was that Campbell was a lifelong Labour supporter. But even more importantly, several MPs who were known as prominent backers of Blair were commending Lobby correspondents at Westminster to go off and read Campbell's article if they wanted to find out what the Modernisers really thought about the state of the Labour Party. Campbell was persuaded to cross the bridge when Blair was elected Leader, becoming his first head of press relations. Some accused Campbell of being a poacher turned gamekeeper, but since he had never sought to hide his preference for propagandising on behalf of the Labour Party, it was more a case of legitimising his role.

A few days after this article appeared John Smith had one of his regular *tête-à-tête*s with Neil Kinnock. Kinnock was always careful not to be a back-seat driver, but he was growing increasingly worried and felt that he might soon have to say something. But he didn't have to. Smith recognised it was time 'to crank it up a bit', and to make the 1994 Party conference the time to set the course and direction for the next general election. The two men discussed tactics, the sort of things that needed to be done in the interim, like the odd speech and lecture over the summer that hinted at what was to come, so that no-one had any nasty surprises in the autumn. They agreed it was important to prepare the ground so that no-one could say it was a panic response to the alarm spreading through the Labour Party. Kinnock left that meeting feeling greatly relieved and reassured.

A few days later, on the night of 11 May, Smith hosted a glamorous £500 a head fundraising dinner at the Park Lane Hotel. It was called a European Gala Dinner and senior socialist politicians from across Europe were in attendance. It was a high point in his leadership: the local elections had been a resounding success; the European elections that beckoned looked as if they might be spectacular; the doom merchants in the Labour Party had started to think that after fifteen years – at last – there might, after all, be a pendulum in British politics and that it might be swinging back in their direction. There was a palpable air of self confidence. John Smith made a speech befitting the occasion. He talked about Britain's place in Europe, of the need to build a partnership between government and industry, and of the importance of getting British men and women back to work.

And he said the climate was set fairer for Labour than it had been for a very long time. He concluded: 'We will do our best to reward your faith in us but please give us the opportunity to serve our country. That is all we ask.'

Those were the final words he uttered in public. The following morning he was dead.

CHAPTER 8

Blood Brothers

'All I have, I would gladly have given not to be standing here today.'

Lyndon B. Johnson's address to Congress after taking over the Presidency following John F. Kennedy's assassination

Politics is often a dimly lit world, in which people talk in code, motives are often dubious, friendships are ordered on convenience and honesty is carefully tailored. But occasionally a shaft of bright sunlight comes in to illuminate it. It happened when Nigel Lawson resigned as Chancellor. That evening the Members' Lobby of the House of Commons became a cauldron of gossip and near blind panic. It happened again after Sir Geoffrey Howe delivered his resignation speech dripping with poison. The ray of light that entered politics on those days tended to show many politicians in their worst possible light: self-seeking, vain and insecure.

And then there was John Smith's death. That too brought honesty, but it revealed MPs in their best light, as the shutters swung open unexpectedly. Of course there was some humbug and hypocrisy mixed in as well – Tories had only days earlier been attacking him, while the Labour Modernisers were despairing and angry with him. But that did not detract from the emotional honesty that the House of Commons revealed that day in a day of powerful images: Ian Lang, the Secretary of State for Scotland, weeping as he spoke to reporters at the Scottish Conservative conference in Inverness; the gasp from the Inverness conference hall as the news was announced to the Tory faithful that John Smith had gone; the dignified and wholly genuine tribute paid by the Prime Minister, John Major, in that extraordinary afternoon sitting of the Commons; the Tannoy announcements in Westminster Underground station expressing condolences to friends and comrades of Mr Smith. This was no ordinary death. The flags at half mast across Scotland at the loss of a very Scottish son were symbols of genuine emotion.

For Labour politicians the date Thursday 12 May 1994 will be etched on the consciousness as 22 November 1963 is engraved on the minds of the Kennedy generation. Tony Blair, the politician who, probably more than any other, had come to symbolise the media-friendly, sound-bite capable, telegenic new Labour man, stood surrounded by cameras and reporters in a state of numbed disarray. Even his clothes seemed strangely inappropriate. He stood in a fawn, lightweight suit, the rims of his eyes red and puffy, talking in a low, lifeless voice. He had gone to Aberdeen on a campaigning stop for the European elections, but, just after his plane touched down, Gordon Brown rang on his mobile phone to say that John Smith was ill and the outlook looked bleak. A few moments later Derry Irvine telephoned to confirm the worst.

Gordon Brown had received a phone call from his oldest friend Murray Elder to tell him the news. Elder and Brown went back a long way – to their nursery school in Kirkcaldy. Elder told him the news was grim. Smith had been taken from his Barbican flat to Bart's hospital, which ironically he had visited only a couple of weeks earlier as part of the campaign to keep the accident and emergency department open. By mid-morning the consultant who had shown Smith around was standing addressing the hundreds of reporters and photographers who had converged on the hospital to announce that the Labour Leader had died of a massive heart attack. It was a morning when phones never stopped ringing. There was barely a moment to collect one's thoughts, let alone grieve. One close personal friend of Brown's rang. Had he heard the news, she enquired. Yes, said Brown. 'What are you doing?' she went on. 'I'm thinking. I'm thinking,' was his reply.

Smith's predecessor, Neil Kinnock, mentor to both Blair and Brown, was at home in Ealing when he was telephoned by his loyal and long-serving PA, Jan Royall, who was already in Kinnock's office at I Parliament Street. She rang Kinnock at 8.45 to say that Smith had been taken ill and that it looked serious. He left home soon afterwards, but as he was driving into Westminster he heard the news confirmed on the radio that Smith hadn't made it. It hit Kinnock hard. He had known Smith and had worked hand in glove with him for many years. But for Neil Kinnock it was a double tragedy that he was now pondering. The night before he had learned of the death of Glenys's mother, whom he had been extremely close to. As Kinnock drove the rest of the way in a sullen and numbed state, he was telephoned in the car by Jan Royall again. The news she gave Kinnock turned his mood from deep sadness to fury in a moment. Two of the leading traditionalists in the Shadow Cabinet were already meeting in a room close to Kinnock's to plot who should succeed Smith. Kinnock is tight-lipped about who they were; all he would say is that they didn't have Gordon Brown and Tony Blair's best interests at heart. Smith, by this stage, had been dead barely two hours.

It was nearly three weeks later that it was announced that Gordon Brown would not be contesting the Labour leadership. Brown and Blair were filmed walking around New Palace Yard at the Commons, with its ornate fountain surrounded by a neatly clipped pergola. As they strolled together, locked in intimate conversation, it looked to all the world that their extraordinarily close friendship had come through without so much as a scratch, as the senior of the two graciously made way for his former Commons room-mate. It was a PR triumph, the *Sunday Times* that weekend noted:

Wednesday's photo-call by Brown and Blair was worthy of Tory Central Office casting. All it lacked was a couple of yapping spaniels at their feet . . . At a time when politicians seem grubby and driven by self-interest, here was

someone prepared to sacrifice ambition for the sake of
friendship and his party.[1]

Brown was rightly commended for his statesmanlike behaviour; his standing was enhanced. Blair now looked unassailable.
But this happy scene concealed much more than it revealed.
Brown was desolate. He felt betrayed by some of those closest
to him. It was the lowest moment in his political career; relationships had been poisoned and the friendship of the blood brothers
had survived, but only just.

The fact is that, while Gordon Brown confessed that he was
thinking, Blair was making decisions. He knew that he would
run; he knew that he would receive widespread backing; he
knew that what he had to avoid at all possible costs was a head-
to-head contest with Gordon Brown. There could only be one
Moderniser in the contest and there is good reason to believe
that Brown's decision, which took nearly three weeks to come,
had been effectively taken by some of the key figures in
the Labour Party on the morning of John Smith's death. And
Blair was absolutely clinical in his dealings with Brown. Blair
made clear that of course the Modernising flag should be waved
by only one contestant, but there was no question of him standing aside. If Brown wanted to run for the leadership, Blair told
him, then that was his decision, but he (Blair) would not be
pulling out.

Two years earlier, in what appears to have been a piece of
crystal ball gazing of the highest order, the political editor of the
London *Evening Standard,* Charles Reiss, wrote an essay called
THE COMING WAR BETWEEN GORDON BROWN AND TONY
BLAIR. It was prescient, almost uncanny.

We know and they must know that this happy friendship
cannot last. By the very nature of politics, they are going
to become deadly rivals. In five years or, who knows, even
earlier, they are likely to be contenders for the greatest prize
in British politics – the leadership of the Labour Party –

followed, they hope, by the premiership of the country. No matter how much they may say they wish to remain friends and work together, only one of them can make it to the top – and only at the expense of the other. Brown and Blair may not admit it, and may not like it, but the build up to the fight has already begun.[2]

When Reiss wrote his piece it seemed as though, if one of the two was to succeed, it would be Brown. And Brown had never stopped believing it would be him. That is why the events of May and June 1994 came as such an agonising shock.

Not many Labour careers started in 1983. It was the Party's worst ever showing in a general election. But Gordon Brown and Tony Blair were immediately seen as the bright boys of the new intake. Both were put on the Labour front bench at roughly the same time; Brown as a trade and industry spokesman, Blair as part of the Treasury team. Both made it on to the Shadow Cabinet within a year of one another, with Blair becoming the Party's Shadow Energy Secretary, while Brown was Shadow Chief Secretary. And so it went on. After the 1992 general election the duo were appointed to two of the most senior front-bench posts shadowing two of the great offices of state. Brown became Shadow Chancellor; Blair Shadow Home Secretary. And, to complete their power base in the Labour Party, both men cruised on to the National Executive at the first time of trying in 1992. But for Labour 'Kremlinologists' it was clear who was ahead. In the 1992 Shadow Cabinet elections it was Brown who topped the poll with Blair coming in second. And in the NEC elections of that year Brown came third behind Neil Kinnock and David Blunkett, while Tony Blair just scraped on in seventh position.

Brown was also a much closer ally of John Smith as a result of their shared Scottish background and all those endless journeys on the shuttle between London and Edinburgh. So it was ironic that Brown's biggest break came when John Smith had his first heart attack after the Labour Party conference in 1988. Brown as number two in the Treasury team had to stand in for Smith. It was billed as a David and Goliath battle as the new boy Brown was pitted against the most intellectually rampant and self-confident Chancellor the Conservative Party had seen, Nigel Lawson. The moment of truth came when Lawson stood up to deliver his 1988 Autumn Statement. The Autumn Statement used to be the occasion when the Chancellor would announce the Government's public spending plans for the year. It came when Lawson had probably just gone beyond the height of his powers. Interest rates were soaring in an effort to curb the inflationary pressures in the economy. Sir Edward Heath, in that memorable phrase, had accused Lawson of being a 'one club golfer' – in other words, the only weapon that Lawson was prepared to use was interest rates to curb the runaway boom in the economy.

But even though some were beginning to doubt that Lawson was a miracle-worker, he still had a formidable hold on the loyalties of the Conservative Party, having been seen as the man who won the 1987 election for his Party. Against that background, Brown's response was extraordinary. He had a command of detail, a lightness of touch and a sure-footedness that delighted the Labour benches. John Smith's biographer, Andy McSmith, recounts how Brown rang Smith in Edinburgh where he was convalescing to convey in half apologetic tones the results of the Shadow Cabinet elections. Smith had achieved his best ever showing, coming second, with 144 votes. But first place had gone to Gordon Brown. It was from that moment on that people started talking seriously about Brown as the next Labour leader.[3]

According to friends who have known him for many years, the Labour leadership has always been Brown's driving ambition; more than that, he felt it was his destiny. He was the coming man. Articles appeared extolling his virtues. It was around this time that the *Daily Mirror*'s political editor, Alastair Campbell, singled out Brown as the man to watch (interestingly his article focused on six up-and-coming politicians. One of the Tory politicians he tipped to become the next Prime Minister was John Major):

> If I was asked to narrow the list of future Premiers to one, Brown would be the man, with Blair a likely Chancellor. They have an instinctive feel for the economy which has won them respect across the political spectrum. They are among Labour's better TV performers.[4]

When Campbell was reminded of this article soon after he had been appointed Tony Blair's Press Secretary, Campbell laughed and muttered, 'So I got it the wrong way round.'

That perception of Brown as, if not heir to the throne (John Smith was clearly the Crown Prince), then at least second in line, persisted until after the 1992 general election. Until then Brown was a mentor figure to Blair, a man whose grasp of the internal workings of the Labour Party made him a man to listen to. And Brown was a politician with not only a very clear idea of what needed to be done, but a realpolitik grasp of how quickly one could proceed with controversial reform proposals. But they were also extremely close friends. One Shadow Cabinet member who knows them both well said they were like Tweedledum and Tweedledee. They had offices next door to each other, and at times appeared to have an interchangeable staff. Other members of the Shadow Cabinet would walk past one or other room and hear raucous laughter echoing out as the two men shared a joke. They always arrived at meetings together. One senior Labour politician said she always saw Brown and Blair as more than just best friends, but also exclusive in their friendship. She said she felt sorry for Jack Straw, who always seemed to be excluded.

They were both admired hugely by Neil Kinnock. It wasn't just that they were bright and able, they showed their leader indefatigable loyalty at a time when others were equivocating. Take to lunch another member of the Shadow Cabinet during the run-up to the 1992 election and one would get barely beyond the starter before they would be talking about the 'Neil problem'. At times it threatened to turn into a serious plot; most of the time it was distracting background noise. But Blair and Brown stayed loyal, and that meant they were drawn ever closer into the leader's inner sanctum.

In 1990, their friendship, mixed with ambition for Labour, took them to Australia. It was a working holiday, mixing meetings with senior Australian politicians like the Prime Minister, Paul Keating, and his predecessor, Bob Hawke, with visits to Blair's greatest friends from university, Peter Thomson and Geoff Gallop. Blair and Brown started in the eastern states of Australia before travelling across to Perth. Thomson recalls a couple of think-tank sessions where all those present came away with the impression that Brown was the senior partner of the relationship, and that Blair was destined to be his lieutenant. Gallop, who has become the deputy leader of the Labour Group in Western Australia, has a similar recollection: 'I think Tony would be the first to admit that Gordon had the greater political depth; all the time they were over here, Tony deferred to Gordon.'[5]

But for all that Gordon Brown was a master of the medium of television, he was eventually to fall foul of it. It became a joke in television newsrooms that it was getting impossible to cover any story without either Gordon Brown or one of his dutiful researchers ringing up the newsdesk to offer Brown up as an interviewee on the subject. It became an even bigger joke that no matter what question you asked Brown, the answer would be the same. Awkward words and phrases tumbled from his lips in soundbite-babble. Brown simply decided what it was he wanted to say, rehearsed it thoroughly before going into the studio, and gave his stock answer. These were tactics that Blair had mastered, but Brown was saying the same thing so often and he looked so lacking in spontaneity that Tories soon started poking fun at him as Mr Soundbite. The editor of one of the BBC's main television news bulletins even tried to impose a blanket ban on Brown because he was on so often and said so little, but was forced to relent when it was pointed out to him that it was not the BBC's job to blackball the Shadow Chancellor of the Exchequer.

Brown had a seemingly unquenchable thirst to be on air. At weekends he would trudge into the Edinburgh studio; during the week he seemed to be a permanent resident of the broadcasters' studios at Millbank, across the road from the Commons. But it created an impression that Gordon Brown was becoming a rent-a-quote politician, which often undermines the seriousness with which a politician is treated. The person, who, whatever the weather, whatever the issue, always had something to say. He horrified the predominantly male newsroom at the BBC's Television Centre one Saturday afternoon by giving up his seat at half-time during the Scotland/England Calcutta Cup match at Murrayfield to nip into the Edinburgh studio, missing the entire second half for a rather banal story. Surely no-one loves politics that much, was the general consensus in the newsroom.

It is always hard to pin-point a moment when the coming man becomes, in the eyes of the media and politicians alike, a waning force; when the bright shooting star starts to burn up in the earth's atmosphere. With Gordon Brown it probably happened after the 1992 general election. Part of it was overexposure. In the blizzard of economic disasters that buried the Government it was inevitable that he would be called upon to comment regularly. But with his somewhat dour appearance, and the strange rehearsed smile that would appear in the middle of his answer for no discernible reason, making him appear a touch enigmatic, he also had a habit of overdoing the gloom. Gordon Brown in private is excellent company with a deep, resonating laugh that displays a sense of fun that isn't much in evidence in his public persona, where he often gives the appearance of a preacher bearing bad news.

After the 1993 budget, Gordon Brown said, 'I will make one budget forecast – that after the budget, unemployment will rise this month, next month and for months afterwards.'[6] It was at that moment that unemployment started to fall. And, similarly, during the Autumn Statement six months earlier he declared that the recession had become a slump, even though that seemed to be the point when the economy had started to grow again.

Brown also had a strong sense that support was ebbing away from him. He became morose and depressed. Those journalists he trusted were invited in for a chat. But it invariably turned into a monologue, as Brown poured out his heart about what was going wrong for him. He felt misunderstood and misrepresented. He couldn't understand why, when he was the hardest-working and most diligent of Labour's front-bench team, people poked fun at his manner. Articles critical of his media appearances also upset him. He became introspective, regularly cancelling lunch engagements. There was a sense that he had become a loser even before John Smith died. Brown at this stage appointed an old press hand from the Engineering Union, Charlie Whelan, to help rebuild his image. But in some ways the die had been cast and it was too late to turn things round. Whelan now jokes that he was the first press officer in the history of the Labour Party to be taken on with the sole brief of keeping his master *off* the television screen as much as possible.

Brown would also worry about what others in the Party thought about him, and he would be alarmed if his position in the NEC or Shadow Cabinet elections showed any slippage in popularity. Blair, whose stock had been steadily rising in the Party, grew impatient with his close friend's preoccupations and told Brown:

> Listen, if you are going to be judged by history at all it will be for what you do when you become Chancellor of the Exchequer. If we don't make it into Government, then the whole project will have failed. In which case, how you did in one set of Shadow Cabinet elections compared to another will be considered a supreme irrelevance.

But Brown was in a cleft stick. No doubt he could have won easy applause from the left and many of the unions by sticking to a traditional cocktail of old fashioned reflationary measures, backed up by Keynesian demand management. But that would have been to negate what Blair and Brown believed was a central task for Labour, and that was the formulation of a new economic agenda. Brown calculated that Socialist planning would have to give way to a warmer embracing of the market if Labour was once and for all to convince its critics that it had broken free of its tax and spend psychology. It was necessarily going to be a slow process, and all the time this economic reformulation was going on there were going to be few plaudits for Brown. No Labour Chancellor or Shadow Chancellor has won much support from his colleagues for uttering the word 'no' endlessly, but this is what Brown had to do. In the 1992 election there was what came to be known as Beckett's law. A simple doctrine, it stated that Labour's only spending commitments were those that had been laid out in the manifesto, anything else was to be disregarded. But Brown was trying to make it an even tighter formulation, insisting that Labour would have no spending commitments at all until the manifesto was written:

> (they) simply do not exist . . . We will not spend what we cannot afford to spend, and only as growth allows. We've made that absolutely clear. I have said there are no manifesto commitments at this stage to public spending.[7]

But such caution did not impress the left of the Party. They wanted to hear the Shadow Chancellor advocate higher public spending funded by borrowing; Brown refused to budge. Instead he offered up emergency job measures, attacks on tax loopholes, the promise of a skills revolution to deal with supply-side weaknesses in the economy, and windfall taxes on the privatised utilities. But the left thought that was window dressing. Gordon Brown had learned the lesson of the last election where Labour had saddled itself with spending commitments two years out from an election which left the Party flatfooted as polling day drew near. In his bid to avoid the same mistakes again, Brown to his parliamentary colleagues often appeared defensive and lacking in ambition for what a Labour Government would do.

Many argue that, had John Smith been struck down eighteen months earlier, there is no question of who Labour's next leader would have been. The *Guardian*'s chief Labour watcher, Patrick Wintour, observed, 'Mr Brown had topped the shadow cabinet poll for five successive years, possessed a compelling personality and could galvanise a party meeting. He was not so much being groomed as the next leader: he *was* the next leader.'[8] Neil Kinnock had some sympathy for that view, but he, more than anyone, knew that politics is a rough trade where you have to ride your luck. Brown's misfortune in Kinnock's view was that the merry-go-round did not stop for him. And Kinnock said the moment he turned his mind to thinking about who should succeed John Smith, he knew in an instant it had to be Blair.

On the morning of John Smith's death, politics was officially put on hold. All debates that day were cancelled and the Palace of Westminster became an eerie place, as MPs wept openly and people walked silently through the normally bustling corridors of power. The dignity of the Commons that afternoon, when MPs paid their tributes to Smith, did much to restore the public's respect for politics and politicians. But, as Neil Kinnock had discovered, in the midst of grief, mourning and sadness there was plotting and scheming too. 'On the day John died I was naturally reticent about even considering let alone raising the question of what is going to happen now. Decency forbids it.' But when he was told of the meeting going on near his office between two other left-wing members of the Shadow Cabinet, all that changed.

> I thought, well, OK, that's the end of the reservation. So I spoke to Tony and to Gordon . . . I said to them 'Listen, let's observe the decencies, but because of what is occurring it is something that has to be discussed.' I said the same thing to both of them that they would have to sort out

between themselves which one of them was going to run, and I wasn't going to offer a view.[9]

Some have sought to argue that, in the immediate aftermath of John Smith's death, Blair still felt that Brown should probably succeed to the leadership (see Martin Jacques in the *Sunday Times Magazine* 17.7.94, an article that Blair, a friend of Jacques, gave much help to). But that is wide of the mark. Blair knew as soon as he heard the news on the tarmac at Dyce Airport in Aberdeen that his moment had come. He has since told friends he felt a confusing range of emotions. He was deeply shocked that Smith had died and immediately felt for Smith's family, but he also knew in an instant what this was going to mean for him, and what impact it would have upon his family. He made two phone calls. The first was to his wife, Cherie. The second was to Peter Mandelson. Mandelson in turn rang Gordon Brown, and said he would be at his flat by lunchtime.

One member of the Shadow Cabinet close to both Blair and Brown recalls that Blair was never in any doubt that he would stand, but that Brown hesitated. At Brown's flat in London, one of his closest female friends, a television journalist who was working nearby had turned up along with his greatest supporter in the Commons, Nick Brown. Mandelson arrived a short time afterwards. They were mourning for Smith and contemplating the future. Although Brown was unusually tentative, he still believed the crown would be his. But, within days, one of the Shadow Chancellor's aides said that Brown was coming under 'undue' pressure from 'prominent figures' to announce by the following Wednesday, two days before John Smith's funeral, that he was withdrawing from the race.

Kinnock spoke to Brown and Blair individually. The former leader recalls that when he spoke to Tony Blair, Blair's only concern was not his relationship with Gordon Brown but what impact being leader would have upon his family. On that score Kinnock was a good person to speak to. Both are deeply committed 'family men'; both dutiful and loving fathers. But Blair wanted to know what sort of life would it be for Euan, Nicholas and Kathryn. How would they continue to enjoy a normal childhood, if, as he hoped, he made it to Downing Street. Kinnock was blunt. It wouldn't be easy, but he said if you believe that you are going to make this country a better place for other people to grow up in, then you must not let that deter you. What Kinnock didn't tell Blair was that he had just been at Westminster Abbey to give a reading at a memorial service. As he signed the visitors' book, he noticed that the signature above his was Chelsea Clinton's, who had been in London on a school vacation without her parents. With the signature of the President's daughter were the signatures of her four Secret Service agents who never leave her side. 'Yes,' Kinnock thought to himself 'there will be a heavy price.'

One of those who Brown came to believe was pushing hardest for him to stand aside, so that only one 'Moderniser' would enter the contest, was Peter Mandelson. The entourage around Brown believed Mandelson was doing Tony Blair's bidding, and there was a strong belief that Neil Kinnock, despite his insistence that he played no role in influencing the decision about which of them should stand, was pulling strings for Blair behind the scenes. And with Kinnock so clear in his own mind that it had to be Blair, it is hard to believe that such a weighty figure in the Labour Party, and one who had been so instrumental in developing both men's careers, did nothing to influence the outcome of Gordon Brown's deliberations. But, in this fraught period, Brown's anger wasn't aimed directly at Kinnock, it was Mandelson whom he saw as all things rotten. Mandelson, for many years an extremely close personal friend, had in Brown's eyes betrayed that friendship. The two fell out spectacularly, and for many weeks did not speak to each other.

But there are many wrinkles in this story. In the days after John Smith died, Mandelson was out and about in his inimitable fashion, beating the Brown drum. He told a number of journalists in a series of conversations that Brown was the brighter of the two, that he had much the deeper feel for the Labour Party and would be the candidate most acceptable to the centre left. It was a tune that Mandelson sang without hesitation or deviation, and with much repetition. After all, for all his closeness to Blair, he knew Brown even better. Journalists faithfully reported those views that night and the following day.

Indeed, the day after Smith died, Mandelson was walking across Parliament Square and by chance bumped into Derry Irvine, who was closely involved with the arrangements for the funeral. After a brief conversation about the shock of Smith's death, the subject turned to the succession. Lord Irvine said the leadership was Blair's for the taking. Mandelson disagreed: 'I am not persuaded of that,' he replied. Irvine was shocked, and contacted Blair immediately to warn him that Mandelson was backing Brown. Blair and Mandelson spoke soon afterwards, and Mandelson explained the delicacy of his position. Blair was sympathetic but firm: 'I understand what you've got to do,' he told him; 'just don't hurt me in the process.'

What Mandelson's motives were at this stage remains something of a mystery. It seems he was in a quandary. Perhaps he genuinely felt that Brown should be the candidate but was later prevailed upon by other people. Or perhaps it was Mandelson's each-way bet. After all, on 12 May it was far from 100 per cent certain that Brown *wouldn't* run, and it was an easy way to cover all the bases. But the most plausible explanation is that Mandelson genuinely thought that Brown should run, and did so until it became clear to him that there was no way of stopping Blair. At which point Mandelson's prime concern became to persuade Brown not to enter a contest that he could not win. After all, Mandelson's whole period as Communications Director had been about trying to back winners, not take up hopeless causes on behalf of people who would lose. But, on the weekend after Smith's death, that judgement had not yet been made. Mandelson, with varying degrees of commitment, was trying to show that he still thought Brown might be a runner. So, on the Saturday when Mandelson was due to appear on

Channel 4's *The Week in Politics,* the former Director of Communications sat in the Green Room saying in a loud voice, 'I must speak to Charlie [Whelan, Brown's special adviser] about how we're going to play the Sunday papers.' The impression Mandelson wanted to create to those journalists present was that he was putting his hand on Brown's shoulder.

But that is not the way the Brown camp saw it. When Mandelson went on the programme and was interviewed live by Andrew Rawnsley, Mandelson gave the impression to many that it had to be Blair, arguing that what Labour needed to do was elect a leader with whom most of the electorate would feel comfortable, and who could win for Labour in areas that hitherto had remained stubbornly Conservative. Charlie Whelan was bleeped at home by another Brown supporter. His pager read: 'So Mandelson's backing Blair.' Mandelson says he was bounced by the question (something hard to imagine for such an experienced media operator), but, whatever Mandelson's intentions, it looked suspiciously to Brown as though Mandelson was throwing his weight behind Blair.

The following day the *Sunday Times* ran a story by Andrew Grice, the chief political correspondent, saying that a non-aggression pact had been agreed between Blair and Brown and that they would not fight each other for the leadership. The source of the story is something of a mystery. Brown's press officer, Charlie Whelan, says it came from Mandelson; Mandelson denies that vehemently. On one level the story was a statement of the near obvious: both men knew that it would look awful for the Modernisers' cause if they were to slug it out in public. It would create the impression that once again two of the Labour Party's leading lights were prepared to challenge each other, not because of policy differences but because of vanity and personal ambition. But there had been no agreement. Blair and Brown had spoken, but at no point did Blair ever indicate that he was out of the race. Instead it seemed that Brown was so confident that he would prevail in this fascinating personality clash that the intended subliminal message of the *Sunday Times* story was that there would be no contest between the two Modernisers because Brown would be the candidate. But on the same day other Sunday newspapers were positively bulging with polls indicating that Blair was out in front with the public and way out in front *vis-à-vis* the Party. If it was Charlie Whelan who had briefed the *Sunday Times,* then it was a tactic that backfired, because the polls combined with the story that there would be only one Modernising candidate pointed to one conclusion: that Tony Blair would be the one. From that moment on, Brown was swimming against a flood-tide. And from then on Mandelson said to Brown that he would help him, but only if there was the ammunition to fight a credible battle.

The weekend after John Smith's death was an extraordinary occasion for Brown. As well as writing a handful of obituaries for different newspapers and magazines, he was also coming under pressure from his supporters to organise a leadership campaign. Brown still believes that he had greater support in the Parliamentary Labour Party than Blair. While it is a proposition that was never tested, it is one that is hard to believe, such was the momentum that Blair built up immediately after his thoughts turned to the succession. Blair and he spoke throughout this period. What surprised Brown was not necessarily his friend's ambition, but the violence with which his supporters were prepared to advance Blair's cause at the expense of Brown's.

Mandelson and Whelan argued viciously throughout this period. Mandelson told Whelan that he must say nothing that did down Blair to any of the newspapers. He argued that, until such time as Blair and Brown had resolved between themselves who would run, then no good could come of pumping one up at the expense of the other. That much the two could agree on. But the reality was that both sides found it an impossible rule to observe. Whelan was in a tricky position because Brown wanted him to say certain things to the press to keep his name in the frame. So when Whelan said that Brown had better links with the trade unions, reporters naturally asked 'better than whom?' And it was much the same on the other side when Blair supporters talked up their man. But what infuriated Brown was his firm belief that Mandelson was not playing by the rules that he himself had laid down. Stories were appearing extolling the virtues of Blair at the expense of Brown, which Brown believed bore all the hallmarks of a Mandelson operation.

Brown's attitude through this period was simply not to talk to Mandelson. According to Brown's advisers, what hurt Mandelson most was Brown's refusal to discuss with him what he was going to do. But, right up until the day before Brown pulled out of the race, he was protecting his position. About three times a week, Brown would meet with his advisers, and two key supporters in the Commons, Nick Brown, the Newcastle MP, and Andrew Smith MP. While Gordon Brown sat back in an armchair in his flat, Nick Brown would read through a roll call of the 270 members of the Parliamentary Labour Party. The Shadow Chancellor would call out three words: they were supporters, opponents, or 'biddable'. Up until Brown pulled out he reckoned he had the support of around ninety MPs with a further fifty who were biddable. They calculated that Blair had around 130 supporters. But all the time Nick Brown believed that Gordon Brown – in theory – could win; not just in the Commons but among the unions and in the constituency parties.

Mandelson was also coming under pressure from senior figures in the Party to get Brown to withdraw from the race. If Neil Kinnock wasn't trying to influence events, others, like Roy Hattersley and Gerald Kaufman, certainly were. On one occasion Mandelson was summoned to Kaufman's Westminster office to be given a typically waspish and pithy instruction:

Now, Peter, the Labour Party is blessed in having two first-rate candidates in Gordon Brown and Tony Blair, however there is only one vacancy, so would you please go and tell Gordon that he will be crushed if he stands against Tony, and that he should therefore announce his withdrawal from the race.

Mandelson smiled, bowed slightly and left the office.

One of the first of the 'inner circle' of friends to declare publicly for Blair was Alastair Campbell, who had written not so long ago how the crown would be Brown's. He upset the Shadow Chancellor by going on *Newsnight* immediately after Smith's death to say it had to be Blair. Campbell was close to Kinnock and someone else from the Kinnock old guard who felt the leadership should go to Blair was Charles Clarke, the former Chief of Staff. Clarke, who had seen both men rise simultaneously in the Shadow Cabinet, felt that Brown's preoccupation with what others thought of him disqualified him as a potential leader.

> I started out believing that Gordon should not run for the leadership, but I have subsequently come round to the view that it would have been better if he had, and actually been beaten. That would have humiliated him and meant that Tony did not owe him a debt. There was never the remotest chance that Gordon would be elected leader of the Party . . . He believed it was all there for him, and it just wasn't.[10]

Brown found the pressure to withdraw intolerable. He spent as little time as he needed to in London, preferring instead his real home in Fife. It was while he was in Scotland that he became aware that a tabloid newspaper had sent reporters up to sniff around his private life. They contacted old friends to find out whether there was anything newsworthy. They found nothing, because there was nothing to find. But Brown suspected that rumours – the sort of scurrilous story that Westminster from time to time wades in – about his sexuality were being peddled by his opponents. Brown has had a number of girlfriends, but because none of the relationships had ended in marriage, his bachelor status became the subject of malicious gossip. 'I'm not married because it's never happened. It could have happened. It just hasn't. Perhaps I've been too busy,' he would later tell an interviewer.[11] This flurry around Brown's private life did matter though for two reasons. First it showed the extent to which relationships had soured in that the Brown camp were convinced (probably correctly) that these stories were emanating from his political opponents within the Labour Party. But perhaps more important in the context of the world of highly packaged politicians, the fact that Blair was happily married with three children served to underline his marketability with the electorate.

But there were many pushing for Brown to stand. If he had entered the race he would have had an impressive band of backers, particularly in Scotland where perhaps the Labour establishment is not as preoccupied about winning in the south of England. Murray Elder, his friend from infant school days, wanted him to run. So, apparently, did Elizabeth Smith, John's widow, although Derry Irvine says that John Smith always regarded Blair as his natural successor. And there were a large number of MPs, constituency activists and union members urging Brown to run. Brown, too, had not given up all hope, even though he must have known in his heart that the forces ranged against him were likely to prove irresistible.

During this period some of the tension boiled over. One of Brown's acolytes, the junior front bench spokesperson, Nigel Griffiths, accused Peter Mandelson of campaigning on Blair's behalf. The Edinburgh South MP said he was 'distressed' that Mandelson was campaigning so soon after Smith's death. There were others who gave vent to similar sentiments. They were quickly put back into line by Brown who realised that such behaviour was foolishly counter-productive. Brown's clearest indication that he hadn't given up on running for the leadership came at the Welsh Labour conference in Cardiff. Blair had also been intending to speak, but pulled out at the last minute for fear that it would turn into a beauty contest. Brown's speech, which came two days after Smith's funeral, bore all the hallmarks of being a personal manifesto, it was a *tour d'horizon*. Brown is, after Neil Kinnock, Labour's most powerful platform orator, and this was one of his most resonating speeches as it sought to define

Labour's role for the future. Inevitably it was treated by the media as a bid for the leadership. And no-one from Brown's side was contradicting that.

It was following that conference that Blair had cause to upbraid one of his over-zealous cheerleaders. Alun Michael had been on the platform when Brown delivered his oration, and while everyone else stood to acclaim Brown's speech, Michael pointedly sat on his hands looking glum and slightly dismissive. When Blair saw this on the television news that evening, according to someone else in the room, he hit the roof. Alun Michael is older than Blair, and treats him like an extremely clever younger brother, but he was shocked to find himself on the receiving end of a tongue lashing that evening.

Contacts between Blair and Brown by this stage were frequent but tense. Only two other people were fully aware of the extent of the discussions that were taking place and the manoeuvring that was taking place, and they were Anji Hunter, and her counterpart in Gordon Brown's office, Sue Nye. Both are formidable political operators in their own right, and neither will speak about what took place. According to a senior member of the Blair camp, Blair eventually steeled himself for a show-down with Brown and told him that there was no question that he was going to stand aside, and it was therefore up to Brown whether he wanted to force a damaging and divisive contest. For the two men who had been the closest of friends and who had shared the same mission for Labour to have engaged in bloody battle would have done untold harm to the Party. Both men knew it; but it was Blair who had called Gordon Brown's bluff. It had become inevitable that Brown would have to fall upon his sword.

Brown and Blair met in Islington on the evening of Tuesday 31 May at a fashionable Mediterranean grill, the Granita, to formalise Brown's withdrawal from the race. It was not the most relaxed dinner the two men have enjoyed. Next to no-one in either office knew the meeting was taking place. Brown had made his decision a few days earlier; now it was a question of ensuring that the manner in which the decision was announced was given the best possible gloss, and to make it seem that Blair and Brown were in control of the agenda. At the time it was claimed that as the price of his withdrawal Brown wanted an assurance that he would have a free hand on economic policy without interference from either John Prescott or Robin Cook, who took a more interventionist view of what Labour should be doing. Their view was that 'seasoning and spice' needed to be added to Labour's policies. But Brown has since told friends that he made no such demand, but it was interesting that, in the first Shadow Cabinet elections after the leadership contest, Cook was moved from Trade and Industry to Foreign Affairs, being replaced at Trade and Industry by Jack Cunningham, while the employment brief (John Prescott's old job) was given to Harriet Harman, a committed Moderniser and previously Gordon Brown's number two. All left-wing influence had been removed from the economic team in the way that Brown had wanted, although Cook (who had wanted Brown's job, but was never going to get it) and Prescott will wield influence on a committee established to look at long-term economic policy commitments.

There was another minor problem to overcome. David Blunkett, who was the Chairman of the Party, insisted, and it was agreed by the Shadow Cabinet, that all the would-be contenders for the Labour leadership, whatever their intentions, should remain silent until after polling had closed for the European elections. But both Brown and Blair took the view that the endless speculation about whether the 'blood brothers' were on the verge of a 'blood feud' was proving such a distraction that an announcement needed to be made.

Once they had paraded for the cameras together, Brown went back to Scotland to lick his wounds. He had, according to all those close to him, found the whole experience extremely painful. There had been misjudgement in that he had failed to appreciate the weakness of his own position. And he had not fully realised the extent of Blair's ambition. But Brown would later find it galling that his decision to withdraw was interpreted by some as a sign of his own weakness. One close friend said

Gordon had revealed for the first time a naïvety about politics. It would have been impossible for Brown to have played a central role in the campaign to have Blair elected, and certainly Blair didn't expect it, but he did help out with some of the big speeches. The irony was not lost on Brown when he picked up his copy of *The Times* midway through the campaign and saw the headline, BLAIR MAKES MARK WITH HEAVYWEIGHT ECONOMIC SPEECH; it was Brown who had written it.

And on the night before the results of the leadership contest were declared, Brown was back in Blair's office helping his friend with the most important speech that Blair had ever made, and the speech which for so long Brown had dreamed of making. It took real courage on Brown's part to be there at such a defining moment. Blair was at his most tense, exploding at one point that the speech needed to be picked apart and started all over again. But as the night wore on, those other advisers present recognised this was just to keep the adrenalin pumping. And soon Brown and Blair had settled down to do what they had always done: sharpening the message, stripping away the verbiage, polishing the phrases and punctuating the speech with applause points. Kinnock walked past the room, and thought about going in, but decided it was best to leave the two of them at it. The next day Blair delivered the speech that Brown had helped craft. It was broadcast live on BBC1, at the end of the transmission there was a poignant shot as Blair walked through the crowd to receive their congratulations. As he did so, he walked past Brown, and Brown, with a wry grin on his face, simply said, 'Nice speech'.

Brown spoke about his decision to withdraw from the race a couple of weeks after Blair had been made Leader. Apparently displaying no bitterness, he said he felt his chances of winning the leadership had been high, but had decided against it because the Party would not have understood.

> Tony and I have worked so closely in the past, developed so many of our ideas together that we could not have ended fighting one another. Personal advancement has got to

come second not just to our chances of winning the election, but performing well in government. If two people who had worked very closely together stood against one another, people would have questioned not just us, but our ideas. It would not have done Labour any good at all. To that extent I have been justified by events. I think the Party has made the right choice.[12]

Those words can't have fallen easily from Mr Brown's lips as he left England for a holiday in Portugal. In the interview he also acknowledged the cost that his economic policies had on his own popularity. 'Obviously the lesson of making changes is that people are distrustful and they blame those who are making the changes.'[13]

A year after Blair had become Leader, Brown and Blair were still working closely together. Blair would tell parliamentary colleagues that there were few strategic decisions taken without first having sought the opinion of Brown. But the basis of their relationship had necessarily changed. It could not be one of equals. Brown had gone from being an intimate and a peer to someone who became part of the Leader's calculations. Having said that, Blair's calculations put Brown in an ever more powerful role within the Party as he was put in charge of day-to-day campaigning, a decision which would arouse jealousies from the other two big names in the Shadow Cabinet, John Prescott and Robin Cook. But Blair had to learn to manage all those key relationships, and where once the only opinion that Blair sought was that of his closest ally, the Leader needed too, the support of Cook and Prescott. As one member of the Shadow Cabinet put it, 'You can have a friendly Leader, but you can't have a leader who is a friend.'[14]

Brown had been humiliated. He had worked from his earliest years to become Labour leader; a year earlier it had seemed as though it would be straightforward. In 1994 he had been tossed aside. One close friend of Brown's since their student days noted that for months after the leadership election he was still very unsettled and difficult to work with. 'The child in him was throwing his toys around the bedroom,' said the confidante. But others say that does not mean his ambition has gone. After all, irrespective of whether Labour win or lose, it is hard to believe that Tony Blair is going to be leader in ten years' time. Perhaps the best summing up of why Labour plumped for Blair rather than Brown was made by one of Blair's closest confidants. He said, 'You have to understand that with Gordon, every muscle and sinew in his body has been developed so that one day he might become the Leader of the Labour Party. Tony's never had that ambition. All he's ever been interested in is becoming Prime Minister.'[15]

CHAPTER 9

The Candidate

REPORTER: What advice do you have for Tony Blair?
PRIME MINISTER: Don't believe what people are saying about you now; and don't believe what they say in eighteen months either.

John Major, 13.6.94

Not for Tony Blair a sweaty Commons committee room to announce his presence in the race for the leadership. No, this most modern politician chose the most deliberately old-fashioned and traditional setting to launch his campaign. In a deliberate piece of completely unstage-managed stage-management, Tony Blair's agent called a meeting of the local constituency association for Saturday morning. The venue: Trimdon Labour Club. The time: 10 a.m. The date: 11 June 1994.

It is a vast sprawling place, which is normally the venue for snooker and darts matches; bingo and dominoes evenings. It is also the meeting place of the Trimdon pigeon fanciers club. By the time Tony Blair arrived at the club in a somewhat battered Ford Escort, around four hundred people had squeezed themselves into the social club. There were pensioners, mothers with children, groups of men, all dressed up in their best clothes for this momentous occasion. It was as far removed from Westminster as it was possible to get. And when Tony Blair came on to the makeshift stage the mood of the audience seemed to turn the occasion from a conventional political meeting into a revivalist rally. 'I am announcing this morning my candidature for the position of leader of the Labour Party.' He looked nervous, his voice was tense and slightly high pitched. His eyes glanced around the room like a child reciting his newly learnt party piece on the piano in front of proud aunts and uncles. The cheers nearly lifted the roof.

'It is now time to complete the journey started by Neil Kinnock and John Smith and move from the politics of protest to the politics of government,' he declared. 'To end the long years of opposition – dark years for us and often for our country and to seek the trust of the British people in shaping their future.' More bursts of applause. And so it went on as Blair skipped through themes and ideas with phrase-making skills that would make the chest of any advertising copywriter puff with pride. 'The world changes; it is changing now. But the principles do not change. They stand for ever as we do, honouring the past but never living in it.' And how to win? 'We must state a new vision of our country, a vision of hope that the world as it is is not the world as it is meant to be.' By the time he sat down, the audience were on their feet. Some were wiping tears from their eyes. Of course, none of this was stage-managed; no stage-manager or director would have ever been able to create a piece of political theatre like this.

Then it was the turn of the audience to stand up and declare their support. 'Tony, I remember you when you came to us as a lad,' started one of the older members of the audience. 'We knew you were something special then and we know it now.' Cheering. An older woman stood up: 'Tony, all I want to say is that I'm right proud of you.' She resumed her seat. And so it went on. One woman was asked by a cameraman on her way into the hall why she had come. Her riposte was instantaneous: 'To hear the next Prime Minister, silly.' If any of these people who had given up their Saturday morning to be at Trimdon Labour club had arrived as sceptics, they left as believers. These images filled Saturday's television screens and Sunday's news-papers, as his campaign team knew they would.

It had been a different story the day before. While John Prescott and Margaret Beckett were unveiling their campaigns in London, Blair's press officer, Tim Allan, had invited film crews to film Tony and Cherie at their home in Trimdon. The idea had been to give the BBC and ITN good library footage of the Blair family *'au naturel'*. There would be domesticated shots of them sitting in the kitchen, and holding hands in the garden. Moody shots of Blair looking pensive in his study. But the whole event turned into fiasco. Cherie arrived back late, having missed her train from London. She was, in the words of one of Blair's aides, 'in a mood from hell'. Blair was tense and kept on telling Tim Allan to send them away because he wanted to get on with his speech. The crews were not surprisingly bewildered by what was going on. 'If this was the most media friendly person the Labour Party had,' the BBC producer complained down a telephone line to her bosses in London, 'I'd hate to see the others.' So filming that had been designed to show the Blairs looking relaxed and loving ended up with both ITN and the BBC gaining footage of them looking stroppy, fed up and distinctly hostile to one another. These were not pictures that conveyed a marriage made in heaven. The Blair camp refer back to it as the Sedgefield massacre.

But if Saturday morning was the public unveiling of Blair the candidate, the campaign itself had started discreetly weeks before, during the European election campaign, when supposedly no electioneering for the leadership was going on. By 9 June, when the starting gun was fired, Blair's people already had a pretty clear idea of which MPs would be backing him, how the Shadow Cabinet would divide and who would be prepared to give up time to join the campaign. Indeed, one of the concerns of the Blair camp was that they were attracting so much support early on that it might have made it impossible for his opponents to gain the required number of nominations from MPs to enter the race. For example, Ron Davies, Labour's left-wing Welsh spokesman, who is in the Shadow Cabinet, nominated John Prescott for the leadership to ensure a contest, but announced at the same time that he was really supporting Blair.

Before the contest started, though, John Prescott held a private meeting with Blair. Stories had been circulating that there might not be a contest, and that, instead of an election, there would be a coronation. Prescott counselled against this. He made two points to Blair: the first was that, having gone through hoops of fire to pass the one member one vote resolution at the last Party conference, the rank and file would not understand if there was no contest. There had been a bloody battle fought to build this new electoral machinery and for it not to be tested would cause bewilderment and resentment simultaneously. The second point he made was that Blair would only have real authority over the Party to carry out whatever reforms he wanted if he had been seen to be elected by the movement. It was sound advice, and led Blair to recognise that Prescott was a cannier politician than he had given him credit for. By that afternoon, Mandelson was busying himself with ringing up the political newsdesks assuring all and sundry that it had never been his master's intention or wish *not* to have a contest.

When nominations closed, over half the Parliamentary Labour Party were backing Blair, while thirteen out of the seventeen members of the Shadow Cabinet had plumped for him (as well as Ron Davies, John Prescott attracted the support of Shadow Cabinet members Michael Meacher and Joan Lestor). Now there was to be a contest, Blair had to pull together a team of workers, researchers and press officers to handle the avalanche of enquiries and demands that would be made of him. One of his most energetic campaigners was Mo Mowlam. She, along with Peter Kilfoyle, had done nearly all the early spade work in the PLP, talking to every MP, acting as a conduit for their particular concerns. Most MPs have a secretary and a researcher; within days Blair had a team of around a dozen bright young things, invariably Oxbridge educated, all eager to help. Tim Allan had been a researcher for Tony Blair for two years before being lured away to television and Channel 4's *The Week in Politics* programme. He came back as press officer for the campaign. David Miliband, the thirty-year-old son of the distinguished Marxist writer, Ralph Miliband, was plucked from the leftward leaning

Institute of Public Policy Research to be chief researcher and speechwriter. The team was knitted together by Anji Hunter, Blair's hugely influential head of the private office, who linked up with him again soon after he entered the Commons.

Hunter and Blair have a relationship of total trust. To get her way on Blair's behalf she will deploy charm and flattery; if that fails she can bully and manipulate. Another member of the office said she was as tough as old boots. When she says no, it is rarely worth bothering to argue. She will also give Blair blunt advice, and few Labour politicians underestimate her importance to him. She works extraordinarily long hours, arriving in the office at dawn and often staying until late at night. Invariably, Blair's political reliance on Hunter will bring comparisons with Harold Wilson's on Marcia Williams (now Lady Falkender) but Hunter does not seek to influence policy decisions. Once a decision has been taken, however, she knows exactly who to contact and which buttons to press to sell whatever needs selling. She also has an astute tactical brain, seeing traps and snares ahead, and advising Blair how best to circumvent them.

The core of the campaign team met in Blair's office in I Parliament Street at 8.30 each morning. The campaign was led by Jack Straw, the former Bennite left-winger who came into the Commons in 1979. Blair asked him to take on the job for tactical as well as personal reasons. Straw was not seen as an out and out Moderniser – his roots were much more mainstream than that – although on the monarchy and on Labour's constitution he was in the forefront of 'modern' thinking, arguing the case for the reform of both. With Straw having a foot in both the Moderniser and Traditionalist camps, Blair saw it as a distinct advantage to have someone leading the team who would reassure the left. Mo Mowlam, the outspoken and occasionally wild Shadow Cabinet member who advocated moving the Windsors out of Buckingham Palace in an ill-judged interview, was Straw's deputy. She also has an irreverent sense of humour, that immediately got her into trouble with the more politically correct members of the campaign. Mowlam's job was to maximise the vote among the women's section of the Party, an uncontroversial enough task until she decided to call her operation 'Bimbos Backing Bambi'. That upset Harriet Harman who complained to Tony Blair that the name demeaned women. In truth, it did little for Blair either, but that didn't seem to be the point.

Aside from the successful harvesting of the votes, the other main priority of the campaign team was to demonstrate that Blair had a governing agenda to lead Britain. While he had shown himself strong on home affairs, and on the unions, there was little sense when Blair entered the contest of him as a politician with an over-arching *Weltanschauung*. He had not spread his wings: where did Blair stand on constitutional reform, on Europe, on welfare reform? All that could be deduced from what he had said until then on those subjects was that he was still working out his position. Therefore a huge amount of Blair's time was given over to formulating policy and speechwriting. Labour MPs joked that Blair was already taking on the demeanour of an American president. As he waited to fly up to Manchester one Sunday morning, he was surrounded by a team of press officers, researchers and speech-writers who were accompanying him. All that was missing were the secret service agents. While Blair's party waited to board the plane, Margaret Beckett arrived to check in. Her sole companion was husband, Leo. It was a striking contrast. But with so many people involved, the campaign was also a costly operation. While many were giving freely of their time, the cost of hotels, flights, rail tickets, etc, soon mounted up. Full colour leaflets were printed in Gujarati and Urdu to maximise the turnout among Asian Labour Voters. The mounting cost was such that Blair's old pupil-master and Labour's Shadow Lord Chancellor, Lord Irvine, sent out letters on behalf of the campaign committee inviting the lucky recipients to donate £100 to the Blair leadership drive, although he went on to add 'you should feel in no way inhibited from sending a lesser sum by my suggestion of that figure.' This, he said, would pay for all those extra little bits and pieces to allow Blair to present his vision of a Labour Government 'of which he will be Prime Minister.'

When it was reported in the press just before the Labour Party conference in the autumn that there had been a row over the huge amount Blair had raised during his campaign – it quoted a figure of £82,000 – one senior aide's response was tart: 'First of all there was no row at the National Executive, and secondly we raised far more than that!' Mandelson was the not-so-secret weapon of the campaign. He was never at any of the campaign meetings, he was never seen around the office. As far as Jack Straw knew, Mandelson was doing no more than tend his Hartlepool flock. But the journalists covering Blair's bid for the leadership knew otherwise.

Because of the enemies that Mandelson had made in his earlier incarnation as Communications Director, it was agreed that the Hartlepool MP would play no public role in banging the Blair drum. He was kept below stairs. John Prescott used to call him 'Mendelssohn, the great conductor': that was among the kinder names that people called him. But melting into the background as an innocent onlooker is not, and never has been, Mandelson's style. The Beckett camp certainly felt that much of the briefing about Margaret Beckett had been orchestrated by Peter Mandelson. His name was not mentioned, but it was clear they had him in mind when angry Beckett backers made a formal complaint about unattributable briefings about her at a meeting of the Parliamentary Labour Party during the campaign.

On the day of Blair's declaration in Sedgefield, Mandelson was at his constituency home in Hartlepool monitoring every word being spoken by journalists. If he didn't like what was being said, then he would bleep the reporter concerned demanding that he or she return the call. 'Ah, thank you for replying so promptly,' he would start before going on to say, 'you need to change that by the next bulletin.' Or 'I liked your first two answers on the *Today* programme, but the rest of it was drivel.' Then, having boxed you around the ears, he would go on to deploy flattery, engaging in enjoyable gossip about how dreadful one or other of your colleagues was.

After one speech in the West Midlands, Blair was being driven away in a chauffeur-driven Jaguar. A film crew was recording his departure. The car came to an abrupt halt, and the electric rear window came down just enough to allow Blair to slide his hand out of the window. He handed the reporter covering the speech a mobile phone: it was Mandelson on the other end of the line with instructions about which clip of the speech needed to be used on the evening news bulletin.

Mandelson's presence was continuous. On another occasion Blair was cornered in 4 Millbank, a lavishly redecorated Edwardian building which is the Westminster home of the BBC, ITN, Sky and a number of other commercial television and radio stations. A gaggle of film crews had gathered to tackle Blair on the strike by railway signal workers that had just started. Commenting on industrial disputes is one of those no-win situations for Labour politicians: sound sympathetic and the Conservatives will dub you the strikers' friend; condemn the strike and you will inevitably incur the wrath of the unions. Blair knew what the television reporters were after and he ran away from the questions – literally. He left Millbank via a side door, and a ludicrous chase ensued, with Blair being chased up Great Peter Street by an assorted gaggle of camera operators, sound-men, reporters and producers. When eventually Blair realised this would do him no good, he stopped and spoke to the reporters, telling them he would make a comment once he had made a call. Inevitably Mandelson became involved, breathing fire down the telephone to producers and editors who might have been tempted to use the film of Blair on the run. The resulting clip was of a shifty answer from Blair that only *News at Ten* used, but the episode, while leading to furious protests from Walworth Road, served to demonstrate both Blair's occasional lack of confidence and – once again – Mandelson's influence as a trusted adviser.

And the campaign ended as it had begun. The BBC had been promised some 'exclusive' filming with the Blairs. The question was what it would be. The political unit wanted to film Blair that morning having breakfast *'en famille'*. Tim Allan, the press officer, came back and said that wouldn't be possible. There would be no filming with the children. But, as a sop, it was suggested that it might be possible to put a camera crew in the car that Blair would be travelling in on the way to the Institute of Education where he was to be anointed leader. However, Allan pointed out that Blair would need some convincing (Blair apparently is not a fan of cameras pointing up his nostrils as he travels in the back of a car) and that it would be best to talk to him in person. He then gave the reporter what he said was a 'highly confidential' phone number where Blair could be found. It was Peter Mandelson's home number in London, and it was Mandelson who answered. They were working on Blair's acceptance speech together.

But for all that Mandelson was instrumental, there was another sense in which his effectiveness was a setback for him. Since before he became an MP he has been trying to cultivate an image as a serious, heavyweight politician. He had sought to put his 'spin-doctoring' ways behind him, even if there is no-one in British politics who practises that tricky art more effectively. And during his short time in Parliament he had made an impact, giving the Government hell over their plans for D-Day, when, quite improbably, Mandelson became the British Legion's best friend. He had campaigned on behalf of those living near the coast who had been born with inexplicable limb disorders and he had made himself an expert on Europe. But, because Mandelson is such a master tactician, Blair wanted to use him to handle the media, and to paint for the press the picture of the Labour Party Blair wanted to create. But if Mandelson was the person who handled the 'image thing', the real work of winning over the constituency activists, trade unionists and MEPs, who would ultimately deliver Blair his victory, was done by the Jack Straw/Mo Mowlam operation. And there was considerable resentment when it looked to them as though Mandelson was trying to take the credit for far more than he actually did.

The success of the operation can only be judged on election day, but, in the immediate aftermath of the campaign, it seemed the Blair message was having a particular resonance with that key section of the electorate: the middle classes. A poll conducted five weeks after he became leader found that there had been a marked increase in support for the Party from the middle classes, women and South of England voters. The figures suggested that, while the Tories had a 30 per cent lead among this group at the time of the last election, not only had this been eradicated, Labour was now enjoying a twenty-point lead. Significantly, much of this change had occurred since John Smith's death. If this had simply been part of a continuing trend then it would have been harder to argue that there was a Blair factor at work with this section of the electorate.[1] One of Blair's big pitches was to argue, *à la* Clinton, that Labour had become the party of aspiration. Blair would maintain this was not an overt attempt to reach out solely to the middle class, but to anyone who was seeking to improve him or herself. However, that was disingenuous; the Blair campaign knew that this message would 'play' particularly well with the middle classes. But one political temptation that Blair resisted was to tailor the message to his audience: the promises and objectives remained the same irrespective of whether he was talking to captains of industry or cribbage players.

Blair was never able to excite a working-class audience in the way that, say, John Prescott can. Blair is more brittle with that type of audience. He is not of them. They know they need him and they respect his brains and his determination. But they don't quite understand him. Nevertheless, as he went from town to town, they knew he was going to win, and enormous faith was invested in him. After one Labour club meeting in St Helens he seemed almost alarmed at the level of trust, hope and belief they were investing in him. 'I only hope they're not expecting too much from me,' he said as he clambered into the car that was to take him on to the next Labour club.

Blair's campaign also had another thing going for it that Kinnock's never had. Sex appeal. It is hard to assess the strength of this, even more difficult to guess at what its significance might be at a general election, if any. But it is there. He is not in the David Owen/Michael Heseltine mould of dashing handsome hero. He has a cheerful, open face and is tall and slim with a twinkle in his eye. As he tried to leave the Windle Labour club in St Helen's one Sunday lunchtime, it would be unfair and untrue to say there were women ripping at his clothes or asking for locks of hair. But there were many who wanted to be kissed, more who wanted autographs and an even greater number who wanted their husbands or boyfriends to photograph them standing next to him. George Robertson, the Shadow Scottish Secretary, said he'd never seen anything like it when Blair visited Monklands during the bitter and divisive by-election. He was the star speaker at the main Labour rally of the campaign. Robertson said that, in all his years, he had never seen a Labour politician – or a politician of any other party, for that matter – treated in such a manner. As Blair finished, a number of women hung around waiting for him to sign scraps of paper. Robertson said he saw one left-wing feminist from his constituency who had always denounced the Shadow Scottish Secretary as politically unsound singing the praises of Tony Blair as if he were a mix of Marlon Brando and Aristotle. A poll carried out for *Forum* magazine found that Blair was the sexiest man in British politics; a statistic that Labour is unlikely to make use of in its party political broadcasts – at least, not directly.

Blair also had youth on his side. His strutting days as a rock guitarist may be behind him, but his love of rock music is undiminished. In his study in Islington lies an acoustic guitar, which he still plays. So, in an effort to reach out to every last voter, Blair readily accepted an invitation to go on Radio 1. Senior politicians' appearances on Radio I see political reporters disappearing into their rooms in the Press Gallery desperate to retune the wireless from Radio 4 to that uncharted territory further up the dial. This is done, not in the expectation of a huge story, but because of the strong likelihood that the politician will make a complete ass of himself as he says something utterly cringe-making about pop music or the concerns of young people (John Smith had been forced to admit that he had not the faintest notion who or what Sonic the Hedgehog was). Blair's young advisers tried to brief him with what the current number one in the charts was. Blair was in need of no such advice. Not only did he know the current number one, he knew the previous one and the one before that.

But Blair is of a pram-pushing generation. A few years back when *Marxism Today* asked what was the first thing he thought about in the morning, the answer came back 'whether Kathryn's nappy needs changing'. Blair is a newish man. He takes his children to school when he can, he marks homework when he can. And he will kick a ball around with his children – again – when he can. But the pressures that piled up when he became Leader of the Opposition meant that his day was stretched at either end, leaving little time to spend at home. But Blair would not boast to pushing a hoover round the house, or cooking a meal. Those tasks he unashamedly leaves for others. Blair is an avid reader. His tastes are conservative, preferring nineteenth century fiction of the Trollope, Dickens and Eliot variety. And he devours political biographies and history books in search of enlightenment and guidance about how political problems were tackled by yesterday's statesmen. Blair has also been an occasional art collector, opera buff, tennis player, wine connoisseur and gastronome which gives him a hinterland that perhaps Gordon Brown lacks. But all of these things found little room in his life once the pursuit of the highest office in politics became his single goal.

His approach is that of the three dimensional chess player, trying to plan a number of moves ahead, and playing several different games at once. There is a pool of people on whom he will suddenly draw for advice: some professional politicians, others not. According to his staff, he will suddenly demand that this or that one is telephoned to find out their view on a subject that he is thinking about tackling. Before big interviews, Blair will have his staff war-game with him the likely questions that will arise, and what the model answer should be. And his campaign for the leadership was designed with the specific aim of appealing way beyond the limited confines of the electoral college that would elect him.

Since the John Smith 'prawn cocktail' offensive was launched at the end of the 1980s, Labour has been desperate to impress the city with its economic policies, recognising that a thumbs down from the financiers, bankers and economists will trickle down very quickly to ordinary voters who have a deeply held mistrust of Labour in office. That made Blair's utterances on issues like taxation, public borrowing and state interference vital during his leadership bid.

The speech on the economy, framed by Gordon Brown signalled in clear tones that Labour's traditional economic thinking had been consigned to the dustbin. It called for a dynamic market economy, and recognised the appeal that Thatcherism offered when Labour lost power at the end of the 1970s: 'The new right had struck a chord. There was a perception that there was too much collective power, too much bureaucracy, too much state intervention and too many vested interests created around it.'[2] It was clear that it had struck a chord with Blair too, who insisted 'the task is not to return to the past. The era of corporatist state intervention is over, the task is to move forward by renewing forms of economic and social partnership and co-operation for the modern world.'[3] Clearly distinguishing himself from the Labour left (and John Prescott), Blair made it clear that he didn't believe that governments could achieve growth and full employment by boosting demand: 'governments and central banks are limited in their capacity to make independent economic policy', concluding, 'macroeconomic policy can do little to change the underlying growth rate of the economy.'[4] What Blair did in this speech was set out an approach. He painted with a broad brush.

Blair didn't win over every businessman who listened attentively to this speech by any means. There were still lurking suspicions that Labour would drive up costs for employers through commitments to the minimum wage and the Social Chapter. There was also the wider concern that a Labour administration would fail to keep the tight grip on borrowing that it was promising, and that inflation would once again lay waste to the British economy. But Blair felt confident enough in interview after interview to declare that Labour had become 'the party of enterprise' and was truly the businessman's friend. When, a few days after Blair became Leader, and stories appeared suggesting that Sir Richard Greenbury, the Chairman of Marks and Spencer wanted to meet the new man with a view to making a political donation, (M and S had bankrolled the Conservative Party for as long as anyone could remember) the Blair camp played the story for all it was worth. There were rumours, too – never denied – that the groceries millionaire, David Sainsbury, had written a substantial cheque to assist the Blair campaign, and when at the beginning of 1995 the Pearson group, which owns the *Financial Times,* announced that it was giving £25,000, Labour sources were quick to seize on it as evidence that Labour now had the imprimatur of the business community.

But there were many questions that Blair failed to answer during his bid for the leadership and in the subsequent months that followed. No opposition politician will write detailed tax plans before an election, but Blair, so anxious not to leave any hostages to fortune, would say next to nothing about even broad questions like what was an acceptable level of borrowing, or whether the aim of the taxation system should be to redistribute wealth from rich to poor. When pressed to explain what or who was rich, Blair would not go beyond saying that millionaires were rich.[5]

On full employment Blair said he too shared the goal of the other leadership contenders, 'It is the goal of any decent society,' he said, but he would define it only as 'high and stable levels of employment'. And he privately made it clear that he thought it would be foolish and unrealistic to set an arbitrary target, as John Prescott had advocated before he became deputy. On the national minimum wage, something he had argued for so resolutely when he was the Party's employment spokesman before the 1992 general election, Blair did not seem to be sticking to his guns: 'It is important to argue the case for the principle of a statutory minimum wage – that there is a level of pay beneath which people should not fall.'[6] But he was a long way from endorsing a level at which it should be set or from deciding the mechanism that would determine it. He was furious when some at Walworth Road put it around that he might be prepared to accept a level of £4.05, something the unions had advocated. Like his tax and spending plans, the level of a minimum wage would have to await an incoming Labour Government, and even then there might be exemptions for young people and some other groups.

Blair put education at the centre of his plans for national renewal, but in doing so he had a problem. The Party's education spokeswoman, Ann Taylor, was one of his supporters, but it is probably fair to say that he was not one of hers. There was a powerful feeling among the Modernisers that, by adopting a position of blanket opposition to testing and league tables, Labour had sent all the wrong signals to parents. In the words of one Shadow Cabinet minister, 'We made it look as though we simply didn't care about standards while the Tories were the guardians of excellence.' There was deep depression among Blair's cohorts when Ann Taylor persuaded John Smith to accept this stance, and while Blair consulted widely before his main education speech of the campaign, his chief sources of inspiration were Gordon Brown (again), and the Party's previous education spokesman and Blair's campaign manager, Jack Straw. There was help too from David Miliband, but precious little input from Ann Taylor who was then the Party's official education spokeswoman, but someone with whom Blair would later clash over education policy. Early on in the campaign Blair hinted that he would keep – in revised form – many of the Government's education reforms, including rigorous appraisal systems and information that would allow parents to compare one school with another,[7] the clear implication being that there would be a place for both opt out schools and league tables. That impression was confirmed after the campaign when Labour launched its education policy paper, in Tony Blair's first engagement as Party leader.

Like the Government, he put the provision of nursery education for all three- and four-year-olds at the top of his priority list. But, even on what would appear to be such an obvious policy winner, Blair's caution permeated Labour's White Paper. He was asked if he would make a commitment to provide universal nursery education within the lifetime of a Labour Parliament. The reply to the question was cleverly formulated, but ultimately meaningless: 'We will make it a priority to make such a commitment.'[8] But, allied to caution about detail, Blair again demonstrated a willingness to think radical thoughts, even if that meant offending traditional Labour client groups like the teaching unions and the local authorities. His support for sacking incompetent teachers drew fire from the second largest teaching union, while his suggestion that all schools should enjoy more autonomy from local education authorities sent shivers through town halls up and down the country.[9]

It was striking at the news conference which launched the White Paper how much more critical Ann Taylor was of the Government's reforms than Blair. He deliberately steered clear of words such as 'scrapping' and 'abolishing', choosing instead the kind of rhetoric that would bring a blue rinse Tory audience to its feet. He wanted greater discipline in schools, the sacking of incompetent teachers, with parents subject to punishment if they failed to control their children. Whatever shortcomings this document had, it wasn't a return to the 'provider-led' policies of the 1960s and 1970s.

The area where Blair recognised that he would be judged most critically on whether a Labour Party led by him really was any different to one led by any of his predecessors was on the question of relations with the unions. During the OMOV debate of 1993, Blair maintained that he was not seeking a divorce, merely a more 'modern' relationship. But that convinced few at the top of the union movement, and as Blair's leadership unfolded, so they would have all their suspicions reinforced. Although it would be some months before Blair revealed just how radical he intended to be, a warning shot was fired when, in his first full day in office, he warned the unions to expect 'fairness not favours'. The unions were disappointed that Blair had raised the issue so quickly, but the new leader was firm:

> They are not going to be shut out in the cold or told they are not a part of our society. They are an important part of the democratic process. But we are not running the next Labour Government for anything other than the people of this country.

And Blair took a similar approach in a speech on the question of welfare reform. Much of the language could have been spoken by a Conservative, so far was it removed from Labour's traditional 'spend–more' welfarism. But it also sought to offer something that would distinguish Labour's approach from political opponents. With strong echoes of Bill Clinton's 'what people want is a hand up, not a hand out', Blair said the welfare system should be geared 'to lift people off benefits into work . . . Britain should become a nation at work not on benefit'. There were echoes of Michael Portillo's and Peter Lilley's insistence that welfare spending couldn't continue to balloon unchecked, adding that the dependency culture was wrecking society. But, while recognising there would have to be a way of controlling welfare spending, Blair shied away from the obvious, but perilous routes of greater means testing and targeting, something the Social Justice Commission would later contemplate. Where Blair parted company with these two ministers of the Thatcherite right was on the role of Government in tackling dependency on the state:

> Labour believes that action by Government can help people to help themselves. The Tories believe that action by Government diminishes individual responsibility. We will use economic success to improve the welfare state. The Tories use economic failure as an excuse to end it.[10]

Where Tony Blair could afford to be a lot more bold was on the issue of constitutional reform. There is no political downside in attacking things like 'the Tory quango state', or saying, *vis-à-vis* the House of Lords, that 'the hereditary principle is without merit'. He set about the task with relish, applying a barrister's mind to what areas should be covered by a Bill of Rights and a Freedom of Information Act. Assisted by Derry Irvine, who would have to take the legislation through the House of Lords, he reaffirmed Labour's commitment to devolution, promising legislation for a Scottish Parliament in the first year of a Labour Government, with legislation too for an elected Welsh Assembly and regional assemblies for those parts of England that want them. It all won easy applause, but would later become the target of a fierce assault followed by a messy Labour withdrawal on the proposal for the English regions. The first sign of trouble came at the 1994 Conservative Party conference in a speech from the thoughtful Scottish Secretary, Ian Lang, who promised that, were Labour elected, the Conservatives would mount the most relentless fight against the legislation. And Lang warned that a devolution bill would grind all other Commons business to a complete standstill. The promise of constitutional reform in the first year of a Blair Government may yet return to haunt him.

But there was little else to cause Blair sleepless nights in his leadership campaign. Blair did not saddle himself with a series of IOUs, but the corollary of that was that he did not make detailed policy commitments either. Some in his campaign team were known to favour the minimalist approach adopted successfully by Mrs Thatcher in 1979, which was to say as little as possible in terms of detail, focusing instead on broad themes (lowering taxes, curbing the unions, rolling back the frontiers of the State). But she came to power on the back of the Winter of Discontent in an election that was a referendum on Labour's record, particularly its final six lingering months in office. The whole purpose of Blair's campaign was to argue that Labour needed to show that it had rediscovered its intellectual self-confidence, with an agenda of its own. And to have adopted a heads-down-and-run-for-the-tape approach would have been a renunciation of much that he stood for in the leadership contest.

Blair won the leadership contest convincingly. His result had been consistent across the three sections of the electoral college. He had won the backing of 60.5 per cent of the MPs and MEPs, 5.3 per cent of affiliated organisations (that includes socialist societies like the Fabians, but is essentially a 'warm words' committee way of referring to the unions) and 58.2 per cent of the votes of ordinary Party members. In each section he had won a clear and decisive majority. Overall he had won 57 per cent of the vote. Nearly a million people had taken part in this unique exercise to elect the Labour leader.

After Blair left the Institute of Education, having been made leader, a party was thrown at Church House for all those who had been involved in the campaign. Blair made a speech where he thanked Jack Straw and he thanked all those who had stuffed leaflets into envelopes. He thanked Anji Hunter and he thanked Derry Irvine. And in the course of what fast came to resemble an Oscar acceptance speech he also thanked Bobby. Only a few people in the room knew who Blair was referring to. Certainly Jack Straw and Mo Mowlam had no idea; nor did any of the other politicians present. In fact Bobby was Peter Mandelson. Such was the secrecy that surrounded his role, that he was referred to in code. There had been an article written likening Blair to John F. Kennedy and the inner circle that surrounded him to JFK's Camelot. One of Blair's secretaries decided that, in that case, Mandelson had better be JFK's brother, and so he was christened Bobby.

All the speeches that Blair had made during his campaign had a common thread running through them, with certain key phrases appearing again and again. There was much talk of 'national renewal', and a repeated insistence that Labour could not and should not seek to turn the clock back to pre-1979. Labour had to be the party of opportunity, the party of hope, it had to speak for people's aspirations. The criticism that what was on offer throughout this campaign was like a menu from a *recherché* restaurant, which lists exotic food with the prices column left blank, was fair.

No leader in Labour Party history had ever been given such a mandate for change; no leader in Labour Party history had wanted to change the Labour Party so much. But as they stood and cheered him at the Institute of Education on 21 July, only a tiny handful of people had cottoned on to just how radical Blair intended to be.

CHAPTER 10

A Loyal Deputy?

'The only danger is that we're going to love each other to death.'

John Prescott

The job of Deputy Leader in the Labour Party has been enshrined in the Party constitution since Clement Attlee decided that he had to find something useful for Herbert Morrison (Peter Mandelson's grandfather) to do. But in all that time it has created more problems than it has solved, and only very occasionally has it been a pathway to the number one job. Michael Foot is the only person in recent memory who has been able to use the job as a stepping stone to the leadership. Most others have found it a passport to nowhere, very few have found political rehabilitation afterwards. Denis Healey described how he had never fought so hard for something he wanted so little. 'It was all for the sake of a job which I found disagreeable and which in itself was not worth having.'[1] And Healey recalls in his memoirs that when Walter Mondale was elected Vice President in the United States his former colleagues from the US Senate gave him a brass spittoon to remind him 'that the job of Vice President isn't worth a barrel of warm spit'.

The job of Deputy Leader in the Labour Party is not even worth as much as that. It is ill-defined and imprecise. It gives the incumbent a seat on the ruling National Executive Committee and a place round the Shadow Cabinet table. But that in itself is not a full-time job for a grown-up. Roy Hattersley chose to carry on as Shadow Home Secretary when he was the unhappy incumbent; Margaret Beckett took charge of much of the Party's internal management and added to that the job of Shadow Leader of the House. Prescott, when he was made Deputy Leader, took charge of campaigning and a membership drive but opted to fulfil no other role. What the job has in abundance though, is the capacity to create trouble. Have the Leader in one part of the country saying one thing and the Deputy in another part expressing a different view, and the following morning the papers will be full of 'Labour Party split from head to toe'. When Roy Hattersley was Neil Kinnock's Deputy he understood that loyalty was everything. Their differences were aired in private; in public they spoke for the most part with one voice. Kinnock recalls:

> If Hattersley was ever called upon, he delivered a 100 per cent. But he never made the mistake of thinking that being Deputy Leader of the Labour Party was important in itself. That's what made him a bloody great Deputy Leader, not just for me but for the Party.[2]

The observation that it is a job which, if done well, achieves nothing, but, if done badly, can do much damage is close to the mark. There were many Labour MPs heard to mutter during the campaign for the deputy leadership that they would vote for the first person who promised to abolish him or herself if elected. But while the job exists it does matter who is doing it, and, in the absence of a clearly stated dream ticket, much speculation was given over to Blair's personal views on his deputy. Tony Blair even refused to vote for the Deputy Leader and his camp were split. Gordon Brown ostentatiously announced that he was backing Margaret Beckett. Those close to the Shadow Chancellor said that he would not have been happy with John Prescott exercising any control over economic policy, and his friends were startled that Tony Blair could even contemplate working with him. Indeed, in the soured atmosphere that prevailed in Peter Mandelson's and Gordon Brown's relationship, Mandelson believed that Brown blamed him for Prescott's victory in the

Deputy Leadership contest, although it has to be questioned whether even Mandelson's mystic powers stretched that far. Others, like Mo Mowlam, though at the centre of the Blair campaign, were backing Prescott. Prescott sought to play things carefully in the campaign, fully aware that he would have to work with Tony Blair at the end of it, but persistent questions about Prescott's intellect, and more particularly, his fiery temperament, would not go away. Some found it impossible to imagine him standing in for the Leader – and they wasted no time in saying so.

Margaret Beckett, on the other hand, had shown that, not only was she competent when she took over at the despatch box, she was highly effective too. And as a campaigner in the 1992 general election she was rock solid. Similar plaudits abounded in her handling of Labour's hugely successful European election campaign in 1994 when she was standing in as acting Leader. But, for all that, doubts about her loyalty and integrity refused to go away in the campaign, and Tony Blair was heard to mutter some of those reservations himself. After one of the leadership campaign's many hustings meetings he told friends: 'She's paying the price for trying to flit between left and right and has only herself to blame if she fails to get either job.'

The magnificent architectural edifice of the Palace of Westminster – or mock Gothic horror – depending on one's viewpoint, can be an awe-inspiring place. But as a working and ergonomically efficient centre for an advanced industrial democracy it is poor. For a politician who wants to do nothing more radical than hold a news conference, there are hardly any facilities. All that ever seems to be available is a cramped, shoebox of a room, the Jubilee Room off Westminster Hall. It is rather gloomy and, once the camera crews and photographers have taken their place, all the reporters who want to ask questions are lined up in rows behind the film crews, rendering them completely hidden from view. By the time John Prescott and, after him, Margaret Beckett launched their campaigns for both the leadership and deputy leadership, the place had become a heaving cauldron.

It was into that seething mass of reporters and photographers that John Prescott had been hoping to make a dignified entrance to announce that he was putting himself forward to run for the Labour leadership. The thickset former ship's steward looked slightly sheepish and intimidated as he barged his way through to the front. There had never been much doubt that Prescott would stand. The difficult tactical decision for him had been to decide what precisely he was going to stand for.

He had already run for the deputy leadership twice. In 1988 he infuriated Neil Kinnock, the then Labour leader, by mounting a challenge to Roy Hattersley who he thought was failing in the central task of halting the erosion of Labour as a nationwide campaigning Party. Rebuilding Labour's base in the constituencies had always been one of John Prescott's burning ambitions. He challenged for the number two job again after the 1992 general election. Then, as well as promising to carry out his missionary work in the parishes, he coupled his message with a promise that he would help Labour rediscover some of its traditional values. At one union hustings he declared, 'It is a sad reflection of the political climate in Britain today that it is necessary for me to say that I am proud to be a trade unionist.'³ Prescott in that contest did as well as could be expected. Running against the Smith/Beckett, man/woman, right/left dream ticket, John Prescott polled a highly respectable 28 per cent of the electoral college, coming second to Margaret Beckett.

Tactics play a big part in any political decision, but what to do in the 1994 leadership contest was more strategically complex than most. First of all there was the 'Gould lesson'. Bryan Gould, one of Labour's most gifted communicators and thinkers, was also one of the Party's most inept tacticians. His decision in 1992 to challenge for both the leadership and the deputy leadership sent confusing signals that helped scupper his chances of landing either job. He seemed to be saying, 'I would like to be Leader, but I don't think I stand an earthly, so you can always vote for me as deputy and I will, I suppose accept that as a consolation prize.' He was given the equivalent of Labour's wooden spoon, gaining neither post and suffering a personal humiliation. Gould later resigned from the Shadow Cabinet, again with the worst possible sense of timing, choosing the eve of the Labour Party conference in Blackpool in 1992 to make his announcement, ensuring that it got maximum adverse publicity for Smith and the Labour Party. And, after a period of sniping at the drift in the leadership, he announced that he would be going back to his native New Zealand to a life of academe and wine-growing.

Needless to say, John Prescott did not want to make the same mistakes. He was also anxious to avoid the barbed personal criticism that marked Gould's campaign against Smith. But Prescott had to second guess what Margaret Beckett would do. She was already in post as Deputy Leader, but her announcement at the first NEC after John Smith's death that she wanted the question of her job resolved at the same time as the leadership question meant there was now the prospect of a wide-open contest. There was also considerable speculation about why Beckett had made her announcement. Only a couple of senior party officials knew that she was going to make it. If Beckett had wanted to, she could have carried on as the Party's Deputy Leader until the autumn, which would then have been the period for someone to mount a challenge. She cited as her reason the fact that it would have saddled the Labour Party with a second huge bill for carrying out an election under the revised one member one vote system (certainly true). This gesture won her warm admiration, but, as with everything that Margaret Beckett did, people were trying to work out what the hidden agenda was. The assumption of most observers was that this was a clever move. She would run only for the deputy leadership, making it more or less impossible for anyone to challenge her after the dignified way in which she had filled John Smith's shoes after he had died. So, much as he wanted to avoid going for both jobs, John Prescott had little option but to do precisely that.

Flanked by his campaign manager, the Trade and Industry Select Committee chairman, Dick Caborn, and health spokesman, Ian McCartney, Prescott set out his stall. He wanted a return to the values of the 1945 Attlee Government but with policies ripe for today's setting. The arch traditionalist gave the sketchwriters a gift when he misread his speech and instead of reading, 'this will be an election about Labour's values, approach, style and direction as we move towards the twenty-first century,' he read it as twentieth century. For those who wanted to paint Prescott as a man wedded to the past here was proof positive! Even Prescott laughed when he realised his mistake.

But he did offer an approach to policy. 'The themes that will form the core of my leadership bid will be those that build on the policy initiatives that John Smith had already set in train: full employment and social justice.' The only potentially sticky moment for Prescott at this news conference came when a *Sun* reporter reminded him of an interview he'd given only weeks earlier for *Esquire* magazine, just before John Smith had died. In typically candid style Prescott responded to the question 'Do you one day want to lead the Party?' with 'Naah. If all the likely candidates were run over by a bus I would do it to the best of my ability and probably make a good job of it. But I am out of that league really.'[4] It is that honesty that makes Prescott so appealing as a politician even if at times it leads him into danger and controversy. In the news conference his pugilistic face dissolved into a wide grin and he declared without any real hint of embarrassment, 'Well, times change, don't they.' Prescott could say little else. But the *Esquire* comments were the truth. He was never, ever playing to become leader. He had gone for the leadership as well because he and Blair had agreed there had to be a contest.

Prescott was also the very model of tact and discretion. Despite repeated invitations from journalists to enter a slanging match with his rivals, he refused to say why the other candidates were worse or less suited to the job than him. Prescott had come to this news conference in a new guise: Prescott the statesman. Not a bad word would pass his lips about either Beckett or Blair. Journalists fidgeted uneasily: this was not the stuff of great copy. And it certainly wasn't designed to get editors or the public sitting on the edge of their seats in rapt attention. This politeness and reserve were also the marks of the one and only televised hustings involving the three candidates. It might have been thought that this kind of behaviour would have been exactly what the image managers in the Labour Party had wanted, but it seemed even this rather anodyne television format was considered too confrontational. The message went out to the various campaign teams that, even though they could and must take part in Party-organised hustings of all the candidates, they must decline invitations to take part in television or radio debates with each other. In the eyes of Party managers, too much had been achieved in terms of Party unity under John Smith to turn this into a white knuckle ride for the sake of lively television.

Prescott, for all the bluff and bluster, is a very thoughtful politician. He had calculated from the outset that, if he was to become Tony Blair's deputy, then he must push his own agenda, but not so far or so radically that it would make it impossible for the two to work together. He set about his campaign with characteristic zeal and enthusiasm. In his surprisingly glossy Policies Into Action document he promised a 'hard headed commitment' towards slashing the dole queues. He would establish a Commission for Full Employment which would report back to the 1995 Labour Party conference, and it would set targets to cut unemployment at the time of the next general election. He was determined that Labour should go into that election with a commitment and promise to slice the jobless totals. This is something Labour refused to do in either the 1987 or 1992 general elections, and would, under Blair's leadership, be destined to have a veil drawn over it, and put in a far away pending tray marked 'forget'. But if one of John Prescott's considerations was to think about future working relationships with Blair, his other concern was to be sufficiently different in policy terms to garner the maximum number of votes from traditional Labour supporters who wanted an alternative to the sharp edged modernisation being offered by the frontrunner. And in his passionate advocacy of full employment, Prescott did just that.

Full employment was in danger of becoming one of those consensual political hooray phrases straddling all the political parties. The Conservatives having spent years defining inflation as the number one enemy, went through something of a change when the Chancellor Kenneth Clarke delivered his June 1994 Mansion House speech. In it he spoke of unemployment as one of the great evils of modern society. And then, during the Labour leadership campaign, the Employment Secretary, David Hunt, was seen to genuflect in that direction when he became the first Conservative minister to address a meeting of the TUC, and spoke of the desirability of full employment. It is a phrase that would not have spilled from the man who went on to be Hunt's successor, the darling of the right and Thatcher prodigy, Michael Portillo. But John Prescott had no doubt about the significance of what Hunt had said. This was the Shadow Employment Spokesman winning the argument on full employment with the real Employment Secretary. And all the time that John Prescott spoke about full employment he was able to say he was honouring John Smith's memory after his speech to the TUC less than a year earlier.

But full employment means different things to different people. The standard definition of it being only 2.5 per cent of the adult population out of work was derived in the Keynesian heyday of the post-war Labour Government (Prescott keeps a 1944 edition of Beveridge's report on full employment on his desk in the Commons). But with the huge growth in the number of part-time workers, and the increasing numbers of women in the job market, this figure is seen by most as not only unattainable but wholly unrealistic. John Prescott, for all his brave talk that Labour must not be afraid to set targets for reducing unemployment, consistently avoided doing so in his campaign. Similarly on the minimum wage – another policy that Prescott set great store by – he consistently refused to say at what level it should be pegged.

As the campaign wore on, it became clearer to the Blair camp that Prescott was going to win the Deputy Leadership, and so the Blair team would pore over Prescott's utterances with great care. Blair and Prescott also saw a great deal of each other, travelling to and from the interminable hustings meetings. But one interview that Prescott gave to *The Times* nearly caused Blair to choke on his cornflakes. Prescott told the paper's Political Editor, Phillip Webster, and Associate Editor, Peter Riddell, that 'I do not agree with many of his [Blair's] views, quite frankly.'[5] His comments set alarm bells ringing in the Blair camp. This was exactly the sort of rash remark that Prescott's detractors had said he would make, confirming their views on his unsuitability to be Deputy Leader. In the course of the same interview, he also went on to detail an economic policy that was not just different in tone to the things that Tony Blair had been saying, it was completely at odds with it. Prescott scorned the 'warm words' committee which he said decreed what could and couldn't be said. So Gordon Brown's insistence that Labour wanted a 'fair taxation' system was seen by Prescott as an evasion. 'If everybody is going to make an effort to get our people back to work, that will involve tax payments as well as the new forms of borrowing.' Prescott argued that if what you are saying is redistribution then you must have the courage of your convictions to stand up and fight for it openly. 'We have had three elections of warm words. I'm not convinced it did us a great deal of good. It does not convince enough of those who want to switch over and it knocks the heart out of our own people.'[6]

The interview brought about a morning of anxious and angry phone calls. Brown was incandescent. Prescott and he had never got on. Brown was firmly of the view that, whatever problems there could be with Beckett, she was at least safe. Mandelson, who was briefing the press on a daily basis, had until then shocked seasoned Westminster journalists by his emollient approach to Prescott (something that had not always been a feature of Mandelson's attitude to the man), but could not disguise either his anger or disappointment at what Prescott had said. Indeed, such was the level of angst that Blair spoke to Prescott directly about it. It seems Prescott was contrite, saying that in some places he had gone too far, in others his comments had been taken out of context – always the last refuge for a politician who has put his foot in his mouth.

But for all Prescott's waywardness, little was made of it. It is as though with John Prescott you know what you are getting, and part of the Prescott package is a rough and tumble way of speaking that doesn't bear close textual analysis. The sketchwriter and former Conservative MP, Matthew Parris, gave a hilarious caricature of John Prescott's vital speech at the 1993 Labour Party conference on one member one vote. It was an address of pure blood and thunder passion. And while everyone present understood what he was getting at, those reporters who had to transcribe their shorthand notes found that much of it was a jumble of syntax, with no coherent meaning. Parris's sketch noted:

Prescott went twelve rounds with the English Language and left it bleeding and slumped over the ropes . . . the very thought of a Prescott transcript is laughable . . . any transcript would be gibberish nouns, adjectives and unattached parts of speech lying among the verbal wreckage like a rose garden after a bulldozer.[7]

Prescott would later joke at the 1994 Labour Party conference, that his wife, Pauline, had played a recording of it – backwards. To affectionate laughter he added, 'she said she understood it better that way.'

Matthew Parris goaded John Prescott about this when he was part of the prosecuting counsel on BBC Breakfast News during the contest: 'We tease you about the ungrammaticalness of your language. You bridle about it. You bridle don't you?' And Prescott duly obliged: 'I didn't have your education. What was yours, Yale and Cambridge and Swaziland . . . I'd love to have had that but I didn't. I'm a secondary modern school lad. But I'll tell you this: nobody ever misunderstands what I mean even if they don't understand the grammar.'[8] In a political age where the dominant colour is grey, John Prescott's campaigning style with its mixture of passion and honesty was a reminder of a bygone era. But the man who had been described as 'an accident waiting to happen', was also confounding his critics by showing a sureness of touch.

The same could not be said of Margaret Beckett. Her entry into the race was a rather odd occasion. She sat alone. There were no supporters by her side. She read a long list of past achievements, but steered resolutely clear of where she stood on questions of policy (something that was to mark her campaign). She spoke at length about how she could lead a united cabinet, bringing all the talents together, but couldn't explain why none of her Shadow Cabinet colleagues had agreed to nominate her. She also played very heavily on the closeness of her working relationship with John Smith and how, for many weeks, she had been carrying out the Leader's job, even though many on John Smith's staff conceded privately that he and Beckett were never close, and that they found her impossible.

In her manifesto 'The Leadership to Win', which she produced a little later in the campaign, she again made great play of what she called her record. 'I wish to put my achievements and experience before you: fighting and winning election campaigns; holding government office; dealing with the Prime Minister at question time; representing Labour at international meetings of foreign leaders [the inside back page of the manifesto had a large colour photograph of her standing with President Clinton]; successfully taking on the Liberals; building and holding together a team drawn from all wings of the Party.' There is no doubt that, in terms of experience, Margaret Beckett had been in the top flight of Labour politics longer than any of her contenders. But, by stressing her track record, it was an open invitation to her detractors to shine a searchlight into the dark alleys along which she has fought some disreputable fights.

The picture that Margaret Beckett presented of herself was one that was hard to reconcile with the same Margaret Beckett who had conspicuously failed to support John Smith when, in John Prescott's words, the leader 'had put his head on the block' over trade union reform and the introduction of one member one vote. Her behaviour at the 1993 Labour Party conference did her great damage, even if it resulted in the strengthening of her position with the left-wing unions. Derry Irvine recalls having dinner with Smith two or three days before the OMOV vote, during the course of which Smith made absolutely clear that he would have resigned if he had lost. This was not posturing, as Smith had no need to posture to his best friend from university. Irvine says his intention had been to take the matter back the following day as a vote of confidence, and, if he had lost, he would have resigned. All of which lends some credence to the story which did the rounds that Beckett believed that, if Smith had resigned, it would have left her on the winning side of the argument and in pole position to take over the leadership.

That Labour Party conference was always going to be a cliff-hanger on trade union reform. For journalists covering these events an enormous amount of time is spent in the hotel bars totting up the votes of the various delegations to see if the leadership is going to secure the required majority. It had been rather taken for granted that Margaret Beckett would be right behind the Leader. However on the eve of conference she gave a radio interview in which her support for one member one vote could only be described as lukewarm. The *Sunday Times* followed this up the next day, much to her irritation, and by now a damaging 'split in Labour leadership' story was running. If ever a politician wanted to maintain a low profile a Party conference is not the place to do it. There are film crews everywhere, and the BBC runs a live conference programme each day examining not just what is taking place in the debates, but what is going on behind the scenes. Just before the critical debate on Composites 55 and 56, Margaret Beckett was pressed on the live programme whether she stood four-square behind John Smith. Her support could not really be described as effusive: 'The resolutions are there before the Party. John Smith has made his position clear. He will speak in the debate and the conference will then make its decision and I think we all hope that the decision will mean that the issue can be resolved.'[9]

Her problems over this issue were compounded when she decided to take out a little box advert in 'Campaign Briefing', the newsletter produced each day of the Labour conference by the hard-left campaign group. It contains short articles on the running debates, notices of politically sound fringe meetings and, on the back page, instructions on how to vote on the key composites. But there, just beneath the call to ignore and defeat the leadership, was a greetings message from Margaret and Leo Beckett!

Her unflagging support for the Labour/union link at the 1993 Labour conference paid limited dividends a year later in the leadership contest when she secured the support of the Transport Union as their preferred candidate for the leadership. With all the ballot papers that they sent out to members came a leaflet from the executive of the T and G setting out about fifteen reasons why Margaret Beckett was the only candidate for them. But, although the members of the union backed her for Deputy Leader, they still went for Blair for the leadership.

Given past form, it was difficult to think of her as the 'unity' candidate, since she had been a leading player in some of the fiercest sectarian Labour politics. Her denunciation of Neil Kinnock, describing him as a 'Judas' for failing to support Tony Benn in the 1981 Leadership contest, is still a part of Labour folklore. And as her detractors were only too keen to remind journalists during the contest, she was hardly the model of sororal loyalty when she happily stepped into Joan Lestor's shoes in 1976 after Lestor resigned from her job as a Parliamentary Under Secretary at Education because of spending cuts. Other instances that sprang to mind included her rejection in 1986 of calls for the expulsion of Militant members from the Labour Party: 'We have always set our faces as individuals against expulsions from the Party on political grounds,'[10] she said. And during the Gulf war she became an occasional member of the 'supper club', an ad hoc left-wing grouping opposed to Labour's support for armed intervention to retake Kuwait.

Blair had never had any problems with Beckett. They had worked closely together as part of the economic team in the run-up to the 1992 general election, and he was impressed by the stubborn way she kept a tight rein on other Labour spokespeople, preventing them from making spending pledges that had not been first agreed with her.

At the last election the Conservatives totted up the commitments made by Labour in speeches and interviews to 35 billion pounds. Margaret Beckett dressed in hair-shirt and wearing a parsimonious demeanour was brought in to dispute the Tories' figures. She insisted that Labour's sole spending pledges were those approved by the Treasury team, and they only included a promise to uprate child benefit and increase the state pension. Pitted against the ebullient, effervescent and often irritating David Mellor, Margaret Beckett sounded like an overbearing schoolmistress as she patiently repeated the incantation that Labour wouldn't spend what it could not afford, while Mellor, the schoolboy in the pantomime audience, was left to shout, 'Oh, yes you would!' In her room, behind her desk hung a notice which read: 'Which aspect of the word "No" is it that you don't understand?'

But one of her first actions in the leadership contest was to tear up Beckett's Law, saying that in the mid-term period of a Parliament it was fair to talk about policy aspirations without having costed out every item. (It's a fair bet that any front bench spokesman who had taken that view in the run-up to the last election would have been the recipient of a fairly severe box round the ears.) But she caused even more alarm in the Blair camp with some of her other pronouncements during the campaign. The morning after the first hustings, she agreed to appear on the *Today* programme. She was tackled on her attitude towards secondary picketing and the Government's trade union legislation. Her answer was revealing:

> There could well be a need just to sweep the board clear and start again ... We need to have legislation which allows a sensible, workable and fair approach to secondary picketing so that people are not treated in the way they sometimes have been in the past, without any regard for reasonable industrial rights which would be enjoyed anywhere else in Europe.[11]

Whatever her intentions, her call for a 'fresh start' on trade union rights set alarm bells ringing in the Blair camp and peals of laughter and delight in Central Office. The Employment Secretary, David Hunt, was quick to issue a statement: 'After days of dodging, Margaret Beckett has admitted Labour would just say "yes" to whatever the trade union bosses decided they want.' These comments will have certainly been taken down by the Conservative Party's highly impressive research department to be used in evidence against Labour at some later date.

As the campaign progressed, the Blair camp grew less and less sanguine about the prospect of Beckett becoming Blair's deputy. Her obvious courting of the left infuriated those on the right that were backing her. And when Tony Blair saw television pictures of the hardline left-wingers Ken Livingstone and Bernie Grant stuffing envelopes on her behalf, he was heard to comment, 'I would have paid good money to have them stay as far away from my campaign as possible.' What Blair was at a loss to understand was why such an experienced politician fought such a ham-fisted campaign.

It was obvious that Margaret Beckett would run for the leadership and not just the deputy leadership. She had been working hand in glove with John Smith, and from the moment of his death onwards barely put a foot wrong in her role as acting Leader. Her speech to the Commons on the day of John Smith's death was perfectly judged and beautifully delivered. Many were in tears as they listened, but her voice barely faltered.

> Opposition politicians also mourn our country's loss, but we grieve for our own. There are few people the announcement of whose death would bring tears to the eyes of everyone who knew him; John Smith was such a man. He was, as the Prime Minister said, a man of formidable intellect, of the highest ethics and of staunch integrity.[12]

From then through to the crowning glory of the European election results, Labour's best showing in a national election for nearly thirty years, Margaret Beckett won nothing but plaudits and bouquets. But, for all that, Margaret Beckett, by going for both jobs, was gambling everything with the risk of winning nothing. It was clear from day one that Tony Blair was way out in front, and many of her male colleagues were at a loss to understand why she had not simply stayed put as Deputy Leader.

If the men in the Party were perplexed by her tactics, many of the women were not. Beckett felt deep hurt at the way in which she had been almost totally discounted as a potential leader by politician and pundit alike when John Smith died. There was no place for her in the script. For a player on the stage of many years standing, that clearly rankled.

> One of my women colleagues said to me: 'They buried you with John.' There is no doubt that I disappeared from the frame as far as most media commentators were concerned. I cannot say I was over-surprised ... A man in my circumstances would not have been assumed not to be a candidate for the leadership. It would probably have been the other way round.[13]

That feeling that Beckett was the victim of unreconstructed Labour male chauvinism was apparent in a letter to the *Guardian* from some of her supporters. 'We are', they declared 'united in our anger at the dismissive sexism meted out to Margaret Beckett in the course of the campaign.' Such 'predictable stereotyping' could be expected from the media, the women complained, but not from a Party of enlightenment.[14]

Pique had become a driving force. The sense of being 'passed over' provoked similar outrage in many of her women colleagues both inside and outside Parliament. In the Labour Party, the job of Deputy Leader is seen as the kitchen sink job. Unglamorous, it requires the skills of an apparatchik and manager toiling away behind the scenes in Walworth Road. Many women members saw her as the sandwich maker in the pavilion while the 'boys' played cricket on the square. Margaret Beckett had had enough of that, and although as Deputy Leader she was brought into the centre of decision making by John Smith, she didn't want to return to that role, and nor did her band of backers.

As the campaign progressed it became clear to both camps that there was no chance whatsoever of overhauling Tony Blair and therefore it had become a battle for the silver medal. Neither camp was admitting that to be the case – and neither camp had any illusions that it was so. But the battle for the runners up prize was going right to the wire. Margaret Beckett, being the incumbent, started as the odds-on favourite, but as the campaign progressed, so it appeared that support was leaching away. The outward veneer of the 'love in' was also cracking as supporters of each candidate sought to shore up support. So stories from 'well placed sources' in the Beckett corner sought to suggest that John Prescott was on the point of throwing in the towel and that he would be urging his supporters to switch to Margaret Beckett. John Prescott's people countered with stories of their own that more than a dozen Beckett supporters in the Commons had 'defected' to Prescott as a protest against the way Margaret Beckett had conducted her campaign.[15]

Margaret Beckett's media campaign was being handled by John Underwood. He had briefly been the Labour Party's Director of Communications, succeeding Peter Mandelson. But he left amid bitter recriminations. At the time there was a lot of poison spread about John Underwood's political judgement. Those doubts were reinforced during Margaret Beckett's campaign when he briefed reporters that she actively didn't want to return to the Deputy's job and that all she was interested in was being Leader. Tactically it was ineptitude writ large. It encouraged Margaret Beckett's supporters to vote for her for the leadership – a post that she had zero chance of winning – while probably supporting John Prescott for the Deputy's job – a post he was most definitely in the frame for.

As the close of polling drew near, there were signs that the Beckett camp was beginning to realise that the wheels were coming off the wagon. A letter in the final week of the campaign was sent out to all Labour MPs from Clare Short, Margaret Beckett's campaign manager. It started 'I am writing in the hope that you have not yet cast your vote in the leadership election'. And it went on to urge MPs to 'step back' from the intense atmosphere of Westminster 'and from what you have read in the newspapers, to consider again the qualities of Margaret Beckett.' The letter also claimed that Margaret had always put leading the Party before the leadership contest.[16]

By the time the votes were counted few were surprised that Margaret Beckett had lost; six weeks earlier it had seemed unthinkable that John Prescott could overhaul her. But in the end it was a convincing victory, with Prescott taking 56.5 per cent of the electoral college votes, and Beckett just 43.5 per cent. Prescott had won in all three sections. When the history book comes to be written of how to steal defeat from the jaws of victory, Margaret Beckett's campaign in 1994 for the Labour Party leadership will be held up as a glorious example. Her supporters wandered around in a daze when the results were announced.

Tony Blair's concern in the immediate aftermath of victory was to bring Margaret back on board as quickly as possible. Outside, she could easily become a lightning conductor for a dispirited left. Blair, with his professed indifference to left/right tags, was keener to lay the emphasis on creating a Shadow

Cabinet of all the talents. But when it was suggested to one of those who had been at the heart of the Blair campaign that all the Leader was concerned about was the Lyndon B. Johnson principle – better to have someone inside the tent pissing out, than on the outside pissing in – he demurred and said the thinking owed more to Don Corleone in the *Godfather* where you held your friends close, and enemies even closer. Whatever, there was considerable relief when Mrs Beckett announced that she would be seeking a place at the Shadow Cabinet elections being held in the Autumn of 1994. And in true Labour tradition where those who have wielded the knife immediately become guilt-ridden, so Mrs Beckett was runner-up in the poll. But, anxious as Blair was to bring her back into the fold, the woman who had been Deputy Leader and then acting Leader was not going to be offered the crown jewels. Her appointment to the middle-ranking Shadow Health Secretary portfolio was clearly less than she had been hoping for, but Blair was not going to budge, even though Beckett went back a second time to see the Leader before accepting what she had been offered.

But what of the Right Honourable John Prescott? His first act as Deputy Leader was to start his mission to recruit more members with his witty acceptance speech at the Institute of Education. 'Write to me, John Prescott MP . . . they'll know where to find me' and sure enough hundreds of letters did find their way to him. He played a shrewd poker game, making it clear where his political soul was, but never going too far that it would make him an impossible deputy to Blair. The two men are not close, but they have a respect for one another and both recognise the need to stay on good terms. Conservative Central Office have assembled bulging folders full of quotes made by John Prescott in his colourful past, and Prescott's detractors could not hide their anxiety that he might prove to be a liability. One of those was Neil Kinnock: 'If John's vanity gland is working as it has done for many years it could be a real nuisance. It may be that Tony has got to do something important in order to squash him a bit, which will be a bloody nuisance . . . The Conservatives have really got the stuff on him, and that may not be a problem three years before an election, but it's another thing when you're sitting together three days before polling day to have what you've said in the past thrown at you: "But you've said, Mr Prescott, and I'll read it out to you . . ." And even if it's only a three-minute squirm on the one o'clock news, it's still a bloody nuisance . . . As the election grows nearer all the tabloids and possibly one or two of the so-called heavies are going to be treating John Prescott as if he's a mixture of Lenin and the leader of the WACO sect. And that could be a problem.'[17]

Prescott's role model in politics is Ernie Bevin, Labour's highly distinguished post-war Foreign Secretary; it is not George Brown, whose bouts of heavy drinking when he was Harold Wilson's deputy were only outstripped by his repeated threats to resign. Prescott understood that loyalty would be an essential prerequisite of a successful partnership with Blair. That is not to say that Prescott learned to burn on a longer fuse. There were a number of squalls in the first few months, but according to both sides they passed quickly. After the leadership contest the Blair/Prescott relationship would become the most critical in the Labour Party. With Blair set on a determined path of reform, Prescott described Blair as the train driver and himself as the guard, wandering through the train reassuring the passengers that the driver really did know where he was going. But Prescott also knew that he could pull the communication cord, and bring the engines to a screeching halt. That meant Blair had to take great care to ensure that Prescott was with him; that in turn gave Prescott something close to the power of veto, a power that Prescott would contemplate using when Blair confided that he wanted to rewrite Labour's constitution. There would be other tensions too, but it seemed the thirst for power was sufficient to keep the lid on some fundamental differences between the two men.

In that context the appointment of Alastair Campbell as Blair's Press Secretary was a shrewd one, because Campbell was popular with both Modernisers and Traditionalists. He knew most

Labour MPs extremely well from his *Daily Mirror* days, and the years spent as a member of the Lobby. He had also been developing a career as a television presenter, radio commentator and all purpose media pundit. Interestingly, Neil Kinnock, who was a summer guest of the Campbells in the South of France, sought to dissuade him from taking the job on the grounds that Campbell would find it endlessly frustrating, particularly the people with whom he would have to deal. Blair, getting wind of his predecessor's views, rescheduled his family's holiday to also visit the Campbells' house near Avignon to correct any misinformation being spread by Kinnock. The former Labour leader had even offered Campbell the job of *chef de cabinet* in Kinnock's new office in Brussels where he had become a European Commissioner. So, for five days during August, the Kinnocks and Blairs stayed at the Campbells' villa discussing the future shape of the Labour Party, with Neil Kinnock seeking to pull Campbell in one direction and Blair trying to pull him in another. When Campbell said eventually that he would take the job he wanted to know first that Prescott had approved of the appointment.

He did. And it was striking, even before Campbell had come on board, how hand-in-glove he worked with both men. Campbell spent a good deal of his time at the 1994 Labour Party conference in Blackpool moving between the Leader's suite at the Imperial Hotel and Prescott's suite. On the Thursday night, Campbell was up in Prescott's room working on his speech. When Blair appointed Campbell he knew he would be getting someone who, irrespective of the closeness of his relationships with many Westminster journalists, would always put Blair first, and who would not be afraid to breathe fire down the collar of any errant journalist. Campbell is a tall, rugged looking, teetotaller who supports Burnley with occasional boorish tendencies – he took delight at an up-market French restaurant in ordering as an aperitif a cup of tea, and then proceeding to dunk the melba toast in the tea to the horror of the wine waiter. His greatest claim to journalistic fame, following a shared experience in a urinal in Washington with John Major, was his exclusive that the Prime Minister tucked his shirt inside his pants. Journalism's loss would be Tony Blair's gain. Campbell quickly established himself as a firm, no-nonsense press secretary. But he would have to perform an even more vital role for his master and that would be to act as shuttle diplomat between Prescott and Blair when the going got tough.

CHAPTER 11

Clear and Muddied Water

'What makes Tony Blair so dangerous for us is that people could
vote for him and forget they're voting Labour.'
                                        Anonymous Tory backbencher

Whatever else Tony Blair's campaign may have lacked it didn't
want for self-confidence. Nowhere was this more evident than
in a willingness to engage in the battle of ideas. Since Margaret
Thatcher came to power in 1979, there had been an intellectual
self-confidence among the right. It first found expression in
monetarism, which then, almost imperceptibly, became
Thatcherism. Privatisation, started in the United Kingdom, is
now a policy emulated across Western Europe. There seemed to
be a profusion of essayists, think-tanks and pamphleteers. No
ideas were off limits – some even became Government policy.
The right was intellectually rampant; bright young academics
found themselves courted by senior Tory politicians. There was
a thirst for ideas.

With the collapse of communism and the crumbling of the
Berlin Wall, the right saw this as almost the final triumph. It was
state control, collectivism, central planning, and the command
economy that had been defeated by its own contradictions – not
capitalism, whose destruction Marxist determinists had said was
an historic inevitability. The intellectual left were in disarray. It
seemed to be game, set and match to the free marketeers. But
another of Mrs Thatcher's missions which she had not achieved
when she left office in 1990 was her stated goal of turning the
Labour Party from an old fashioned socialist party into a modern social democratic one. That was starting to happen under

Blair. Blair never sought to hide his admiration for Margaret Thatcher's leadership qualities, if not for all of her policies (although it is remarkable how few he would seek to reverse). His approbation of her was part genuine, and part good politics. By praising the queen across the water, Blair was also reaching out to disaffected right wingers who loathed John Major's more collegiate style of operating which they saw as a sign of pitiable weakness. But Blair could not have imagined how the compliment would be repaid. In the Spring of 1995, the second volume of her memoirs was serialised in the *Sunday Times*. On the first week of serialisation there was a less than coded attack on how in her mind John Major had lost direction and had given in to Brussels too much; on the second week she gave an interview and spoke about Blair. Conservative strategy hitherto had been to dismiss Mr Blair as no more than a 'soundbite' politician. Lady Thatcher's assessment was different:

> He is probably the most formidable leader we have had since Hugh Gaitskell. I see a lot of socialism behind their front bench, but not in Mr Blair. I think he genuinely has moved.[1]

For the same reason that it made good politics for Mr Blair to salute Lady Thatcher, there was a rationale for Lady Thatcher praising the new Labour Leader. But for those who were active combatants in the parliamentary dog-fight there was no room for such niceties. And the question for both Liberal Democrats and Conservatives was how best to tackle Blair's new model army.

The problem for Conservative ministers – and there were few who were complacent about the threat that Blair posed – was that as soon as they debated what was to be done, they were faced by a question that risked awakening the ideological differences in the Conservative Party that had sapped so much of John Major's time and energy. If the 1992 general election introduced the tags Modernisers and Traditionalists into the Labour Party, the threat posed by Tony Blair brought two new names to the Conservative Party: the Radicals and Consolidators. For the cognoscenti of politics it was also confusingly called the 'Clear Blue Water' versus the Coke strategy. The Radicals and Clear Blue Water supporters believed that only by pressing ahead with the Thatcherite revolution would the Party win power for a fifth term in a row. That meant putting as much clear blue water between Labour and the Tories as possible. The Consolidators on the other hand argued that the only place to stand was where the Conservative Party from Disraeli onwards had always stood, and that was just to the right of the centre circle of British politics. The Coke strategy was so called because the Conservatives would go into an election with the message that 'we are the real thing', while Labour were offering a pale imitation.

Conservative Central Office seemed entirely unfocused on what to do about Blair. A previously unpublished six-page document was sent out by the Party's research department on 14 July, a week before the end of the Labour leadership campaign. The paper observed that

> having calculated that his image will do enough to win him the leadership, his objective is to dupe the electorate into thinking that the Labour Party under his leadership would be a different beast. His method is to employ warm words about the challenges of the future, but to evade discussion of the nuts and bolts of Labour policy.

The rest of the document is a trawl through old files to try to show that Blair is a man with dubious left-wing baggage.

Ian Lang the Scottish Secretary gave the question of how to tackle Blair the first serious airing during the Labour leadership campaign where, even though Blair wasn't mentioned once, his presence seemed to permeate every page of the speech. Giving the Conservative Party's annual Swinton Lecture, Lang said that the Tories would only win if they stuck to the centre ground of British politics. And that meant refusing to budge on the themes that Blair was trying to steal like the relationship between community and individual rights and responsibilities. 'We must be alert to the fact that there can develop in politics an impulse for change which if unheeded can become inexorable.'[2]

To those on the Tory right who wanted to carry the Thatcherite torch into the 1990s he had a blunt message:

In searching for an answer to the question why we have such a full diet of policy initiatives yet are perceived to be drifting, I think it would be wrong to settle on an ideo- logical approach as the solution to our problems. Ideology can become a substitute for thought and an ideologically driven party ultimately becomes a pastiche of itself, entirely in the grip of ideologues applying uncritically yesterday's answers to today's problems.

As coded messages go this wouldn't have required the skills of the Bletchley Park decipherers to shed light on what he was say- ing. Lang was warning those on the right of the dangers of 'going that one revolution too far'.[3]

In Conservative euphemism, this was the speech of a Consolidator. Consolidators included one-nation Tories like Douglas Hurd, Kenneth Clarke and even ministers thought to be of the right like Gillian Shephard, who, on becoming Education Secretary, went out of her way to reassure parents – but more particularly teachers and their unions – that the Government's revolution in the classroom had ended. Hers was a mission to soothe ruffled feathers. The Radicals include obvi- ous right-wingers like John Redwood, Michael Portillo and Peter Lilley – the troika of 'bastards'.

One of the most prominent Consolidators was the Chancellor Kenneth Clarke. He echoed many of the themes set out by Ian Lang, although he swapped Lang's tap dancing shoes for his customary steel-capped hush puppies. In a series of speeches and comments, Kenneth Clarke accused Blair of being a political transvestite. A cross-dresser who was remark- able only for his attempts to steal Tory clothes. He pledged that the Conservatives would not be moved from the 'hard centre' of British politics.

By coincidence both Clarke and Blair were due to tackle the question of welfare within twenty-four hours of each other, just before the Labour leadership campaign drew to a close. On one Tuesday evening in July, Kenneth Clarke fulfilled a long-standing diary commitment to speak at the London School of Economics. The following morning Blair was due to deliver a keynote speech on welfare in Southampton. Clarke's text was pure 'one nation' Toryism. It sought to address the growing anxiety and insecurity felt by the middle classes. It was, he said, 'idle to think that middle England does not sometimes feel worried'. And he went on:

> Imagine the private sector or public sector middle manager in middle England who may be told that his organisation is being downsized. He will want to feel that there is a high quality health and education system on which his family can depend. He will also want to know that there is a modernised, affordable welfare system which will assist him with the means to re-train and find new employment.[4]

The Blair speech the next day could have hardly been more similar: 'Insecurity, once the preserve of the underprivileged few, is now the common experience of the many.' And he continued in a way that would suggest that both men were employing the same speechwriter:

> A functioning economy and labour market needs stability. That means the middle manager needs to be able to count on the stability that comes from the opportunity to get another job if the previous one disappears and the stability that comes from a secure home and family.[5]

If the early 1950s saw 'Butskellism': the similarity of policies pursued by Rab Butler and Hugh Gaitskell; then the 1990s could produce One Nation Labourism, made up of the largely shared agenda between Kenneth Clarke and Tony Blair. These speeches were a graphic illustration of the need felt by the Tory left to scent-mark the territory they had traditionally occupied and were in danger of seeing confiscated by a predatory invader. But it also marked a shift on to the most important electoral battle-ground, the fight for the middle classes.

What made these two speeches significant was the unambiguous attempt to woo a section of the electorate which poll after poll had shown were feeling sore and in a mood for political retribution. It was as if the two main parties had stumbled upon an important discovery: that the Conservatives could no longer take these people for granted; and that for a Blair-led Labour Party here was a group to be courted.

Blair's overtures to the middle classes came at a time when it seemed that a group of people who always appeared self-perpetuating and recession-proof were feeling the cold as never before. And as the pollsters and marketing men moved in to take their pulse and check their temperature, churning out a mass of statistical data all pointing to a patient in need of care, so the politicians started to think seriously about what the political consequences of a disaffected middle class could be upon the electoral map of Britain. All the vices of society that the middle classes had been able to hide from in the past were now crowding in: they were increasingly the victims of crime; drugs were for sale in their children's playgrounds; unemployment or the fear of unemployment was a constant companion; the value of their houses crumbled; their mortgages were larger than the value of their houses; and they were in debt. At the very moment that every economic indicator was pointing in the right direction – low inflation, low interest rates, sustainable growth (the elusive virtuous circle of economic management) – so confidence in the Conservative Party seemed to be at its lowest ebb. Politicians sat up and took notice as the professional classes emitted a variety of alarm signals. Robert Reich, Bill Clinton's Labor Secretary, on a visit to London described this group of people as the 'nervous class'.

The 'Blair factor' was also ringing alarm bells in Central Office. A poll conducted for *The Times* showed that, midway through the campaign, Labour's poll rating stood at 52 per cent and would rise to 55 per cent if Tony Blair became Leader. The poll findings also suggested that the Liberal Democrats were particularly vulnerable to 'Blair-appeal'. Their support, already down, would slip still further to 18 per cent. And this poll also showed Labour with a commanding lead over the Tories among middle-class voters. But a Gallup poll for the *Daily Telegraph* taken soon after Blair became Leader was even more dramatic. It showed Labour enjoying a standing in the polls that had never been seen in the polling organisation's fifty-seven-year history. The Party's lead over the Tories was also by a record margin. The poll contained other astonishing findings. Apparently 53 per cent of Conservative voters would either be delighted or sanguine about a Labour Government. Polls mid-term in retrospect are best used to show how far an electorate can change its mind when it comes to polling day – in other words, they can be dismissed as largely irrelevant. But there is no doubt that as class-based politics have declined and the bonds of traditional tribal loyalties have loosened, so the voter has become much more promiscuous, willing to sleep around with whichever party seems the most attractive.

That worked to the advantage of the Conservatives in the heyday of Thatcherism as the traditional working class embraced the Conservative Party, at first tentatively and then in droves as they themselves became part of the aspirant middle class. But the nightmare scenario for Conservatives was that it could now work the other way round, with the middle classes abandoning the Tories in favour of Labour without stopping at the Liberal Democrats *en route*. In the 1945 election and the two elections of the 1960s it was the middle classes who were the swing voters making a Labour victory possible.

If poll findings can be easily dismissed (and who can blame a Conservative for scoffing when polls at general elections have consistently underestimated their support), the evidence of the European elections was harder to ignore. Admittedly, turnout was low, and people were not voting about crunch issues like how much money either Party would be taking out of their pay packets to fund their programmes, but Labour were winning in places they had not done well in since the 1960s, and in some places even before that. There were gains in Essex, Suffolk, Norfolk, Hertfordshire, Shropshire and Kent. What was also remarkable about these results was that this was the first time that Labour had matched its poll rating with votes actually cast in ballot boxes. The Tory share of the vote was the lowest in any election this century. Conservatives looking around for crumbs of comfort sought refuge in the explanation that this was a sympathy vote for Labour following John Smith's death; but others saw it as something much more ominous: a willingness to give Labour a chance in advance of a Party recast in Tony Blair's image. And these fears were heightened by the evidence of the huge numbers of voters who switched direct from Conservative to Labour without registering their vote of dissatisfaction with the Liberal Democrats.

But if the response of the Tory left was to say 'here we stand', there will be no surrender of political territory, the response of the Conservative right was altogether different. If Clarke and Lang represented the Consolidators' school, then Portillo was the standard bearer of the right. His fans – and, curiously for a politician, he attracts the same kind of fervour and devotion as a pop star – on the Thatcherite right reproduced a collection of his speeches which they called 'Clear Blue Water'. Clear Blue Water was also what John Major told his backbenchers he wanted when they huddled together in Committee Room 14 of the Commons to bang their desks at the traditional end of term address before they went off for their 1994 summer holidays. Major's advisers believed there were three critical areas of Labour weakness that Blair had not found answers to. One was predictable, namely

Labour's ambitious plans for constitutional reform. The other two – taxation and Europe – were more surprising because they were precisely the issues that had caused the Conservatives so much grief since the 1992 general election.

If an analysis had been done on the one sentence that Labour politicians used more than any other during 1994 it would have undoubtedly been 'the Tories will never be trusted by the voters on taxation again'. It was chanted so often that many Labour MPs even started to believe it. But despite the mistrust and sense of betrayal towards the Conservatives that voters were reflecting in opinion polls, Labour's private qualitative polling showed that Labour was held in even lower esteem on the taxation question. When small groups of voters were spoken to, the research findings revealed deep-seated fears about what Labour in government would do. That was a shock for Labour coming after the 1993 budget when the Conservatives had introduced the biggest package of tax increases since the nation was at war with Napoleon. The refrain that whatever Labour did the Tories would still be the party of *lower* taxation was one that would resonate for the Conservatives.

This research explained the extensive and ceaseless campaign by Labour leaders to drive home the message that Labour had been converted to the cause of low inflation and low taxation. It was a campaign that culminated in the annual Mais Lecture which Blair had been invited to deliver just under a year after he had become Leader. He promised that he would not allow tax rates to rise higher than the international average, and he said for the first time that the objective of any government was to lower rather than increase the burden of taxation. Low inflation would be the cornerstone of Labour's policies, he told his city audience. And he went on, 'I can already hear Conservatives claiming that they agree with these objectives.'[6]

The other area where Tory strategists believed that Labour was vulnerable was on the subject of Europe. The argument was put that even though John Major had been to hell and back trying to manage his party, Labour's newly found pro-Europeanism was at odds with the mood of the country, and that given the choice, voters would prefer John Major's brand of constructive Euro-scepticism to Blair's acquiescence to Brussels. But this was an argument predicated on a false hypothesis, namely that the Conservatives would find an agenda on which they could unite. All too frequently, Cabinet Ministers went on the radio to push their own agenda; one would stress that he would hesitate for an eternity before accepting a single currency, others warned that Britain could not afford to be left behind if others went ahead; some would say it was a question of the utmost constitutional importance. Kenneth Clarke said there was no constitutional question raised. When eight Conservative backbenchers defied the Government on a vote that John Major said was a question of confidence, they were denied the whip, and were told they would only be given it back when they made amends. Far from recanting, they organised themselves into an effective group, and eventually it was the Government which buckled, allowing them back in without so much as an apology.

There was a rich irony that went undetected when Blair delivered his keynote speech on Europe at the beginning of 1995. He went to Brussels accompanied by senior party figures who mingled with leaders of the European business community. It was one of the most pro-European speeches delivered by a leader of either of the two main parties for many years. It had been researched, drafted and written by Jonathan Powell. It was as pro-European as Margaret Thatcher's famous Bruges speech had been Euro-sceptic. That had been drafted by Powell's big brother, Sir Charles Powell (who used to insist the pronunciation of his surname was Pole) when he was the Prime Minister's foreign policy adviser. It begged the headline 'Powells Apart', but it was never used.

The question of Britain's sovereignty was central to the issue of constitutional reform. In the view of John Major, the ambition of Blair's plans was only outstripped by their stupidity. The Prime Minister used speech after speech to dismiss as teenage madness talk of English regional assemblies, reform of the Lords, etc. And on giving tax raising powers to a Scottish Parliament, Major invoked the West Lothian question that so dogged Labour the last time it was in power in the 1970s. Tam Dalyell, then a Labour MP for West Lothian raised the logical inconsistency of how it could be fair for him and Scottish colleagues once they had their own parliament in Edinburgh to vote on matters at Westminster soley affecting England, when English MPs would have no say over matters decided by the Scottish Parliament. It was telling how quickly Labour retreated over the question of English regional assemblies when the Conservatives turned the heat up, confirming to Tory strategists Labour's vulnerability.

But the Tory right were busy setting out their own agenda on how to beat the Blair threat. In fact it wasn't so much how, but who. The arch plotter of the disaffected Thatcherites, Sir George Gardiner, produced a booklet called, predictably enough, *Clear Blue Water*. The booklet that took three months to pull together was less a policy document than a manifesto for Michael Portillo. With a regal looking portrait of Mr Portillo on the front cover, it was a collection of his speeches, articles and thoughts on a variety of subjects. Sir George was commendably frank about why he had produced the book.

> As the Conservative Party reached the depth of its unpopularity in 1994's by-elections, local elections and then Euro-elections, the Labour Party elected a new Leader who quickly left no doubt of his intention to appeal directly to those former Conservative voters who had come to feel estranged from the Party. So the cry was raised by Conservative activists to see established 'clear blue water' between the policies we stand for and those espoused by the Labour Party.[7]

The extent to which the Conservatives had slid into a parlous political state was highlighted by a leaked internal document from Conservative Central Office, written by one of the deputy chairmen, John Maples. Its impact was the greater because it had been written for internal consumption in language that would never be heard in public from this smoothest of political operators. He had spent the summer conducting in-depth qualitative market research, working with small groups of voters in four areas and the message that Maples reported from this group of disaffected Conservative voters could not have been blunter. On Tony Blair, Maples reported, 'If Blair turns out to be as good as he looks we have a problem'; on the economy Maples said:

'Although in the 1980s the Conservatives seemed to promise a classless society of opportunity, the reality is now that the rich are getting richer on the backs of the rest who are getting poorer.'[8]

And it went on in similar vein about the government's standing on the health service (here Maples said the best thing that could happen would be for the Conservative Party to gain zero media coverage on the subject for the following year), and on privatisation which his research found that disgruntled Tory voters had grown tired of.

The seriousness with which the Prime Minister had thought about the Blair threat became apparent in his keynote speech to his 1994 conference. For this speech there was no big advanced billing. Instead it was quietly pointed out that this would be the occasion where the real John Major stood up. There was no mention of Blair, nor of his inexperience in real decision making. Instead Major dispensed with all the normal accoutrements of a modern speech – there was no auto prompter, and Major moved out on to a sort of pontoon to speak to the faithful so that he was closer to his audience. And what he presented was a man of quiet and deep competence. A patient man who got things done, a man who was in the business of government, not fancy flights of oratory. Major wanted to be judged by results, not adjectives. Peace in Ireland will be the most startling manifestation of that dogged determination.

But Major's speech with its rejection of 'change for the sake of change' was clear evidence that he was throwing in his lot with those seeking a less turbulent political life. There would be no surrendering of traditional Conservative ground in a bid to heighten the perceived differences between a Major-led Conservative Party and a Blair-led Labour Party. Significantly after Major's speech, when the Cabinet traditionally come down from the platform to gush about the contents of the speech to the assorted film crews and reporters, only one minister refused requests for interviews: Michael Portillo, the Employment Secretary. Major is going to fight Blair on the centre ground of British politics. (Although the partisan *Daily Mirror*, the day after the speech, accused Major – with some justification – of being the 'hokey-cokey' Prime Minister: one year he puts his right leg in, the next year his left.)

The extent to which the Conservative Party had become a party of consolidation after its 1994 conference became apparent when the one 'big cat' in the cabinet, Michael Heseltine, was forced to abandon his controversial plans to privatise the Post Office which was to have been the flagship legislation of the 1995 parliamentary session. Heseltine blamed a dozen or so portly Tory has-beens and never-will-bes, but he was thwarted by those of his ministerial colleagues who wanted to lead the Conservative Party into calmer political waters. The Tory Whips' Office, far from threatening thumbscrews and torture to the would-be rebels, seemed to be offering covert support and succour. It was a decision replete with ironies. The person who had fought to carry the Thatcherite torch of the 1980s into the 1990s was Michael Heseltine, who had been responsible for her downfall; while her chosen successor, John Major, was cast in the role of a previous Conservative Prime Minister, Stanley Baldwin, whose motto, 'safety first' helped him hold on to power in the inter-war years.

The Baldwin comparison was one that frightened Labour. Their research showed that in spite of the series of serious set-backs that afflicted the Prime Minister, the British people still liked and trusted him. They felt sorry for John Major, and they did not blame him personally for all that had gone wrong. Where Labour strategists believed the Government's problems were more deep-seated was in the sense felt by the public that they had run out of steam. The quote from Norman Lamont's resignation speech when he accused the Government of being in office, but not in power, would be replayed again and again by Labour.

The other problem for the Government – and it was related to that sense of exhaustion – was the steady flow of stories involving Conservative MPs acting dishonourably. Allegations that Conservative politicians had been taking money for asking questions in the Commons, had been involved in dubious share deals or were tabling amendments in the names of colleagues to avoid declaring their own interests in a subject, all contributed to a sense that the Conservatives had grown bloated on power, unable to distinguish between party and national interest. John Major's appointment of the Scott Inquiry to look into whether ministers had breached the Government's own guidelines on sales of weapons to Iraq, and Lord Justice Nolan's investigation into standards in public life, were a clear mark of the concern felt in Downing Street. But the theme of the decline in standards in public life was tailor-made for the Opposition. It was one that John Smith had made his own, and Blair early on signalled that he intended to do likewise:

Let me tell you I would expect ministers in a Government I lead to resign if they lie to Parliament. I would expect ministers to pay their own legal fees if they get into personal difficulty. I would not allow foreign businessmen to bankroll a political Party while not even paying any taxes in this country. And I would expect to know that if a Member of Parliament in the Labour Party asked a Parliamentary question they did so out of duty to their constituents not because £1000 has been sent to their home address.

Conservative strategy was confused on how to get at Blair; indeed there were times when it seemed the Tories wanted to leave him well alone, and concentrate instead on some of the left-wingers around him. But some of the most effective attacks on the Labour Leader were on his change of stance on key issues. As with Kinnock before him, Tory researchers had been through their files digging up evidence of past socialist commitments. Michael Howard, who spent many years facing Blair across the despatch box, said that if it came to a choice between Major and Blair, Major would come out on top:

> How do you judge a leader of the Opposition, particularly one who has never been in Government before? One of the main things that one wants from a Prime Minister is political courage, and it is an attribute that Tony Blair claims, but how do you test political courage? Surely one of the ways in which you test it is whether somebody is prepared to speak out for what they believe is right. But, in his time in Parliament – whether it is trade union reform, Europe, or the minimum wage – he has not been prepared to speak out against the current position of his Party's leadership, whatever it may have been at the time. This may be because he agreed with it, in which case he now concedes he was wrong on all these vital issues, or it was because he wasn't prepared to stand up for what he thought was right, so taking up a position apparently at odds with what he was thinking privately. And that is a very, very serious state of affairs.[9]

If the Conservatives had to decide the ground on which they were going to attack Blair, the Liberal Democrats were presented with a rather different problem. The arrival of Blair, for some commentators, was akin to a thunderbolt crashing through the roof of the Liberal Party's Cowley Street headquarters, raising in an instant the question of whether their Party had a role left to play in British politics. The Liberal Democrats had always had a mission. It was long-term, it wasn't making remarkable head-way, but it was reasonably clear. It was to replace the Labour Party as the main party of opposition. But Sir David Steel's cry of 'Go back to your constituencies and prepare for government', suddenly seemed absurd, as opposed to only slightly absurd when Blair arrived. Admittedly the project launched with such fanfare and gusto in 1981 by the Gang of Four (Roy Jenkins, David Owen, Shirley Williams and Bill Rodgers) started to look a little wobbly as early as 1983 when only five of the Party's thirty MPs survived the rigours of the general election campaign.

But as each Parliament passed, each marked by spectacular by-election wins, their spirits never sank completely. And, although a mixture of the voting system and circumstance meant they never made the breakthrough that their leaders had spent so much of their time dreaming of, nor had Labour regained the trust of enough of the voters to secure victory single-handed. And less remarked upon were the steady, relentless advances that the Liberal Democrats were making in local government. Tory or Labour authorities became hung councils; hung councils sur-rendered to Liberal Democrat control – by the time Tony Blair came to lead the Labour Party the Liberal Democrats had 4,500 councillors in town halls across Britain. But, like the athlete who always promised so much in training, the Liberal Democrats were never really able to show their form when it came to big events like general elections, or the European elections. In the 1992 European election there was a breakthrough of sorts in that the Party won its first two Euroseats, but it was well short of the hatful that some advisers had been predicting. And in that election their national poll showing was well down on what they had achieved a month earlier in the local council elections.

Paddy Ashdown was not for the first time in his career furi-ous at the way the BBC and the press had covered his Party's results – playing down what he saw as a significant achievement. In the immediate aftermath of the results, Lord Rodgers, for-merly Bill Rodgers, and one of the key strategists of the SDP, went to see Ashdown in his rooms in the Commons off the main committee corridor. He wanted to know how Ashdown intended to meet the threat posed by a new and vibrant Labour leader. Ashdown was uncertain. Rodgers said he needed to go out and make some big-hitting speeches explaining why there was still a place for the Liberal Democrats in the premier league. In the event, Ashdown proclaimed that the Liberal Democrats were still distinctive and still no closer to Labour than they were to the Conservatives. Rodgers told friends that 'Paddy had made a bloody fool of himself' by taking this line when it was patently obvious to anyone that there was precious little in policy terms to separate Labour from the Liberal Democrats.

But worse was to come for Paddy Ashdown. First Shirley Williams and then Roy Jenkins and finally Bill Rodgers all went public to extol the virtues of the new man in charge of their erstwhile Party. Baroness Williams and Tony Blair both attended a weekend conference organised by the *Guardian,* an occasion that called for magnificent stage management skills as it was made perfectly clear by Blair's office that at no time must any of the photographers or cameracrews be able to get a shot of Williams and Blair in the same frame. So, in scenes that would do credit to the distinguished history of a Brian Rix farce, timings had to be managed so that as one door closed heralding the departure of Shirley Williams another opened to bring in Tony Blair. Williams argued that Blair's elevation to the leadership of the Labour Party made the case for greater co-operation between the two left of centre Parties not only compelling but essential. Lord Jenkins penned an article for *The Times* that was so fulsome in its praise for Blair that it was almost as if one was reading about the great man's prodigal son. And finally Lord Rodgers joined in, telling *The World at One* that the Liberal Democrats had to abandon the ambition of becoming the principal Party of opposition and that Blair was the right man to lead the country into the second half of the 1990s.[10]

Rodgers went even further. While he would not countenance a return to the Labour Party, the former gang of four member said that he would work for a Labour victory. 'I want Blair to succeed, there's no question about that, and I would like to help him. I would be very pleased if I could play some part in helping him draw up his plans for government.'[11] With the Blair camp aware that they needed to garner all the votes available, they sat back contentedly as the Labour Party's former tormentors made their noises of reconciliation.

It was an extraordinary political turnaround that these words passed the lips of Messrs Williams, Jenkins and Rodgers. There was no way that any such overture would ever have been made to John Smith when he was Leader because the scars of battle from when they left the Labour Party were still too fresh. But, equally, the fact that Blair was able to greet these comments from one-time traitors with such equanimity wouldn't have been possible were it not for the fact that Blair had entered Parliament after these upheavals, and never had the same feelings of malice and even hatred that some others had towards them. Indeed some of that feeling spilled over when Jack Straw, Blair's campaign manager, went on the radio soon after the gang of three had cosied up to the new Labour Leader.

It is a bit rich for the people who left the Party and then waged war, not on the Conservatives, but on Labour for twelve years to say, 'The Labour Party has changed and we would like to be welcomed back with open arms.' I don't think we are going to hang out the flags for the fact that twelve years on, the people who sought to destroy the Labour Party are now going through the funeral rites of their own approach.[12]

Interestingly Jack Straw had spoken to Blair's office before going on air about what line to take. It was agreed Straw should strike a fairly neutral 'well, you know where we are if you want to join us' chord. But once in the studio all the hostilities towards those who founded the SDP spilled over uncontrollably. An aide to Blair said it was not the sort of language he would have chosen.

For weeks after Blair's election Paddy Ashdown was strangely silent. He was eventually cornered on the subject at a Westminster news conference where the normally ebullient Liberal Democrat Leader was remarkably tetchy. He said there was an old saying in the Middle East that 'If a dog barks, British Intelligence is behind it.' He said it now seemed as though if anything happened in British politics it was because of Tony Blair. That was not the case, he insisted testily. And Ashdown went on to say, yes, Blair did indeed have some fine qualities, but that didn't mean the Liberal Democrats should favour him over John Major. The dance to stay, in the public mind at least, equidistant from the two main parties was not about to change.

The threat to the Liberal Democracts was obvious. The worst-case scenario as far as they were concerned was that the seats – ostensibly in the West Country where they were the main challengers – would stay Conservative because a resurgent Labour Party would split the anti-Conservative vote. Those fears seemed to have a grounding in the wake of the 1994 European elections, where a split opposition vote allowed the Conservatives to squeak home in a number of Euro constituencies. But a year later it was the Conservatives who had cause to feel the greater level of anxiety. The 1995 local council elections were exceptional in that it appeared as though tactical voting had finally come of age. Ward by ward, council by council, there was an impression that voters were out to punish the Conservatives; they coolly took the decision as to which party was best placed to beat them, and placed their vote accordingly. That meant that far from disappearing from the electoral map, the Liberal Democrats reinforced their hold on local government in the areas where they had traditionally done well.

It was shortly after these election results that Paddy Ashdown announced a highly significant shift in Liberal Democrat strategy. He buried equidistance. He made clear for the first time in public that in the event of a hung parliament, the Liberal Democrats would not help prop up a Conservative administration. It was an announcement that had been a long time coming. To many, unable any longer to tell the difference between Liberal policies from those of a Blair led Labour Party, the decision seemed unremarkable. But that was to underplay the extent to which Paddy Ashdown had to manage the feuding edges of his own party.

In the Liberal Democrats there has always been an inherent tension between the grassroots and the elected MPs. The strongest tradition inherited from the Liberal Party was a belief in 'pavement politics'. So, far from Westminster politics being the height of every Liberal's ambitions, it was something to be eschewed. What these people sought was influence over the local neighbourhood, with power devolving downwards, not concentrated in the Palace of Westminster. And to these political streetfighters, the establishment enemy – particularly in the North – was the Labour Party, where they had held sway over the municipal boroughs for as long as anyone could remember. When the Liberal Democrats held their first party conference after Blair's election as leader, there was bitter resentment from many party activists at the suggestion from the SDP wing, particularly from grandees like Shirley Williams and Bill Rodgers, that there should be some kind of accommodation with Labour.

Blair came to play the part of Banquo's ghost at the feast in Liberal Democrat circles in the months after his election to the Labour leadership. At their Party's conference in 1994 the degree to which they should abandon equidistance was the backdrop to all discussion. And in private, key figures like Ashdown, Menzies Campbell, Charles Kennedy and Alex Carlile recognised that the political landscape had changed beyond all measure, and that the really burning question was what kind of co-operation there could be between Labour and the Liberal Democrats, and at what price. Because, for all the studied indifference that Labour displayed towards the Liberal Democrats, Tony Blair was only too happy to see the Liberal Democrats win seats in the South West at the expense of the Conservative Party – seats that Labour alone would never have stood a chance of taking. There was another factor to Blair's thinking. With his strong centrist views that many on the hard-left of his own party find hard to take, he calculated that a strong Liberal Democrat presence in a future Parliament of which he was Prime Minister could act as a vital bulwark against those from within Labour like the campaign group who would be demanding more hardline policies.

Blair and Ashdown get on well – both arrived in the Commons at the same time in 1983, and have on occasions had informal discussions. The lack of hostility felt by the Labour Leader towards the Liberal Democrats was shown in an interview that Blair gave to the *New Statesman* magazine. When asked about the involvement of Labour backbenchers in a planned discussion group of MPs from both parties, the Labour Leader said, 'It doesn't trouble me at all: it's sensible'. He was equally relaxed about working with the Liberal Democrats in Government:

> The most important thing is that we have a government that doesn't just say, 'We're the masters now, things have changed,' but is deliberately trying to change the politics of the country – and that requires working to achieve the broadest possible basis of consent.[13]

CHAPTER 12

The Project

'The Tories have lost the nation's trust. But that does not mean we inherit it automatically. We have to work for it. We have to earn it. Above all we must show not just that they have failed, but how we can succeed.'

Tony Blair, 21 July 1994

Tony Blair and his advisers were much given to talking about 'the project' either side of the leadership election. At its crudest, it was of course about winning the next election, of ending Labour's wilderness years. But when Blair talked about this or that one being a supporter of the project, or against the project, he meant something more than the simple question that was asked during the Thatcher era, 'Is he one of us?' The project was about designing a left-of-centre agenda that gained the trust of the British people. For Blair it was about seizing the political highground, and redefining what it meant to be a socialist in post-Thatcherite society. It was about framing a coherent set of policies that would make people want to vote for Labour, not simply vote against the Conservatives. In his first year as Leader he set about his task with a clear-minded determination. Nothing, he decreed to his Shadow Cabinet with an authoritarian streak, would be allowed to get in the way of the project.

A graphic illustration of this came in Blair's first significant managerial act as Party Leader. To no-one's great surprise, Blair decided it was time for Larry Whitty to hang up his minutes book as the Party's General Secretary. He had been in post for nine years, had turned around Labour's perilous financial position, but was generally seen as being 'of the old guard'. Blair moved

259

quickly and decisively against him, pushing him into a political siding. It was speedy and firm.

Blair had already decided who Whitty's replacement should be, and from that moment worked to secure his services, even though, technically the decision was one for the National Executive to take. Blair wanted Tom Sawyer who was then General Secretary of the National Union of Public Employees. Despite a Bennite past, and the famous 'no say, no pay' remark, Sawyer was considered to be one of the union movement's leading and most articulate Modernisers. The day an advertisement for the post appeared in the *Guardian*, Jack Dromey telephoned Blair to enquire whether he should apply. They spoke on the telephone for some time. Blair was courteous, even mildly encouraging, but said that on balance it might be better for Dromey to stay where he was as one of the Modernisers on the left-wing dominated Transport Union executive. In fact the conversation was a charade. Blair had already approached Sawyer, and Sawyer had agreed to take on the job.

The day after Whitty's dismissal, as Blair travelled North to his constituency, on a train that broke down suspiciously in John Major's constituency, he arrived in Trimdon to find his fax machine burning red hot. The Joint Trade Union Committee at Walworth Road had met, were angry and had agreed the following resolution:

'The JTUC Officers are most concerned at the decision of Tony Blair, Leader of the Labour Party, to seek the removal of Larry Whitty from the post of General Secretary. After a long period of unease, unrest and low morale within the Party staff following two periods of major restructuring and reorganisation, the staff are at present beginning to become settled with the new establishment . . . It is most regrettable to put at risk the present settled environment within the Party by introducing unnecessary managerial changes and the subsequent possibility of further alteration to the staffing structure.'[1]

It was signed by Roy Hill, Lorraine Hopkinson, Cathy Parry, Bob Smith and Ann McDowell. As they fulminated against their new leader, Blair turned to officials from his local Party and said, 'Now I know I was right to move Larry.' There then followed a series of separate faxes, first from the GMB at Walworth Road saying they hadn't been consulted, and then another from the NUJ condemning the actions of the joint trades unions. It was the Labour Party of old; conservative, resistant to change and disputatious. Luckily for Blair, none of these resolutions found their way into the press, and the argument did not spill into the public domain.

No doubt those who signed the motion criticising Blair did so as a warning shot across the bows to proceed no further. But Blair had not even begun. An even more vivid example of his bold, even cavalier approach came when he visited the TUC conference soon after he had become Leader. When Blair travelled to Blackpool there was a delicious moment during a photocall with John Monks the TUC General Secretary when a photographer asked them to stand closer together. Blair's body language said it all. He froze on the spot, kept a seemly foot apart from Mr Monks and then smiled a smile which said, 'I know exactly how close I want to be to Mr Monks and it is this far and no further.'

Later, when Blair was doorstepped by a group of reporters, he was asked, 'Do you regard the trade unions as just another pressure group?' His reply was instructive. He said that Labour would govern for all the country and would therefore treat them in the same way that Labour treated business.

> 'We have got to get away from the notion that we can keep re-living the battles of the past. I want to move the country on but I will do that not only for the trade union movement but for business and for others.'[2]

Admittedly the original notion that the Labour Party would act as the political wing of the trade union movement went some time ago, but no Labour leader has been quite so blunt in putting the unions in their place. Blair had been provoked by an article by the leader of the GMB, John Edmonds. In it Edmonds had taken a number of swipes at Labour's Modernisers and wrote that the Labour Party's relationship with the unions was one of the 'defining links' in British politics. He also said that Blair spoke a different language that many in the movement found unsettling.[3] Blair wasted no time in disabusing him of that view when he spoke to the press, and by all accounts was even blunter with union bosses when he spoke to them in private. The late Harold Wilson once pleaded with Hugh Scanlon and other union barons to move their tanks off his lawn; in a Blair-led Labour Party the intention is not even to allow them up the drive.

Blair was given a mandate to carry out his reforms that no Labour leader in history had had. Blair's leadership campaign gave no quarter to the sections of opinion within the Party that normally needed stroking. But in politics memories are short, and Blair calculated that if he was going to make use of his mandate to change the Party he would have to move with greater speed than caution. He could not make the same mistake that Smith had made over One Member One Vote and delay everything for a year, allowing time for forces resistant to change to regroup. Traditionally left-wing constituencies had voted for him; every union bar one – whether left or right – had thrown their weight behind him; even some MPs traditionally seen as being from the 'hard' left had backed him.

But Blair had something else as well as a mandate. He had a quite unprecedented inheritance. He came to the battlefield after some of the most difficult fights had been fought. If the period of John Smith's leadership was marked by a certain torpor and inaction, his very presence as a reassuring and safe figure on the national stage did much to give Labour back that most nebulous but vital thing: trust. But Blair had also been bequeathed the reforms pursued by Kinnock in the mid 1980s in which he addressed all the difficult internal questions and points of policy which dragged Labour on an Odyssey to become a modern political Party. That left Blair in a position to reap the benefits of his predecessor's work; it also pointed up the extent to which the new Leader was untested.

Blair's *Who's Who* entry before he became Leader did not list the various front bench posts he had held. When asked why this was so, Blair was disarmingly honest: 'Well, they're not proper jobs are they?' he said. The tests that he had confronted he had passed. But when he became Leader Blair was like one of those British boxers who looks all rippling muscle but has never had to take a punch. It was not that no-one had laid a glove on him, it was more that he had not fought a defining battle. His persuading the unions to accept the end of the closed shop could not be put on a par with, for example, John Major's travails to place the Maastricht Treaty on to the statute book. But Blair had already decided to embark upon a battle that would be a test of his muscularity, stamina and cunning. It was something that no leader had dared do in thirty-five years, and that was to rewrite the Labour Party constitution.

During the Labour leadership campaign, Blair was asked by David Frost what he intended to do about Clause IV, section iv of the Labour Party's constitution. 'I don't think that anyone actually wants that to be the priority of the Labour Party at the moment,' said Blair.[4] But it was his one disingenuous moment during the leadership contest. He had already started sketching out a strategy to bring the question of Clause IV to the surface.

In the wake of Lord Wilson's death in May 1995 there were many attempts to compare the inheritance bequeathed to Harold Wilson in 1963 when he took over after the untimely death of Hugh Gaitskell and Tony Blair's in 1994. There were some striking similarities. The Conservative Party in Wilson's time had been in power since 1951, but their final years in office had been marked by scandal and a pervasive sense of disintegration. Wilson was a great television communicator and media operator. He promised to harness the coming technological revolution. He led a Labour Party equally hungry for power after so long in opposition. But there were differences too, the most striking of which was the relative state of the Labour Party in 1963, and its position in 1994. The Labour Party in the early 1960s was painfully divided between left and right, between unilateralists and multi-lateralists, and although Aneurin Bevan had died in 1960 and Gaitskell in 1963, there were still many in the movement proud to wear the badge of either the Bevanites or Gaitskellites. It was a tame, almost neutered beast that Blair took charge of.

Rather than comparing Blair to Wilson, perhaps the most instructive comparison is with Hugh Gaitskell. They shared a similar public school and Oxbridge background, and both had the aim of being 'reformist leaders'. While the passage of time changes policy and approaches to policy-making, the direction in which Blair sought to lead Labour is the one that Gaitskell and his acolytes had mapped out at the end of the 1950s. But it was to end in such dismal and humiliating failure that it would be another thirty-five years before anyone tried again.

When Harold Macmillan won the general election in 1959 for the Conservatives, it was the third defeat for Labour in a row. Gaitskell, the Labour Leader, went that autumn to a sombre Party conference, and gave the delegates a frank assessment of what had done Labour most harm and where the Party had gone wrong. He put his finger on what until then had been considered one of the jewels of Labour in office, public ownership. The tone of his remarks suggested that he knew he was walking into a lion's den:

> There seems no doubt that if we are to accept the majority view of those who fought this election, nationalisation – on balance – lost us votes. No-one suggests it was the main cause but anything which appears to have swung votes against us deserves careful, and as far as possible, dispassionate study . . . Some of the existing nationalised industries are unpopular . . . Thousands and perhaps millions of voters were induced to think that we intended to nationalise any and every private firm.

Gaitskell then went on to try to define what he saw as the essence of democratic socialism. He listed a number of points. Firstly, it was about representing the underdog in society; it was about social justice (by this he meant an equitable distribution of wealth and income) – 'We do not demand exact equality,' he said. His socialism was the belief in a classless society; about fundamental equality between the races; it was concerned with putting the public interest before the private interest. And then, at the end of these remarks, the punchline; Gaitskell called for the rewriting of Clause IV of the Labour Party constitution:

> It seems to me that this needs to be brought up to date. For instance can we really be satisfied today with a statement of fundamentals which makes no mention at all of colonial freedom, race relations, disarmament, full employment or planning . . . Standing as it does on its own, this cannot possibly be adequate. It lays us open to continual misrepresentation. It implies that common ownership is an end, whereas in fact it is a means.[5]

It is worth pointing out that before Gaitskell made this speech, no-one had taken that much notice of Clause IV, which read:

> *To secure for the workers by hand or by brain the full fruits of their industry and the most equitable distribution thereof that may be possible upon the basis of the common ownership of the means of production, distribution and exchange.*

But once Gaitskell made his speech, a whole new campaign was born devoted to the retention of the Clause to which the Labour Leader had given sudden prominence. Gaitskell came up against a coalition of forces that was to be his undoing. Right-wing union barons, suspicious of Gaitskell's motives and even more fearful of what it would mean for their own powerbase in the Party, linked arms with the traditional left in an unholy alliance which would force Gaitskell to retreat. In truth, Gaitskell played a bad tactical game, failing to prepare his case and build support before making his speech. A year later, the Labour Party adopted Gaitskell's set of aims and values, but they were very much an adjunct to, and not a replacement of, Clause IV. So, far from destroying that part of the constitution, Gaitskell's activities resulted in the birth of Clause IVism.

The Labour Party constitution was drafted by Sidney Webb in 1918, revised in 1926, and in 1994, when nearly every other outdated sacred cow had been taken out and shot, was still found on the back of every Labour Party membership card. Not since Gaitskell was forced to retreat had any Labour leader even dared challenge this – until Tony Blair. Originally seen as a piece of right-wing revisionism in Britain to counter the distant thunderclaps of Bolshevism and Lenin's dictatorship after the 1917 revolution in the Soviet Union, Clause IV had for the left become the most important symbol of enduring socialist values. For what it represented was not a lofty statement about ethical socialism; it was about socialism as an economic theory and a way of delivering a more equal society. Its implied support for mass nationalisation may have commanded little support – even among left-wingers – but it was seen by a wide section of the Labour movement as a holy text of democratic socialism (even if the words seemed entirely anachronistic to modern Britain) the questioning of which was to strike at the heart of the Labour Party and amounted to nothing less than an act of heresy. Arthur Scargill called upon all those metaphors to declare that Tony Blair was no different from a bishop ripping up the ten commandments and should therefore be a candidate for excommunication. The battle that Blair chose to fight was therefore about nostalgia as much as it was about the tools of economic management.

Tony Blair and Gordon Brown had first talked about the need to get rid of Clause IV after the 1992 general election, when they and Peter Mandelson met at Blair's house, two days after the election defeat. It was one of the burning issues that the Modernisers felt had to be addressed, along with one member one vote. But the whole package of reforms around the constitution, like the organisation of the Party conference and the working of the National Executive, John Smith made clear he was not going to touch with a bargepole. It was a debate too far for him. But when Blair took over, it assumed primacy in the new leader's thoughts.

There were four critical conversations in the summer of 1994 that took place before Blair felt sufficiently confident to announce that the Labour Party constitution would be reviewed. The first person he outlined his thinking to was Gordon Brown who had all along shared the view that, if Clause IV misrepresented what Labour was going to do when in government and all it did was hand ammunition to the enemy, then why keep it? But Brown, who has never got on with John Prescott, said that it was vital to have Prescott alongside. Brown told Blair it was not enough to have Prescott sympathetic to what the Leader wanted to do. He had to be a 100 per cent behind him. Anything less would result in stories appearing about splits in the Labour leadership, but of greater long-term significance, it would have emboldened opponents to mount a counter-attack. The vital thing, said Brown, was to deter large numbers of people from hoisting the flag for Clause IV.

During Blair's summer holiday in France, Blair discussed it with Alastair Campbell. Blair wanted to know how Campbell would handle it professionally, in terms of presentation; but more importantly, he wanted to know how Campbell thought Prescott would react. Campbell says that it was at that moment that he knew he was going to leave his well-paid job on *Today*. If Blair was going to try to get rid of Clause IV, win or lose, he rationalised, he wanted to be part of it. To the specific question of how Prescott would react, Campbell guessed that he would be against the idea, and would take some convincing.

When Blair returned from holiday, the next person he spoke to was Mandelson. For two people who meet so often, Mandelson unusually took the decision to keep a note of their discussion. Blair, using Labour's private polling, said it was quite clear that the Party's problem was that voters did not believe that the Party had changed sufficiently, therefore expunging Clause IV would be a vital step towards convincing them. Blair said the evidence seemed to suggest that, while people supported him as Leader, they weren't sure that was what they would get with Labour in Government. Blair said to Mandelson, 'There is still too great a fear of the unknown as far as the Labour Party is concerned. They still think it is a risk to vote for us, they're saying "what you are saying about the Labour Party is fine, but are we actually going to get you, or are we going to get someone else." ' When Mandelson discussed the potential pitfalls, Blair was brusque: 'The Party is not worth leading if it's not leading to government.'

It was about a week later that Blair invited Prescott round to his house in Islington to discuss the conference. They met on Sunday evening, about three weeks before the conference. Blair said that he wanted to include a passage in his speech about reform of the constitution; Prescott knew immediately what his Leader was driving at. Initially Prescott was hostile. He said he thought the Party had too strong an emotional bond to Clause IV, and would not let it go easily. He also argued that it was an unnecessary diversion for the Party in the run-up to an election to be debating internal questions like the Labour Party constitution, which would sap too much energy. Prescott also made a correct assessment that he would be the person who would be blamed by the mainstream/traditional/left-wing elements of the Party. After all, they had voted for Prescott as deputy as an insurance policy against Blair's wilder modernising excesses. But, as they sat in Blair's drawing room, Prescott significantly did not say no.

What followed then was a regular exchange of drafts of the final section of Blair's speech. It was batted from Blair to Prescott to Campbell to the head of the policy unit, David Miliband, and back round again. No-one else was sounded out. Only a handful of people knew, although union leaders, like John Edmonds, were given an early hint of what was in Blair's mind. But even in this tight circle it was hard pounding. Prescott still was far from happy, and debate centred on how much to say in the speech and on what sort of timescale to operate.

When Blair travelled up to Blackpool for the conference he spent his whole time on the plane going through the speech with Campbell. He was extremely tense. The normally relaxed smile had gone. They still hadn't agreed a final form of wording with Prescott, and that was number one priority. Blair already had a long passage in his speech about trust, and how the only way to tackle the growing disillusionment that ordinary people felt towards politicians was to be honest about what could and could not be achieved: 'When we make a promise, we must be sure we can keep it. That is page 1, line 1 of a new contract between Government and citizen.'[6] And in the course of saying that Labour had to sell its message about what it stood for he said there should be 'No more ditching. No more dumping. Stop saying what we don't mean. And start saying what we do mean.'[7] Prescott said that if all of that was going to stand in the speech then it was incumbent on Blair to be clear about where he stood on the constitution.

Labour history is littered with deals where the i's had not been dotted and the t's not crossed, and where at the first whiff of grapeshot those who were party to the agreement went scuttling off in different directions. Blair and Prescott were not going to let that happen in the first real test of their relationship, but it wasn't until late into Monday night, just over twelve hours before Blair was due on to the platform to deliver his speech, that agreement was finally won. And even then there was a hiccup on the morning of the speech. As Blair sought to alert other key people in the Party what to expect (he spoke to Bill Morris of the Transport Union, John Edmonds of the GMB, Clare Short MP and certain members of the Shadow Cabinet), Robin Cook, then the Party's Trade and Industry spokesman, was appalled at what Blair intended to say. He went straight to Prescott's room to try to dissuade him from supporting Blair, and Blair, who was tipped off about what Cook was doing, got straight on the phone to Prescott and demanded that he come immediately to the Leader's suite. It was the only row they had, but Prescott came while Cook fulminated.

In fact the passage in the speech which dealt with the constitution was very brief, and Clause IV was not even mentioned. But Campbell took one other safeguard to ensure that hostile elements weren't tipped off about the speech in advance. There were no embargoed copies handed to the newspaper journalists, and the television reporters were given copies with the last three pages missing. It was said this was because the speech had been finished late. That was true, but that wasn't the reason. The key passage read:

> It is time we had a clear up-to-date statement of the objects and objectives of our Party. John Prescott and I, as Leader and Deputy Leader, will propose such a statement to the NEC. Let it then be open to debate in the coming months. I want the whole Party involved. I know the whole Party will welcome that debate. And if it is accepted then let it become the objects of our Party for the next election and take its place in our constitution for the next century.[8]

It was a remarkable speech, given a thunderous ovation. Later, George Robertson, the wry Shadow Scottish Secretary, said ten minutes after Blair had sat down the only noise that could be heard outside the hall was the sound of pennies dropping. Before he had spoken, Blair and Campbell had gone through all eventualities. They had decided what to do if there was booing; Blair had even asked what the chances were that his leadership would be dead in the water by 10 o'clock that night. 'Oh, about a 5 per cent chance,' said Campbell helpfully. But Blair, for all the tension and nervous energy that had been expended in advance of the speech, was unmoved afterwards. He just wanted to get on and carry on the selling job. He neither seemed pleased with himself nor worried. It had been done.

The following day the press was extraordinary. Every paper sang Blair's praises as a man of vision and of depth and of courage. And so they went on. But two days later, through lax Party management and inexperience, Blair suffered a defeat in which the same conference that had cheered him to the chandeliers and gilded ceiling in the Empress Ballroom of the Winter Gardens on Tuesday, voted to keep Clause IV on Thursday. There was a strong suspicion in the Blair camp that the outcome of the vote was Robin Cook's revenge. Cook had chaired that particular session of the conference, and eyebrows were raised at the speakers he chose to come to the rostrum. There was a definite tilt in favour of those who favoured retaining Clause IV, and much muttering about Cook could be heard afterwards. But it didn't take Cook's delphic antics to send Blair the message. It could be seen in the 1994 NEC results, there was a hint of it in the Shadow Cabinet elections too: the Modernisers were not going to have it all their own way. There was a schizophrenia in the mind of many Labour activists that while they voted for Blair because they knew he stood a better chance than anyone else of winning the next election for Labour, they didn't actually like his approach to policy.

As Blair set about working out what should replace Clause IV, tying in Prescott to whatever decisions were made was an essential pre-condition to success. But following the open hostility shown at the Party conference towards Blair's plans to tinker with the constitution by some members of the Shadow Cabinet (opposition that was partly born of pique at not having been consulted, and partly ideological), Blair took care to consult widely with key Shadow Cabinet and union leaders before drawing up his draft proposals.

The new draft wording in the consultation document of 30.11.94 showed the radical change in thinking with its acceptance of 'a competitive market economy with a strong individual and wealth generating base'. The document accepted that services such as the NHS and schools had to remain in the public sector, but went on to say: 'It does not follow that common ownership is our reflex answer to all market failures.' Instead Blair wanted tighter control of the privatised monopolies that were in state control. The Blair/Prescott document also marked a shift in the standard socialist definition of equality as understood by traditional Labour supporters. While they argued that Labour needed to maintain its commitment to equality of opportunity, and recognised the need to reduce the material inequalities between rich and poor, they go on to write: 'We do not believe in absolute arithmetic equality.'

But the extent to which the left remained suspicious of both Blair's agenda and accumulation of power became evident immediately after his election as leader when a broadside was fired by the mainstream left-wing newspaper *Tribune* at suggestions that Blair now had 'presidential' powers:

> This dangerous nonsense will have to be resisted by the left at Westminster and in Trade Unions. Once more – as so often in the past – the left will be the guardian of democracy within the Labour Party. Tony Blair has become the leader not because of untrammelled enthusiasm among the Party activists . . . but because the Labour Party and the trade unions are groaning under the yoke of an extreme Conservative Party.[9]

And it was to that audience that the Labour MP Peter Hain was playing when he wrote a damning article in the *New Statesman* (which was picked up by all the other newspapers) in which he alleged that the modernisation of the Party was destroying the activist base and creating 'an empty shell of a Party'. The article may have had more to do with the Neath MP's attempts to secure a place on the Party's National Executive (which he failed to do), but his criticisms of what a Labour Party cast in Tony Blair's image would be like struck a chord with many Party workers.

It is fashionable to pretend that activists don't matter . . .
Of course activists are wanted at election time to deliver
leaflets or knock on doors in the wet and cold. They are
also urged to respond to endless phone calls for credit card
donations. But the rest of the year they are expected to put
up and shut up. So why join the Party at all? It is hardly
surprising that activity rates have fallen sharply, that branch
meetings are badly attended and general committees barely
quorate.[10]

Much the same point was made in a study of what sort of person becomes a Labour activist. In the book *Labour's Grass Roots*,
the authors conclude,

There are those in the Labour Party who envisage a
reduced role for both members and activists. They may
concede that members help to provide funds, and give the
Party a sense of political legitimacy. But there is a suspicion
that members are also a nuisance because they intrude into
the process of political packaging.[11]

There was no evidence at the 1994 Labour Party conference
that that process had taken hold. The motions submitted for discussion by the activists in the constituencies clung to familiar
themes like soaking the rich, and rejecting any move towards
ending the principle of universality in welfare payments. The
many thousands of traditionalists who held office at all levels of
the Labour Party were making clear that they weren't writing
Blair a blank cheque. But in his desire to rewrite Clause IV Blair
wanted to do something else, and that was to remove an inherent tension between the activists and the Leader.

No Labour Leader had ever believed that Clause IV could be
implemented wholesale – even Sidney Webb, writing a year after
the constitution was adopted, expressed the view that the Clause
was not prescriptive and could be adopted flexibly – but because

it stood there unchanged, the activists were forever able to beat their breasts and accuse the leadership of having betrayed the Party's principles. By removing the old Clause IV, Blair wanted to remove a source of tension that had dogged all Labour Leaders. But it was certainly true that Blair wanted to widen the membership base of the Labour Party so that it would no longer belong to the activists. Their political outlook was invariably to the left of the leadership, and certainly to the left of most voters, even though they were the Party's stolid foot-soldiers in election after election.

From the occasion when Blair was mauled at a public meeting he had attended with Dennis Skinner in Sedgefield just after he had been elected an MP, the Labour Leader became aware of what he called a 'culture of cowardice' that ran through parts of the Labour movement. By that he meant those people who preferred opposition, because it meant taking no difficult decisions.

> Someone knocks on Dennis Skinner's door and says 'Sign this petition', and Dennis will always sign it. That's not bravery. Being brave is being able to say no to people. Being brave is standing up for what you believe in, even if it makes enemies or brings you into conflict with other parts of the Party.[12]

Blair is an old-fashioned disciplinarian. At one Shadow Cabinet meeting he told those present that if any one of them got into trouble with the press, they must take responsibility themselves. The 'Bambi' tag that some had attempted to hang round his neck was soon dispensed with. He doesn't shout and rail in the Kinnock manner, but the long, loose leash that John Smith allowed members of his Shadow Cabinet went. When days after Blair became Leader and Ann Taylor discussed how they would present her new education policy document, Blair, according to one adviser present, picked it apart. When Joan Lestor presented to Blair her policy document on the family, Blair called for it to be completely rewritten. And on the day that the

IRA announced their ceasefire, Kevin McNamara, the Party's Northern Ireland spokesman, beetled into the BBC's Humberside studio to give his reaction, only to be told by the Leader's office that he was not permitted to speak, and that any reaction to the ceasefire would come from Blair himself. It was a humiliating rebuff to McNamara. He had already got through to *The World At One* studio and the presenter was about to start the interview when the gagging order from the Labour Leader's office was delivered.

Blair in the first two months of his leadership moved the Labour Party from being an organisation which forever seemed to be reacting to a world that was moving faster than it could keep pace with, to a Party that sought to lead public opinion. In his determination to fight the Clause IV battle, Blair showed himself to be something of a gambler and risk-taker. But the decision on where Tony and Cherie Blair would send their eldest son to secondary school was to reveal in Blair a streak of naïvety about his party matched by a stubbornness that some of those closest to him found exasperating. Indeed, this one decision was to cause much more angst and adverse comment than any other political decision that he had taken.

During the Labour leadership contest, the *Daily Mail* had revealed that among the many schools that the Blairs were looking at to send their son Euan was the Oratory in Fulham. It made ripples not waves when it was disclosed that their preferred choice of school was outside their own borough of Islington, and it raised eyebrows that it was an 'opt out' school, in other words one that had opted out of local authority control. The Blairs had first thought about sending him to this highly regarded Catholic school when Blair was Shadow Home Secretary. He and his wife had assessed that it would perhaps lead to a paragraph being written about it in the *Guardian*. But when the *Daily Mail* went back to the story a few months after Blair became Leader, and confirmed that Euan had been offered and had accepted a place at the school, the heavens opened.

Just before this happened the Blairs were entertaining Tom

Sawyer and his wife to dinner with some other guests when the subject of schools came up. According to one of those present the Blairs were aghast when the Sawyers said quite casually that they had sent their children to the local comprehensive school near where they lived in Lewisham. The story might have grown in the telling, but the Blairs were apparently asking the sort of incredulous questions about life in an inner city 'comp' that used to face nineteenth-century explorers when they came back from overseas with tales of the strange things that the natives did in the jungle. Sawyer, who is from an ordinary working-class background and had thought it hitherto an unremarkable decision that he and his wife had taken concerning their children's education, reasoned that it was a peculiarly middle-class trait, firstly, to talk endlessly about schools and schooling, and secondly, to feel the need to justify why the local school was not quite good enough.

The Oratory school in West London, about eight miles from where the Blairs live, had been one of the first to take advantage of opting out of local authority control when the Conservatives introduced their education reforms aimed at widening choice for parents. But Labour policy had been to oppose the Government, believing that the flowering of grant maintained schools would be a Trojan horse to assist the return of selective education. Those schools that opted to sever their links with the local education authority and receive their funding directly from government received preferential treatment, with more money to spend on books and school fabric. Labour believed the Government were seeking to bribe parents into voting for their children's school to opt out. They also thought it was part and parcel of a long-standing government plan to centralise control and reduce further the powers enjoyed by town halls. Local Labour Party branches up and down the country had linked up with the main teaching unions to fight nearly every proposal to move a school out of local authority control.

Ordinary party members, and not just the activists, felt they had had the rug pulled from underneath them by none other than their Leader. There was great anger at Westminster and outside. The reservoir of goodwill that existed towards Blair when he became Leader was draining away fast; many of his supporters found the decision quite inexplicable. For the first time there were serious tensions within the Leader's office. Alastair Campbell had warned Blair how the press would treat the subject, even down to the type of screaming headlines that would confront him. But Blair was not to be put off. He told friends that he would not have been able to live with himself if he had taken a decision affecting his son's education merely out of political expediency. But Campbell was furious, both that his professional advice had been ignored and that Blair was sending his son to an opt out school. What was required in news management terms seemed to him to be the defence of the indefensible, and he told Blair that he wanted nothing to do with handling the press on this issue. Instead it was left to David Hill, then Labour's Director of Communications at Walworth Road and one of Campbell's juniors, Tim Allan, to put the best possible gloss on the decision.

The day the *Daily Mail* article appeared, Blair's office rang the newspaper offering an article of reply by the Opposition Leader putting his side of the case. The office faxed the piece over, but it never ran. When Blair's office rang to find out why, the *Mail* said they had sent it too late and missed the copy deadline. Eventually a piece appeared a few days later in the *Sunday Mirror*, but that had the effect, so long afterwards, of looking defensive, particularly as it was in a Labour supporting paper.

The Labour Party Press Office tried to argue that it was no different from someone receiving treatment at a Trust hospital. Labour had vigorously argued against the Government's health service reforms, but had never said that patients should boycott them and insist on going to a non-trust hospital. They also insisted that the school was still a state school, that entrance was not based on an examination, and that his Islington junior school was a 'feeder' school for the Oratory. More persuasive was the argument that many of Euan's friends were going to the school and it was where he wanted to go.

The story ran for days and Blair seemed genuinely affronted that he should be tackled on the subject when he appeared on the normally cosy daytime television show, *Good Morning with Anne and Nick*. He said he hoped his choice of school was not going to be made 'a political football', and went on to add that he would not make a choice 'on the basis of what is the politically correct thing to do. I want to do it on the basis of what is the right school for him. We would have sent him to this school whether it was grant maintained or not'.[13]

But a football it had become. Graham Lane, the Labour Education Chairman of the Association of Metropolitan Authorities, questioned why it had been necessary for the Blairs to send their son to a school so far away: 'I understand there are several good schools of this type nearer to where he lives. I do not understand why someone would want to send his child across 4 London Boroughs.'[14] The General Secretary of the National Union of Teachers, Doug McAvoy, pointed out that the Oratory had also opted out of the national system of fixing teachers' pay and conditions of service.

Blair throughout his political career had sought to protect his family from the media glare, but his eldest son had taken centrestage. Accusations of hypocrisy abounded from the Conservative benches and elsewhere. John Major did not criticise Blair directly, but he did not need to. He limited himself to saying that it was sad that people who were taking advantage of the increased opportunities offered by the Government were at the same time trying to deny them to millions of others.

It was said of Tony Blair that when he got up in the morning he wouldn't even tie his shoe laces without calculating what the political consequences would be. So how had someone so conscious of his media image found himself in this position? Blair's friends say that he genuinely did not believe that he had been acting hypocritically. But they also pointed to something else that Sawyer witnessed when he dined with the Blairs: middleclass guilt. According to close friends the Blairs felt that with their stretched lifestyles and careers, they were not able to spend as much time helping their children with the homework and the like as they would have wanted. So, the explanation goes, rather than doing nothing they assuaged their guilt by sending their children to schools where class sizes were that bit smaller, discipline was that bit stricter and teaching standards were that touch higher. Whatever their own shortcomings as parents, in carefully selecting a school for their children, they contented themselves that they were still doing their best for them – even though that meant running the gauntlet of the press who accused the couple of hypocrisy, while the Party shouted 'betrayal'.

But there was an unintended spin-off from this episode, which was picked up by that most disaffected of Thatcherites, Alastair McAlpine. As he sat reviewing the papers one weekend on *Breakfast with Frost*, the *Mail on Sunday* had splashed with a story about some aspect of the furore surrounding the Blairs and the choice of school. McAlpine, when asked for a comment, said he thought it would send thousands more disillusioned middle-class Tory voters over to Labour as this would convince them more than any policy document could ever do that Blair was just like them. For every Labour supporter who was disgusted, there seemed to be a Conservative who was quietly impressed.

David Blunkett, who was by then Education Spokesman, was left to pick up the pieces. He had to try to smooth things over in the Labour Party where the sense of anger and disappointment was most acute; Blunkett also had the thankless task of seeking to explain the mismatch on television and radio between the actions of the Leader and Labour Party policy as it then stood. Only a week before the row had blown up Blunkett had told the Commons that Labour was opposed to grant maintained schools. That position was not going to last. A blond haired, Manchester United-supporting eleven-year-old named Euan Blair had been responsible for a significant shift in Labour Party policy. But Blunkett, having come to the rescue of his Leader, was to find himself embroiled in a separate education row at the end of 1994 that seemed to set off a chain reaction of mishaps.

CHAPTER 13

A New Clause

'For what has one profited if they shall gain the whole world and
lose their own soul?'

Matthew 16.26

Tony Blair's Press Secretary, Alastair Campbell, as befits a Scot
(or at least an Englishman with Scottish ancestors) traditionally
celebrates Hogmanay by piping in the New Year. His bagpipes
have graced the newsrooms where he has worked and his New
Year parties were never complete without a quick blast. But the
only blasting that was taking place on New Year's Eve, 1994, was
down a telephone line as Campbell and David Hill sought to
track down David Blunkett to find out what it was that he had
said to the *Sunday Times* that allowed them to run a story in their
New Year edition saying that Labour was considering imposing
VAT on school fees paid by parents. Campbell was on a train,
returning from watching a football match at Burnley, with a
mobile phone whose batteries were running flat, while Hill had
just returned from ten days in St Petersburg.

The report was highly damaging to Labour's attempts to portray itself as the Party of middle-class aspiration as well as of the
dispossessed, with its suggestion that the Party wanted to punish
those parents who had decided to send their children to private
schools by adding 17.5 per cent to the fees. In addition, the closer
the idea was looked at, the more it smacked of the politics of
envy, because for such a controversial measure it would have
raised a comparatively paltry amount for the Treasury (about
£100 million). And in terms of practical politics, it seemed to fly
in the face of Labour's greatest campaigning success after fifteen

years in Opposition that had taken place only a month earlier under the direction of Gordon Brown: the defeat of the Government over the imposition of the higher rate of VAT on heating and fuel. Conservatives seized on the school fees story as proof that Labour, too, had its own agenda for extending the scope of VAT. But try as they might to nip this story in the bud, Hill and Campbell could not raise Blunkett, which left them unable to deny the story to other news organisations; they had no idea what Blunkett had said or where he was.

As they considered the various options that New Year's Eve, they recognised that many on the left would have approved of such an idea. It might have discouraged many of those articulate middle-class parents from shunning the state system, and instead, devote their considerable energies to driving up standards in the local comprehensive. And the thought flickered through their minds that Blunkett, keen to re-establish his credentials with the left after he had baled his Leader out over the Oratory, could have been tempted by such a policy.

But where Blair's Press Secretary and the Labour Party's then Director of Communications failed, one of the BBC's political correspondents, Nicholas Jones, succeeded. Early on Sunday morning, Blunkett gave Jones a telephone interview which ran on the morning bulletins. In it the Education Spokesman did not deny that it was a possibility that VAT could be put on school fees. 'I'm ruling nothing out at this stage because we want to look at the two issues of charitable status and VAT on private school fees together so that we can see what would be fairest.'[1]

As they say in newsrooms, the story had grown legs, and was up and running. By now though, Gordon Brown and Tony Blair had become embroiled, as well as Campbell, Hill and Blunkett, all anxious to cut the story off at its knees. Brown particularly was incensed that Blunkett had gone well beyond his brief to talk about an area that was none of his business, namely taxation policy. There was a round of telephone calls on how to sort out the mess. It was decided that Blunkett should go on Radio 4's *The World This Weekend* that lunchtime to set the record straight.

The line was agreed that Blunkett would say that while policy was being formulated all options were open, but that it was unlikely that VAT would be put on school fees.

While Blunkett was making his way to the studio, David Hill, who had also been given his instructions, rang the BBC and the Press Association to issue a statement on behalf of the Labour Party. It said quite unequivocally that the Labour Party had ruled out extending the scope of VAT to school fees. This was not communicated to Blunkett and the first he learnt of it was when he was sitting in front of the microphone listening to the news bulletin which preceded his interview. Not surprisingly, Blunkett was at his most elliptical during the interview, uncertain whether the BBC had got its facts wrong in the news bulletin or whether the policy had changed in the hour and a half since he had spoken to Tony Blair. It was the latter, but his tone suggested that he was not prepared to take the rap for it: 'The Shadow Chancellor and the Leader of the Party think it is helpful to rule out that possibility in order to avoid confusion, and I accept that decision.'[2]

But that was not the end of it. Later that afternoon several journalists were briefed by a senior Labour figure to the effect that the Economic Commission (which draws up policy), under Gordon Brown's chairmanship, had ruled out that option the previous November, but no-one had told Blunkett. The sheer incompetence of having kept the Party's Education Spokesman uninformed was gleefully picked up by all the newspapers the following day. However, Brown would later deny this to be true and it was suggested by sources close to the Shadow Chancellor that the briefing had been given in order to make Brown look as though he was the villain of the piece for not having told Blunkett what was going on.

It was still January the first, and 1995 had got off on the wrong foot. This episode was to be a taste of what was to come in the following couple of weeks. Whatever the issue, there was an impression that while one senior figure nudged policy in one direction, another was always on hand to shift it in another. Over constitutional reform, Jack Straw seemed to be saying one thing, and John Prescott something quite different. At a news conference to set out Labour's priorities for the forthcoming parliamentary session, Blair was tackled on whether Labour would renationalise the railways. The previous October at Labour's annual conference, Frank Dobson, the then Transport Spokesman, had been clear: 'The next Labour Government will reverse the break up and privatisation of the railways.' But early in 1995 Blair was boxing much more cautiously, giving an answer that was interpreted as a U turn: 'I am not going to get into a situation where I am declaring that the Labour Government is going to commit sums of money to renationalisation several years down the line . . . I am not about to start spraying commitments as to what we are going to do.'[3] But the next weekend Blair's Press Secretary, Alastair Campbell, steered the policy in another direction telling the *Observer*'s political editor, Anthony Bevins, that John Prescott was looking at ways of pledging to take the railways back into public ownership.

Press secretaries traditionally lurk in the shadows, anxious to stay out of the limelight. They prefer to see themselves referred to as 'reliable sources' rather than by their name, but the morning the *Observer* story appeared, Campbell was a guest on *Frost on Sunday*, and was busy standing up the story that he had given to Bevins a day or so earlier. Campbell had been an extremely high-profile journalist, but when he crossed the bridge to work for Blair, most thought his days of media appearances were over. There was resentment within the Shadow Cabinet that a non-elected servant of the Party was appearing on television and radio to do the job that elected politicians thought was rightly theirs. Campbell also never left his master's side when the cameras were around. It became the butt of jokes in Labour Party circles. On one news bulletin when the Opposition Leader and Campbell were seen walking together one of Blair's staff turned to another and said, 'Who's that bloke you keep seeing alongside Alastair Campbell?'

The policy hiccups were worrying in themselves, for they

revealed a number of weaknesses in the Labour operation. But Blair thought they had a wider significance. At the end of the first week in January Blair called his senior people together for a crisis meeting. Among those present were John Prescott, Tom Sawyer, Anji Hunter, Alastair Campbell and staff who would later play a key role in the Clause IV campaign, like Sally Morgan and Margaret McDonough. One said Blair was panicky. 'He had gone to Prague, but was on the phone to us all the time. And when he came back he was upset at the raggedness of the operation. That first meeting in January had a real feel of panic about it.'[4] The national press had been given ammunition, and were firing it. But what particularly worried Blair was the extent to which this was impinging upon his campaign to rewrite Clause IV. What can loosely be called the 'activist press' had also grown restive. Papers like the *Guardian* and magazines such as the *New Statesman* and *Tribune* were brimming with hostility. 'If we are not careful,' Blair told those in his room, 'we are going to lose this thing. What's required is a massive reaching out to the Party.'

The anti-Clause IV campaign was gathering support in the constituencies, and among ordinary members. The argument that what Blair had embarked upon was an idiotic diversion, was being made with increasing force by his opponents. Early in January, Blair had been scheduled to go to Brussels to make a high-profile speech and meet senior businessmen from Europe's multi-nationals. The speech was to come the day after a major news conference at which Blair had set out Labour's campaigning priorities for the year. The aim had been to show Labour's unity of purpose; instead, as Blair prepared to leave for Brussels, one of his press officers came in to alert him to an advertisement that had been taken out on the front page of the following morning's *Guardian*. Its headline read: 'Labour MEPs Defend Clause IV'. Beneath it read:

Common ownership has been a key part of Labour's pro-gramme to give ordinary people a decent future. With

Britain and much of the world in crisis, this is no time to jettison this powerful weapon for social and economic justice. We are opposed to privatisation and believe that common ownership should remain part of Labour's core beliefs and values.[5]

The initial reaction in Blair's office was one of fury. The advertisement claimed the support of over half of Labour's MEPs. It was calculated to do maximum damage to the leadership. It completely overshadowed Blair's Brussels speech that was coming up, and buried reports about Labour's campaigning aims for the year ahead. But it also presented Blair with an opportunity. In the pantheon of Labour politics none is less popular than the MEP. Elected by a small percentage of voters to do a job that most see as worthless and irrelevant, the MEP is seen as leading an expenses-bloated lifestyle, eating in Brussels' best hostelries and inns, junketing round the world and deciding only upon whether bananas ought to be straight or curved. Class heroes they are not to Labour's rank and file.

When Blair met them the day after the advertisement had appeared, it had been decided, in the words of one of his advisers, 'to kick some ass'. At a private meeting of Labour's sixty-two MEPs he told them first that they had been guilty of 'gross discourtesy'. They had blunted Labour's New Year offensive, and he then accused them of being a bunch of 'infantile incompetents'.[6] When an old friend of Blair's, David Hallam, the MEP for Hereford and Shropshire, stood up and said that Labour should commit itself to renationalising the public utilities, the Labour Leader told him to 'grow up'. Throughout these exchanges, Alastair Campbell was running in and out of the room, like a prefect reporting back on the thrashing that the headmaster was giving to the naughty fourth-formers, feeding titbits to the press about the latest admonishment that Blair had delivered to his errant flock.

The newspaper reports the following day went some way to making up the ground lost over the previous two weeks, with headlines like 'Bambi bears his fangs' and ' "infantile" MEPs get scolding from Blair'. Someone else who would have similar treatment meted out to her was one of Labour's Foreign Affairs team, Anne Clwyd. She had gone off to Turkey without first having told the Chief Whip of her planned absence. She missed a key vote, and was away from the front-bench for a session of Foreign Office questions. She was sacked by Blair without further ado. Indiscipline was something Blair was not going to tolerate. But not all the problems could be put down to the behaviour of others; there were systemic weaknesses, too. He instructed Jonathan Powell, his Chief of Staff, to look at Labour's 'command and control' structure which had been found badly wanting. Blair told the Shadow Cabinet that front-benchers must watch their public statements much more carefully, and not make 'policy on the hoof'. The Powell review would also result in the establishment of a weekly campaign management meeting chaired by Tony Blair and a daily media and tactics meeting. The carving up of responsibilities among the big three in the Shadow Cabinet saw Robin Cook charged with long-term policymaking, while John Prescott was made responsible for national campaigning. Gordon Brown would be given responsibility for day-to-day strategy, taking charge of a daily meeting which decided media tactics.

Few doubted that Brown had been given the most powerful job, and that quickly aroused jealousies between the rival camps. While Blair individually had got on reasonably well with Robin Cook, John Prescott and, of course Gordon Brown, the relationships between Prescott and Cook, Prescott and Brown, and Brown and Cook, had tended to be fraught, mistrustful and cool. 'Complex' was the only word that one senior Blair aide would use to describe the relationship between the three most senior members of the Shadow Cabinet. Tensions were exacerbated when it looked as though Prescott had been shut out of the day-to-day meeting, and he insisted that his special adviser should also be able to attend the early morning meeting held in Brown's office at 7 Millbank each day.

From the Mandelson days in the 1980s Labour's press operation had consistently outstripped anything offered by Conservative Central Office. With the Tories in government, ministers had at their disposal the weight of the civil service machine and the Government Information Service. That left Central Office dramatically undergeared. At weekends, when newspapers and bulletins were awash with political stories, the Labour Party would be on the phone to journalists and newsdesks non-stop, spinning a line, offering a spokesman, giving background briefings. At Central Office there would be one press officer on duty who would not speak unless he was spoken to, and when he was spoken to he would tend to know nothing about the subject because he was out of the Government loop. But in the Labour Party the problem was the reverse.

The number of press officers, spin doctors and advisers had multiplied, but often these people did not see themselves as working primarily for the Labour Party but for the individual member of the Shadow Cabinet who had appointed them. The result was that too much time was spent briefing, not against the Conservatives, but against each other. Politics may be the stuff of high ideas and lofty ideals, but its practice is often muddied by personal animosity and fragile egos. On one occasion during the 1995 local council elections, a Party Election Broadcast (PEB) had powerfully accused John Major of being a liar. It sparked a huge row, with Blair unhappy that its tone was impossible to reconcile with the 'new' politics that he had spent so much time advocating. The finger of blame was quickly pointed at Joy Johnson, who had shortly beforehand been appointed as the Party's Director of Campaigning and Communications. The Prescott camp were suspicious because she was seen as a Gordon Brown appointee (she had in fact been appointed by the NEC, but it had been Brown who had pushed her candidature); even someone in Blair's camp only half jokingly said of her: 'it's good that Charlie Whelan [Brown's press officer] has got a new assistant'. And as the flak flew one press officer confided in a handful of journalists that Blair had seen the script of the PEB and that it was not their fault that he had 'wobbled' over the broadcast. It was pointed out that he only became unhappy when the press had turned nasty over its contents. The picture painted by a Labour press officer was that Blair was a slightly weak, vain man whose prime concern was what the newspapers were saying about him.

But for all that was going wrong at the start of the year, there were some brilliant recovery operations. One weekend, before the new command and control structure had come into place, John Prescott was to be the lunchtime guest on a new political programme on ITV to be hosted by Jonathan Dimbleby. The rival, *On The Record,* getting wind of this invited Blair on the programme as a 'spoiler' and he duly accepted. When the two men compared their diaries pandemonium broke out. There was a serious and unnecessary risk that the two would diverge on something, and that the evening news programmes and next day's papers would be full of Prescott/Blair split stories. Campbell rang *On The Record* and invented a family event which Blair had to attend which would mean he could only pre-record the interview at around 10.00 a.m. They accepted. At the end of the interview the Blair entourage raced back to Westminster where Prescott had been waiting for them in his office. Campbell had recorded the entire interview on a little Dictaphone, and he played it back to Prescott to ensure that the Deputy Leader did not depart from the text when he gave his live interview later that morning.

The party machine showed itself to be a more effective fighting force when it came to the battle to rewrite Clause IV. At the start of 1995 Blair had grown uneasy at the headway being made by his opponents. On 16 January he called key officials together from his own office and Walworth Road to decide what to do. They hit upon the idea of a nationwide tour, with Blair and Prescott going to speak to ordinary Labour Party members at least once in every region of the country. Mandelson, who had remained semi-hidden during the leadership contest when he was simply referred to as Bobby, was now out in the open as a trusted Blair adviser.

It was Mandelson who persuaded Blair of the need to take the Clause IV campaign out around the country. Blair's office wanted it to be the biggest consultation undertaken in the Party's history. A strategy of sorts was worked out. Anji Hunter drew up the itinerary. While Margaret McDonough was put in charge of the detailed arrangements for each event, Sally Morgan took charge of liaising with the unions. Blair would later tell friends they were the unsung heroes of the Clause IV campaign. Each visit would be accompanied by a regional media onslaught. Local radio stations would be offered a phone-in, the TV station a sit-down interview. The biggest selling newspaper in the region would be granted an 'exclusive' interview, and so it went on. When the tour ended, after two engagements a week for twelve weeks, Blair reckoned that he had spoken to 30,000 party members, many of them people who had only joined when he became Leader.

Blair knew he had to reach out beyond the activists if he was to win a popular mandate for his revised constitution. Success at the special conference to be held at the end of April, delivered by the union barons with their block votes, would have been a pyrrhic victory. It was the outcome the Conservatives forecast and wanted. On 21 February John Major predicted a big victory for Blair saying the Labour Leader was sure to win 'because he will have the support of the unreconstructed trade unions in doing so'.[7] Major had every reason to make the prediction; Blair had every reason to fear it. After all, it had been the constituency section of the Labour Party which voted for the retention of Clause IV at the end of the 1994 Labour Party Conference only two days after Blair had announced his intention to rewrite it.

Blair wanted it to be a genuine and open debate, without rancour. But when Bill Morris, the General Secretary of the Transport Union which is the biggest single affiliate to the Labour Party, had warned that he would not support 'woolly and fudged words' as a replacement for Clause IV, he was to be on the receiving end of a less than fraternal embrace. On the television news that evening Morris stood accused of being 'confused, muddled and pusillanimous', by 'a source close to the Labour Leader'.[8] This was not the way Blair wanted his opponents to be played, and asked Campbell to set up an enquiry to find out who had been responsible. Campbell received blanket denials from everyone he spoke to although he thought it bore the hallmarks of Peter Mandelson. Mandelson denied responsibility, too. Once again stray bullets were being fired, with the leadership unable to discover who was doing the shooting. Morris would later complain about creeping intolerance in the Party. 'We have got to be trampled, crushed, humiliated. All this week I have been waiting for the men in white coats to take me away because I was diagnosed as muddled and confused.'[9]

The first stop on the Clause IV roadshow would be Gateshead on 26 January. But the day before Blair left to travel to the North East there were two important pieces of business to transact. First was a meeting of the NEC which came out with a recommendation that local parties should ballot their members on whether to accept a new Clause IV, rather than leaving it to the activists on the General Management Committee to decide. It would later prove to be one of the key decisions of the campaign. The second was a speech that would give Blair's campaign a significant political boost. The intervention of Robin Cook was timely. Cook, one of Labour's most senior left-wingers, and certainly the most articulate, had originally set his face against change, dismissing attempts to rewrite Clause IV as a silly irrelevance. But now he was calling on the left to embrace a new statement of aims 'that is a fuller, richer statement of our ideology . . . The objective is not to drop common ownership, but to focus it on the circumstances where it is appropriate.'[10]

As Blair set out on the start of his roadshow he made a declaration that he would not be satisfied unless he won a majority in the constituency section of the electoral college. Part of the reason that he felt able to say that was because he knew that many constituencies would ballot after the lead given by the previous day's National Executive, but another part of him wanted to up the ante – to focus the minds of those who were considering voting against him. Blair's enduring faith (from when he first entered the Labour Party nearly twenty years earlier) that the membership was of a different political hue to the activists was to be fully tested. As they travelled to Gateshead for the first meeting with ordinary members, what none of his entourage knew was whether they were going to be cheered and applauded, or torn limb from limb.

In the event, Blair got a warm reception. The questions he was asked were the questions that came up again and again across Britain. The hostile questions came in three varieties. The first was: why do it when no-one ever discussed Clause IV on the doorstep? To that question Blair would retort, 'But why aren't we raising our values and what we stand for on the doorstep? We're not raising Clause IV because it is no longer relevant to where we are and what we stand for. We should be raising what we stand for, and we'll be able to when we have a new statement.' The second question was a variation on the first. Many expressed the view that with Labour enjoying thirty point poll leads over the Tories, to embark on a divisive internal party battle was misguided. To that, Blair would pause, and then launch into a lecture about the dangers of complacency. 'It sends a shiver down my spine,' he would say, 'whenever I hear people say we're so far in front we don't need to do any more.' He would then lecture his audience on the poll lead that Labour had when the poll tax was at its most unpopular, and how quickly that evaporated. The final charge that he had to face was that he was asking the Party to give up socialism. It would be wrong to say these events were stage-managed, although it was surprising how that question always seemed to come up at the end, and gave Blair the chance to launch into a summing up. He told the Party that it must be clear about what it meant by socialism. If it meant a simple economic doctrine requiring a command economy with massive nationalisation, then he agreed that socialism was dead. But then he would talk about community, solidarity, and that there was more to society than 'I'.

Like any well-structured piece of drama, the battle to rewrite Clause IV even came with its own comic scene to alleviate the tension. The *dramatis personae* were the so-called Labour 'luvvies'. They had their heyday in the Kinnock era, but were in danger of falling into disuse by the Party under Blair. He saw no particular need for their big kisses on both cheeks. But Blair had accepted an invitation to the home of Ken and Barbara Follett. They, more than any two people, symbolised the glitzy Labour luvvies: him the millionaire thriller writer, with the £160,000 Bentley and the Cheyne Walk home in Chelsea; her the top image consultant who made her money from telling MPs what clothes to wear and what make-up to apply. In Kinnock's day they adorned all the big gatherings. Luvvies were courted and adored, lending the drab business of politics some showbiz lustre. The deal seemed to be that where Kinnock got glamour, the luvvies got *gravitas*. But when the Blairs arrived at the Folletts' home by the Thames, the *paparazzi* were camped out on the pavement, flashbulbs popping. This was not the image Blair wanted to project, and he let his disquiet be known.

Whether by coincidence or not, soon afterwards the *Sunday Times* ran a story indicating that Labour's celebrity supporters were turning against Blair. It quoted the film maker Ken Loach, actress Juliet Stevenson and a host of others all expressing their disillusionment with the rightward drift of Blair's leadership.[11] That weekend the leadership was at the Party's Young Labour conference in Brighton, and it was made clear that Blair was not overly concerned. Campbell told reporters that Blair was not keen on having the luvvies playing a role in the Party. Follett, who had marshalled Labour's celebrity supporters at the last election, asked to see Blair. They met. The author wanted a public reconciliation, but according to a source close to Blair, 'Follett was told to go and get stuffed'. Soon afterwards Follett resigned from the 1000 Club, an organisation where membership is only conferred on those who donate a thousand pounds or more towards Labour Party funds.

It was a trivial spat in itself but with Blair seeking to win over the ordinary members, the calculation in his office was that this would go down a treat. But as Blair scurried around the country reaching out to the rank and file, Campbell was trying to get Blair to sit down with a pen and a piece of paper to marshal his thoughts into a form of words. Various speeches were signalled by Blair's office as being 'significant' in that they contained some clue as to what the new Clause IV would feel like, but no draft had been formally written. The cut-off point for deciding the new form of words would be 13 March 1995, the date the NEC met to finalise its recommendation to the special conference. Sufficient time had to be given to the constituencies for them to ballot their members.

In the preceding weeks there was a series of drafting sessions involving a revolving cast of senior characters in the Party, each chipping in with his or her own favourite theme or idea. By 8 March there was a new draft that had been the result of extensive consultation, but it was shredded. According to one source, it said that Labour would work as happily with employers' organisations (ie the CBI and the Institute of Directors) as it would with the unions. This was a piece of modernisation too far, and the line was scrubbed. But the draft seemed to Blair to be likely to maximise opposition in the Party without inspiring. The biggest political battle would be over full employment, with Prescott wanting a clear commitment that would be compatible with the position he had adopted during the leadership contest. The big unions too, wanted an unambiguous statement about Labour's stance on full employment and a minimum wage but they were to get neither.

But before the NEC meeting Blair and his team travelled to Inverness for the Scottish Labour conference. It was a nervy time for the Labour Leader, because the smart money seemed to be riding on the conference voting to retain Clause IV. Blair was worried this would have a domino effect within the Party, leading others to follow the example set by the Scots. According to one of those travelling with him he was agitated and irritable. Though he often looked as though he played at politics as effortlessly as David Gower used to square-cut to the boundary, in private Blair was more like Linford Christie in the way he would concentrate and focus on the task in hand. The morning of his speech, as photographers and camera crews waited for him to emerge, Blair, Anji Hunter and Alastair Campbell had slipped out from a side door to go to a house just outside Inverness that belonged to an old friend of Blair's to write the definitive version.

In fact the Scottish Labour Party backed Blair, and that weekend he returned to London. He was to have one final meeting with John Prescott that Sunday evening before the final wording was put to the National Executive. While Prescott and Blair sat in Islington, Jonathan Powell and Sally Morgan were in the Commons ringing round union leaders and other members of the NEC to give them a detailed run-down and explanation of what the new clause said. The following day the NEC voted overwhelmingly to recommend the new clause to the special conference. It read:

1. *The Labour Party is a democratic socialist party. It believes that by the strength of our common endeavour, we achieve more than we achieve alone, so as to create for each of us the means to realise our true potential and for all of us a community in which power, wealth and opportunity, are in the hands of the many not the few, where the rights we enjoy reflect the duties we owe, and where we live together, freely, in a spirit of solidarity, tolerance and respect.*
2. *To these ends we work for:*
*   *A dynamic economy, serving the public interest in which the enterprise of the market and the rigour of competition are joined with the forces of partnership and co-operation to produce the wealth the nation needs and the opportunity for all to work and*

prosper, with a thriving private sector and high quality public services, where those undertakings essential to the common good are either owned by the public or accountable to them;

* *A just society, which judges its strength by the condition of the weak as much as the strong, provides security against fear, and justice at work; which nurtures families, promotes equality of opportunity and delivers people from the tyranny of poverty, prejudice and the abuse of power;*

* *An open democracy, in which government is held to account by the people; decisions are taken as far as practicable by the communities they affect; and where fundamental human rights are guaranteed;*

* *A healthy environment, which we protect, enhance and hold in trust for future generations.*

3. Labour is committed to the defence and security of the British people, and to co-operating in European institutions, the United Nations, the Commonwealth and other international bodies to secure peace, freedom, democracy, economic security and environmental protection for all.

4. Labour will work in pursuit of these aims with trade unions, co-operative societies and other affiliated organisations, and also with voluntary organisations, consumer groups and other representative bodies.

5. On the basis of these principles, Labour seeks the trust of the people to govern.[12]

There was no doubt that this marked a radical break with Sidney Webb's formulation. But it did not win universal acclaim. Some parodied it as being no different from the kind of 'mission statements' that were the stock in trade of American hamburger chains and similar organisations ('we undertake to make the finest possible hamburgers in an environment friendly to our staff and our customers according to the best culinary principles . . .' etc). Others said the new wording would endure the test of time for the sole reason that it was so anodyne there was nothing that any fair-minded person could really take exception to. And for those who were hoping for fiery poetry to inflame the senses, there was disappointment.

There was bitter disappointment too, on the left of the Party that the nearest the new clause came to endorsing full employment was that phrase 'the opportunity for all to work and prosper'. It had nothing to say about the minimum wage. When Blair later wrote about his position on a minimum wage and full employment, he said: 'They must be implemented in practical and sensible ways, not chanted like some mantra designed to come true simply by the amount of repetition.'[13] But the talk of community, solidarity, duty and partnership was consistent with the Christian socialist ideas that Blair had encountered when he had been a dissatisfied undergraduate at Oxford. By the time the new clause had been adopted there was little doubt that Blair would win, but it was the scale of victory that remained unknown.

Just before Easter the leadership had suffered a set-back when Unison, which had through its block vote 11 per cent of the total, announced at the special conference that it would be against the new Clause IV. The voting arrangements gave the unions 70 per cent of the total vote and the constituency parties 30 per cent. Unison had not balloted its members, and the decision was taken by the Political Committee which was made up of around 50 activists. Unison, which draws its membership from low-paid public sector workers, had been one of the organisations pushing hardest for a commitment to a minimum wage. The following week though, there would be an important confrontation between old and new Labour when the Assistant General Secretary, Rodney Bickerstaffe, went to see Blair. According to Blair's office Bickerstaffe had come to deal. They say he wanted the nod from Blair that Labour would back a £4.05 minimum wage, and in return Bickerstaffe said he would do what he could to persuade the Unison delegation to change its position. Blair was having none of it. Bickerstaffe, who disputed the account given of the meeting, was sent away empty handed, and he would later deliver an amusing, but bitter, speech at the special conference in which he argued that he was being treated as the sacrificial lamb to be taken out and slaughtered because his union had rejected change.

As the conference drew near the results that were flowing in from the constituencies strengthened Blair's hand against the die-hard unions that had refused to ballot. Over 500 constituency Labour parties in Britain balloted their members. Only three voted to retain the old Clause IV; everyone else opted for the revised wording. This was a vindication beyond Blair's wildest dreams of his views about how to bring the ordinary members closer to the leadership. They had fallen in behind a political agenda that owed nothing to the left-wing totems of yesteryear. But these results had sharpened the battle considerably between the modernisers and the union bosses who did not ballot. They stood accused of being fundamentally undemocratic and out of touch with their membership. After the Clause IV debate that charge would result in a challenge to Bill Morris's leadership of the Transport Union by Jack Dromey, husband to Labour's Employment Spokeswoman, Harriet Harman. It was seen as another move by the Blair camp to consolidate their already powerful position in the Labour movement, by taking over the biggest union affiliated to the Party. Indeed Dromey made Morris's handling of the consultations (or lack of them) over Clause IV one of the central issues. But there were good reasons to believe that Dromey's challenge did not have Tony Blair's 'blessing', even though Dromey was considered a moderniser, and certainly that was how he presented himself in an ill-tempered campaign. Blair did not want to be seen to be taking sides, but he also did not want to open up another front, and remained studiously impartial.

The one day special conference at Methodist Central Hall in Westminster was where the original Clause IV had been adopted in 1918. Those wanting to retain Clause IV knew they had been out-gunned and out-manoeuvred. But few could have expected that figures like Arthur Scargill, whose mere appearance at a Labour rostrum used to bring certain sections of the audience to its feet, would be roundly booed when he sought to challenge whether changing the constitution was constitutional. One woman from Bristol produced a contorted argument that it was undemocratic that ordinary members had had so much say in determining the outcome because they did so much less for the Party than the activists. She said Labour didn't need extra members because it would make Labour more right-wing. Rodney Bickerstaffe in his speech made a misjudgment when he said that John Smith would never have found it necessary to rewrite Clause IV. 'Tasteless,' said many afterwards. But 'new' Labour had learnt some of the tricks from the old. It seemed that those people who spoke against Blair had been carefully chosen in the knowledge that they would make the worst possible case for retaining Clause IV as it was. Blair would later praise Margaret McDonough for her stage management skills even though he made it clear that he did not wish to be told how she had done it.

Blair made two speeches that afternoon. The first, his formal opening of the debate, set out the case for embracing the new form of words.

I can be the first Leader in our history to stand up and say I will implement Clause IV, part four of our constitution. It is radical. But it is also relevant, sensible and modern. Definitely new. Definitely Labour. For far too long Conservatives have defined what it is to be a democratic socialist. It is time we defined our socialism for ourselves.[14]

He would later make another speech after the result had been declared. Overall, 65.23 per cent voted in favour, while 34.77 per cent voted against. In the constituency section he won the backing of 90 per cent of the local parties; among the unions he won 54.61 per cent support. When Blair returned to the microphone, he toyed with his audience. 'Let me turn now to the name of the Party . . .' He left a long pause before saying with a big smile, 'it stays as it is'. But then there was a 'hand on heart' passage in which he said that while he had not been born into the Labour Party, it was the Party he would die in. He had chosen Labour out of intellectual conviction. It was said to reassure those who still mistrusted him, who believed that Blair had a hidden agenda. But as the celebrations got underway among the modernisers, it was clear that those who had been on the losing end of the argument, or who had given their support only reluctantly, were looking for something more. They wanted Blair to draw a line in the sand and say, 'this far and no further', on the question of reforming Labour's links with the unions.

But in the Blair camp there was something akin to the mood that must have been present among the allied commanders at the end of the Gulf conflict after they had retaken Kuwait. The question was whether to continue the rout and march on to Baghdad. It was decided that there could be no resting on laurels, but no triumphalism either. However, that was not the way it appeared the following Monday after Blair had given interviews to the *Guardian* and *Daily Mirror*. In the *Guardian* interview Blair hinted at further changes to come. Since he had become Leader, Labour had gained another 100,000 members, taking the total membership to over 300,000, and that meant it was time to look at reducing further the unions' block vote at party conferences to 50 per cent. That had been envisaged when the One Member One Vote reforms were passed in 1993, but now Blair was spelling it out quite clearly. But he was straying onto other territory too. He hinted that in future unions would not be able to avoid balloting their members. 'There is no doubt at all that the system needs to be looked at again, especially with the larger unions. Because I do not believe anyone seriously believes that had there been ballots the members would have voted against the change'.[15] He also indicated a strong preference for reforming the membership of the National Executive, a body dominated by the unions, to ensure that a wider cross section of people sat on it.

* * *

The morning those stories appeared, John Prescott was at the BBC studios in Millbank to be interviewed on the phone-in programme, *Westminster On Line*. During one answer he gave a warning again that there must be no triumphalism. 'People have got to remember that we have to move together, even those who are for something and those who are against something. And those in victory should remember that.'[16] That was quickly picked up and interpreted as a warning shot at Tony Blair after his comments in the newspapers. Later that morning Mr Prescott denied that he had meant any such thing in a statement to the Press Association. But he had. It soon leaked out that off-screen Prescott had been incandescent, saying of Blair and his courtiers 'they're taking the piss', and he proceeded to unleash a stream of furious invective against the Party Leader for having apparently reneged on the deal agreed between them over the weekend. By all accounts his mood had brightened none when he confronted Blair and Alastair Campbell about it later that morning. The row was patched up quickly but it served to underline the different political cultures from which each man stemmed.

In the aftermath of a comfortable victory it was easy to forget what a gamble Blair had taken in seeking to rewrite Clause IV. If he had taken the advice of some of the most seasoned Labour Party hands around him, he would either never have embarked upon it, or proceeded with such a degree of caution that victory, when it came, would have been a lot more hollow. But if the Labour Leader had shown himself to be courageous and bold in handling his own Party, many were to arraign him for being caution incarnate in the area of policy making.

When accused of stealing Conservative clothes (as he frequently was), Blair would demur, arguing that there was a 'new' division between left and right, forever seeking to redefine the battle-lines of British politics. The differences that Blair identified were real enough, in terms of economic management, schools, the health service, law and order and the like, but they were not the profound ideological differences that had once separated the two main parties. And on a range of policy issues the first year of Blair's leadership was marked by a certain defensiveness. Policies such as the minimum wage were to be put on a back burner until after an election; the constitutional reform package was watered-down. Economic policy was still undergoing a tactical repositioning, with Labour anxious to prove that it was ready to wear the jacket of fiscal probity. There was concern for consumers, and a redefinition of the role of the Bank of England. On Europe Blair did stick his neck out, saying that Britain would join a single currency providing the convergence criteria, as laid down by the Maastricht Treaty, had been met and on the condition that decisions were economically and not politically driven. But Blair would grow irritated when it was suggested that Labour had no policies. Labour's traditional problem was not that it had too few policies, but that it was positively bulging with policy documents. But key spending decisions were not going to be taken until an election, and that allowed critics to say that Labour was full of good intentions but no commitments. During his first year in office Blair's priorities were to build trust in Labour as an alternative government, and to sell the 'vision thing'.

In 1963, Harold Wilson sold a vision in his famous Scarborough 'White Heat of Technology' speech. His biographer Ben Pimlott noted: 'Wilson, too, made the kind of rousing, modernising speech delegates wanted to hear. Like Blair he announced that Labour was "redefining and restating" its socialism. After the Scarborough speech, everyone spoke of a new dawn, Labour's coming of age, a party of the future.'[17] Labour went on to win the election a year later, bringing to an end thirteen years of unbroken Conservative rule. But it was an extremely close-run thing, Labour scraping home with a majority of just 5. The 1964 election also pitted the brilliant technocrat, Harold Wilson, against an ageing Scottish aristocrat, Sir Alec Douglas Home, who had taken over the Conservative Party Leadership after a broken Macmillan had bowed out. The scandals that were befalling the Conservative Party, put in the context of the prevailing moral climate of the early 1960s, made the problems that beset the Conservative Party's fourth term in office in the 1990s look somewhat less menacing. If the 1964 result was a brilliant result for Labour and Harold Wilson in particular, it could easily be argued that almost equally remarkable was the extraordinary resilience of the Conservative vote in the face of such unpropitious circumstances.

After one of the many regional Clause IV meetings, Blair and his entourage drove from Bournemouth to Salisbury where they were to stay overnight before setting off for Bristol the next day. Over dinner in a private room, and after a few drinks, Blair looked into the abyss and contemplated defeat at the next election. He launched into the sort of humorous monologue that he had performed in reviews at Fettes and Oxford: 'If we lose at the next election, I would become a political phenomenon. I would be sought-after on the international lecture circuit, explaining to wide-eyed wonderment how, through cunning ineptitude I managed to lose a general election having been consistently thirty points ahead in the polls. I could peer over the lectern and tell students of politics why, when the government of the day was making a mess of everything it touched, Labour still lost.' Everyone round the table laughed. Blair's naturally self-confident bearing made it clear that he did not believe this would be his fate, but the thought had obviously crossed his mind more than once.

Glossary

Politics in general and the Labour Party in particular are rich in jargon, factions, and acronyms. A few of the most commonly encountered are:

Campaign Group: The Campaign Group of Labour MPs was founded in 1982, to bring together the more left-wing members of the PLP (qv). After Tony Benn just failed to beat Denis Healey for the Deputy Leadership some MPs felt that the Tribune Group (qv) was no longer left-wing enough to represent their views. Campaign endorsed Margaret Beckett for the Leadership, which was widely regarded as harming rather than helping her chances.

CLP: There is a Constituency Labour Party for each of the 634 Parliamentary constituencies in Great Britain (the Labour Party does not organise in Northern Ireland). Seven members of Labour's NEC are elected at Conference by the CLPs – the so-called Constituency Section. Once the preserve of Bennite left-wingers, the CLP Section has in recent years tended to be made up of people loyal to the Leadership. Blair was elected to the NEC in this section in 1992. In 1994 the CLP Section was elected for the first time by OMOV (qv), and contrary to expectations two left-wingers (Dennis Skinner and Diane Abbott) were successful.

CLPD: The Campaign for Labour Party Democracy was founded in the 1970s with the express aim of making the parliamentary party responsive to the demands of activists. It aimed to do this by requiring all MPs to face reselection by their GMCs (qv), once during each Parliament, by giving activists on GMCs and in trade unions votes in the election of Party Leader and Deputy Leader, and by giving control of the manifesto to Party Conference.

CSJ: The Commission for Social Justice was set up in 1992 by John Smith to review Labour's policies on the Welfare State. Chaired by Sir Gordon Borrie, it was administered by the IPPR (qv) to put it at arm's length from the Party. One of its objectives was to establish a modern approach to welfare that did not saddle the Party with heavy spending commitments. Its final Report was published on 25 October 1994.

Entryism: A tactic employed by some Trotskyist groups which began life as revolutionary socialist organisations, remained committed to revolution and to their own distinct programme and structure, but felt that they could gain greater legitimacy and power by operating covertly within the Labour Party (see Militant). To combat this the Party maintained a list of proscribed organisations, membership of which was incompatible with that of the Labour Party. This proscribed list was scrapped in 1973, leading to a resurgence of the problem. The Labour Party now requires organisations within the Party to be registered and disciplinary problems are referred to the National Constitutional Committee.

Fabians: Founded in 1884, the Fabians brought together left-wing intellectuals who believed in a gradualist rather than a revolutionary approach to socialism, and took their name from a cautious Roman general from the Punic Wars. Now largely seen as a right-wing Labour grouping cum think-tank.

GMB: The General, Municipal and Boilermakers Union is one of the largest unions affiliated to the Labour Party. Its present General Secretary is John Edmonds who is worried about the direction being taken by the Party in recent years, particularly in apparently weakening links with the unions. The Union was, with the T and G, at the centre of opposition to the proposals to introduce OMOV (qv) at the 1993 Party Conference. However, in the North East the GMB has been a bastion for the Right, and the union sponsors Tony Blair.

GMC (GC): The General Management Committee, now the General Committee, of each CLP (qv) is composed of delegates from Party Branches, local trade unions and from socialist societies such as the Fabians, Women's Sections and the Co-op. In the days before OMOV these were the key Party activists who ran the CLP, monitored the work of the MP, elected the delegates and sent resolutions to Party Conference. The GMCs in many areas became more left-wing partly in reaction to what were seen as the failings of the Wilson-Callaghan Government 1974–1979, and sometimes as a consequence of entryism (qv).

GPMU: The Graphical, Media and Paper Union was formed in a merger between the Society of Graphical and Allied Trades (SOGAT) and the National Graphical Association (NGA). Both unions were strong supporters of the closed shop, engaging in a number of disputes, most notably with Rupert Murdoch at *The Times* when the Wapping plant was set up.

IPPR: The Institute of Public Policy Research, left-of-centre think-tank set up to counter the influence of the free-market bodies which had seized the intellectual agenda throughout the 1970s and 1980s. David Miliband, appointed Head of Policy in Tony Blair's office in August 1994, was research fellow there, where he was also secretary to the Commission for Social Justice (qv). Patricia Hewitt, formerly adviser to Neil Kinnock, was deputy director until 1994 and also on the Commission. Prominent Fabian Baroness Blackstone is Chair.

LCC: The Labour Co-ordinating Committee was established in 1978 as a left-wing organisation within the Labour Party. However, it fell out with the hard left over Tony Benn's candidacy against Denis Healey for Deputy Leader in 1982. Thereafter it became the leading 'soft left' activist group within the Party, moved closer to the Kinnock Leadership, and has been seen as enthusiastic for the 'Moderniser' cause.

Militant: One of the splinter groups in direct descent from Leon Trotsky's Fourth International, which in Britain established the Revolutionary Communist Party in the 1940s. The RCP splintered, one fragment becoming the Revolutionary Socialist League which then became Militant in the 1960s. It became one of the most assiduous of the entryist (qv) groups, and achieved notoriety over its running of Liverpool Council. Expulsions began in 1983 but only really gained impetus after Kinnock's impassioned attack on them in his 1985 Conference speech.

MSF: The Manufacturing, Finance and Science Union was formed from the merger of ASTMS (Association of Scientific, Technical, and Managerial Staffs) and AEUW-TASS. Originally led by Communist Ken Gill, he was replaced in 1992 by Roger Lyons, a supporter of John Smith. The union was crucial in Smith's victory on OMOV in 1993, changing its position at a lunchtime meeting, just hours before the vote.

NEC: The National Executive Committee is Labour's ruling body and is elected at the annual Party Conference. It comprises the Leader and Deputy Leader (ex-officio), the Trade Union section, the CLP section (qv), Socialist Societies, the Women's section, and the Party Treasurer.

NGA: National Graphical Association (see GPMU).

NUPE: The National Union of Public Employees has now merged with the health workers (Cohse) and the Local Government white collar union (Nalgo) to form UNISON. Once clearly on the left it supported Kinnock in his attempts to modernise the Party and was one of the driving forces behind the Policy Review after the 1987 General Election defeat. Its then Deputy General Secretary, Tom Sawyer, was appointed General Secretary of the Labour Party in October 1994.

OMOV: One Member, One Vote is the system that has been proposed, and partially introduced, for elections within the Labour Party. Parliamentary candidates used to be selected by the activists on the CLP GC (qv) but are now elected via a ballot of all the Constituency members. The principle is being extended to voting for the Party leadership and for positions on the NEC (qv). Its proponents believe that, by involving the wider membership, it will reduce the influence of the hard left, who are able to dominate small meetings. The main stumbling block has been the traditions of the trade unions which have rarely involved their membership in direct ballots on Labour Party matters.

PLP: The Parliamentary Labour Party.

Shadow Communications Agency: Created by Peter Mandelson when Director of Communications for the Labour Party, it brought together advertising and marketing professionals willing to give their services free of charge to the Party.

Solidarity: Taking its name from the Polish trade union grouping led by Lech Walesa, Labour Solidarity was set up by right-wing Labour MPs in 1981 who had no intention of defecting to the SDP but who wanted to combat the Bennite left. John Smith, Jack Cunningham and Roy Hattersley were all members.

TGWU (T and G): The Transport and General Workers Union is the largest trade union in the UK, and has always had the largest vote at Labour Party Conference. Its leaders have been in the first rank of Labour movement barons, and they regard the proposals to change the relationship between the Party and the unions with deep suspicion.

Tribune Group: Once the main left-wing grouping of Labour MPs, it is now more centre-left and contains many leadership figures including Tony Blair, Gordon Brown and Neil Kinnock. Its drift to the centre during the 1980s prompted the formation of the Campaign Group by MPs who opposed the changes. Not to be confused with . . .

Tribune newspaper: A weekly left-wing newspaper, not officially linked to the Labour Party but aimed at Labour and Trade Union activists. In the absence of an official Party newspaper *Tribune* has become the unofficial house magazine for the Labour Party.

Chronology

6 May 1953	Tony Blair born, Edinburgh.
1964–71	Attends Fettes School in Edinburgh.
1972–75	St John's College, Oxford.
Autumn 1975	Tony Blair joins Labour Party.
1976	Called to Bar.
3 May 1979	General Election. Conservatives sweep to power after winter of discontent.
29 March 1980	Tony Blair marries Cherie Booth.
2 April 1982	Argentina invades Falkland Islands.
27 May 1982	Blair contests Beaconsfield by-election, coming third with 10 per cent share of the vote.
February 1983	First expulsion of members of the editorial board of *Militant* newspaper from Labour Party.
20 May 1983	Tony Blair selected as Parliamentary candidate for Sedgefield.
9 June 1983	General Election. Conservative landslide. Labour returns 209 MPs, the lowest since 1935 with a 27.6 per cent share of the vote. Tony Blair elected member of Parliament for Sedgefield with a majority of 8,281 votes.
8 March 1984	Miners' strike begins.
1984	Tony Blair appointed to Labour's front bench within seven months of entering the Commons.
1984–87	Opposition Spokesman on Treasury and Economic Affairs.
5 March 1985	Miners return to work.
11 June 1987	General Election. Labours share of the vote is slightly increased.
1987–88	Tony Blair promoted to Opposition Spokesman on Trade and Industry.

1987	Gordon Brown is elected on to the Shadow Cabinet.
1988	Tony Blair is elected on to the Shadow Cabinet.
1988–89	Shadow Energy Secretary.
1989–92	Shadow Employment Secretary.
17 December 1989	Tony Blair announces Labour is to abandon support for the closed shop.
11 February 1990	Nelson Mandela is released.
2 August 1990	Iraq invades Kuwait.
22 November 1990	Margaret Thatcher resigns.
9 April 1992	General Election. Conservative majority is cut but Labour's share of the vote is still lower than 1979.
13 April 1992	Neil Kinnock resigns.
18 July 1992	John Smith is elected Leader of the Labour Party. Margaret Beckett elected Deputy.
16 September 1992	Britain withdraws from the ERM.
Autumn 1992	Tony Blair is elected on to NEC.
1992–94	Shadow Home Secretary.
January 1993	Blair and Brown visit Washington.
21 May 1993	Blair says Labour will be 'tough on crime, tough on the causes of crime' *The World This Weekend, BBC Radio* 4.
October 1993	Labour conference votes for OMOV but with a compromise proposal.
12 May 1994	John Smith dies after a heart attack.
1 June 1994	Gordon Brown withdraws from Labour Leadership contest.
9 June 1994	European elections. Labour win 62 seats on the European Parliament with a 44.2 per cent share of the vote.
11 June 1994	Tony Blair launches his Leadership campaign.
21 July 1994	Tony Blair elected Labour Leader. John Prescott elected Deputy Leader.
31 August 1994	IRA announces ceasefire.
4 October 1994	Blair announces review of Clause IV.

Notes

CHAPTER 1

1 *Daily Mail*, 27.5.94
2 ibid.
3 author's interview with Leo Blair
4 author's interview with Tony Blair MP
5 author's interview with Mike Gascoigne
6 author's interview with Nick Rydon
7 *Sunday Times*, 19.7.92
8 author's interview with Alastair Campbell
9 *The Mail on Sunday*, 22.5.94
10 *Evening Standard*, 18.7.94
11 *Isis Magazine*
12 *House* magazine, 2.4.90
13 author's interview with Mary Harron
14 author's interview with Marc Palley
15 *Newsnight*, BBC 2, 10.6.94
16 *Sunday Times*, 17.7.94
17 author's interview with Alistair Burt MP

CHAPTER 2

1 author's interview with David Fursedon
2 author's interview with Peter Thomson
3 *Newsnight*, BBC 2, 10.6.94
4 author's interview with Tony Blair MP
5 *Sunday Times*, 17.7.92
6 author's interview with Derry Irvine
7 author's interview with David Fursedon
8 *Stroll On*, Tony Booth, Sidgwick and Jackson
9 *The Time of My Life*, Denis Healey, Michael Joseph, 1989
10 author's interview with Tony Blair MP
11 author's interview with Charles Clarke
12 *Guardian*, 17.8.94
13 *Discipline and Discord in the Labour Party*, Eric Shaw, Manchester University Press, 1988

14 author's interview with Mike Davis

CHAPTER 3
1 author's interview with Baroness Gould
2 Tony Blair's Australian Lecture, 1982
3 ibid.
4 ibid.
5 ibid.
6 author's interview with Peter Brookes
7 *Today*, BBC Radio 4, 15.9.94
8 *Sunday Times Magazine*, 17.7.92
9 *Sunday Times*, 17.7.92
10 *The Times*, 15.5.93
11 *Alan Clark Diaries*, Weidenfeld and Nicolson, 1993
12 *Hansard*, 6.7.83, column 320
13 *Hansard* 17.7.84, column 165
14 *Hansard* 23.10.84, column 552
15 ibid.

CHAPTER 4
1 author's interview with Neil Kinnock
2 *The Scotsman*, 16.11.87
3 *The View From Number 11*, Nigel Lawson, Bantam Press, p.404
4 *Guardian*, 9.5.85
5 Neil Kinnock's speech to Labour Party conference, October 1983
6 *Labour Rebuilt – The New Model Party*, Colin Hughes and Patrick Wintour, Fourth Estate, 1990, p.54
7 *The World This Weekend*, BBC Radio 4, 5.7.87
8 *The Week in Politics*, Channel 4, 11.7.87
9 *The Times*, 29.9.87
10 ibid.
11 *The Scotsman*, 16.11.87
12 author's interview with Eric Illsley MP
13 author's interview with Cecil Parkinson

CHAPTER 5
1 *On the Record*, BBC 1, 23.4.89
2 author's interview with Neil Kinnock
3 ibid.
4 author's interview with John Monks
5 ibid.
6 author's interview with Tony Dubbins
7 Tony Blair's speech to Sedgefield Labour Party, 17.12.89

8 author's interview with Charles Clarke
9 *Looking to the Future*, The Labour Party, 1990
10 ibid.
11 *On the Record*, BBC 1, 27.5.90
12 ibid.
13 *Looking to the Future*, The Labour Party, 1990
14 *Guardian*, 19.12.89
15 *Hansard*, 8.11.83, column 208
16 *Hansard*, 8.11.83, column 210
17 author's interview with Michael Howard MP
18 *New Statesman*, 5.10.90
19 author's interview with Peter Mandelson MP
20 Labour Party Press Release, 4.7.91
21 author's interview with Charles Clarke

CHAPTER 6
1 author's interview with John Monks
2 *Election 92*, BBC Books, p.145
3 *On the Record*, BBC 1, 5.7.92
4 author's conversation with Roy Hattersley MP
5 *Sunday Times*, 17.7.92
6 ibid.
7 NEC report, 1992
8 *Guardian*, 8.5.82
9 *The Independent*, 13.6.92
10 *Renewal*, October 1992, number 4
11 *Guardian*, 14.4.92
12 Kenneth Clarke MP, 7.8.92
13 ibid.
14 *Newsnight*, BBC 2, 20.7.94
15 *Newsnight*, BBC 2, 20.7.94
16 *Tribune*, 8.1.93
17 ibid.
18 *Financial Times*, 5.1.93
19 *The Times*, 11.2.93

CHAPTER 7
1 author's interview with Neil Kinnock
2 confidential interview with author
3 *ITN*, 4.12.92
4 author's conversation with Roy Hattersley MP
6 *The Independent on Sunday*, 28.2.93
7 *Channel 4 News*, 4.2.93

8 Tony Blair's speech to Wellingborough Labour Party, 19.2.93

9 *The World This Weekend*, BBC Radio 4, 21.1.93

10 *Reclaiming the Ground*, Spire Press, 1992, p.9

11 ibid.

12 ibid.

13 *The Mail on Sunday*, 21.3.93

14 John Major at the Conservative Central Council, 6.3.83

15 Tony Blair's speech to the Police Federation Annual Conference, 20.5.93

16 *Daily Mail*, 31.7.93

17 author's interview with Baroness Gould

18 *Guardian*, 9.6.93

19 *On the Record*, BBC 1, 11.7.93

20 *Fabian Review*, Sept./Oct. 1993

21 Tony Blair's speech to the Labour Party Conference, 30.9.93

22 Michael Howard's speech to the Conservative Party Conference, 6.10.93

23 *Gallup Political and Economic Index*, Report 382, June 1992; Report 392, April 1993; Report 404, April 1994

24 confidential interview with author

25 *Guardian*, 23.6.94

26 *Spectator*, 30.4.94

CHAPTER 8

1 *Sunday Times*, 5.6.94

2 *Evening Standard*, 28.7.92

3 *John Smith: Playing the Long Game*, Andy McSmith, Verso, 1993, p.130

4 *Sunday Mirror Magazine*, 11.9.88, p.21

5 author's interview with Geoff Gallop

6 *Hansard*, 17.3.93, column 289

7 *Today* BBC Radio 4, 28.1.95

8 *Guardian*, 2.6.94

9 author's interview with Neil Kinnock

10 author's interview with Charles Clarke

11 *Mail on Sunday*, 16.4.95

12 *Guardian*, 4.8.94

13 ibid.

14 confidential conversation with author

15 confidential interview with author

CHAPTER 9

1 MORI, *The Times*, 26.8.94

2 Tony Blair's speech to the Engineering Employers Federation, 30.6.94
3 ibid.
4 ibid.
5 BBC *Breakfast News*, 12.7.94
6 *Panorama*, BBC 1, 13.6.94
7 *On the Record*, BBC 1, 26.6.94
8 BBC *One O'clock News*, 26.7.94
9 *Daily Telegraph*, 23.7.94
10 *Reforming Welfare: Building on Beveridge*, 13.7.94

CHAPTER 10
1 *The Time of My Life*, Denis Healey, Michael Joseph, 1989, p.482
2 author's interview with Neil Kinnock
3 *John Smith: Playing the Long Game*, Andy McSmith, Verso, 1993
4 *Esquire*, June 1994, p.85
5 *The Times*, 29.6.94
6 ibid.
7 *The Times*, 30.9.93
8 BBC *Breakfast News*, 13.7.94
9 BBC *Conference Live*, 27.9.93
10 Minority Report on the Liverpool Labour Party, 26.2.82
11 *Today*, BBC Radio 4, 19.6.94
12 *Hansard*, 12.5.94, column 431
13 *The Times*, 21.6.94
14 *Guardian*, 7.7.94
15 *Observer*, 10.7.94
16 letter from Clare Short MP to all Labour MPs, 12.7.94
17 author's interview with Neil Kinnock

CHAPTER 11
1 *Sunday Times*, 28.5.95
2 Swinton Lecture, CCO, 3.7.94
3 ibid.
4 Kenneth Clarke, 12.7.94
5 Tony Blair, 13.7.94
6 Annual Mais Lecture, 22.5.95
7 *Clear Blue Water*, Conservative Way Forward, 1994, p.9
8 *Financial Times*, 21.11.94
9 author's interview with Michael Howard MP
10 *The World at One*, BBC Radio 4, 3.8.94
11 author's interview with Lord Rodgers, 3.8.94
12 *The World at One*, BBC Radio 4, 5.8.94

13 *New Statesman*, 28.4.94

CHAPTER 12

1 statement issued privately by JTUC officers on 2.9.94
2 *The Times*, 7.9.94
3 *The Times*, 6.9.94
4 *Breakfast with Frost*, BBC 1, 12.6.94
5 Labour Party Conference Annual Report, 1959
6 Tony Blair, 4.10.94
7 ibid.
8 ibid.
9 *Tribune*, Hugh MacPherson, 29.7.94
10 *New Statesman*, 12.8.94
11 *Labour's Grass Roots, The Politics of Party Membership*, Patrick Seyd and Paul Whiteley, Clarendon Press, 1992, pp.218–219
12 author's interview with Tony Blair MP
13 *Good Morning with Anne and Nick*, 1.12.94
14 *Daily Mail*, 2.12.94

CHAPTER 13

1 BBC Radio 4 bulletin, 1.1.95
2 *The World This Weekend*, 1.1.95
3 *Daily Telegraph*, 10.1.95
4 confidential interview with author
5 *Guardian*, 10.1.95
6 *Daily Mail*, 12.1.95
7 *Hansard*, 21.2.95, column 153
8 *BBC Television News*, 21.1.95
9 *Spectator*, 2.2.95
10 *The Times*, 26.1.95
11 *Sunday Times*, 5.2.95
12 statement agreed by Labour Party NEC, 13.3.95
13 *Observer*, 23.4.95
14 speech at special conference, 29.4.95
15 *Guardian*, 1.5.95
16 *BBC Westminster On Line*, 1.5.95
17 *Observer*, 9.10.94

Index